Collected Poems

Also by Carol Ann Duffy in Picador

The Other Country

Mean Time

The World's Wife

Feminine Gospels

New Selected Poems

Rapture

Mrs Scrooge

Love Poems

Another Night Before Christmas

The Bees

The Christmas Truce

Wenceslas

Bethlehem

Ritual Lighting

Dorothy Wordsworth's Christmas Birthday

The Wren-Boys

AS EDITOR

Hand in Hand

Answering Back

To the Moon

Collected Poems

CAROL ANN DUFFY

PICADOR

First published 2015 by Picador
an imprint of Pan Macmillan
20 New Wharf Road, London N1 9RR
Associated companies throughout the world
www.panmacmillan.com

ISBN 978-1-4472-3143-1

Copyright © Carol Ann Duffy 2015
Textual artwork © Stephen Raw 2015

The right of Carol Ann Duffy to be identified as the
author of this work has been asserted by her in accordance
with the Copyright, Designs and Patents Act 1988.

All rights reserved. No part of this publication may be reproduced,
stored in a retrieval system, or transmitted, in any form, or by any means
(electronic, mechanical, photocopying, recording or otherwise)
without the prior written permission of the publisher.

Pan Macmillan does not have any control over, or any responsibility for,
any author or third party websites referred to in or on this book.

1 3 5 7 9 8 6 4 2

A CIP catalogue record for this book is available from the British Library.

Printed and bound by CPI Group (UK) Ltd, Croydon, CR0 4YY

This book is sold subject to the condition that it shall not, by way
of trade or otherwise, be lent, hired out, or otherwise circulated without
the publisher's prior consent in any form of binding or cover other than
that in which it is published and without a similar condition including
this condition being imposed on the subsequent purchaser.

Visit www.picador.com to read more about all our books
and to buy them. You will also find features, author interviews and
news of any author events, and you can sign up for e-newsletters
so that you're always first to hear about our new releases.

Contents

Standing Female Nude – 1

Selling Manhattan – 65

The Other Country – 125

Mean Time – 179

The World's Wife – 227

Feminine Gospels – 301

Rapture – 367

The Bees – 431

Ritual Lighting – 509

Christmas Poems – 529

Index of titles – 561
Index of first lines – 573

For Ella

Lineage

Child, stardust, small wonder
you look up tonight
to wish on old light.
I sense my mother's spirit
in the room. Time
has made her a prayer for us.

A wish and a prayer at Christmas
and you either or both.
I hoped for nothing more.

The ancient law:
the mass cannot be sung
without the wax
because the lineage of bees
is from Paradise.

TODAY WE HAVE A POET IN THE CLASS.

Girl Talking

On our Eid day my cousin was sent to
the village. Something happened. We think it was pain.
She gave wheat to the miller and the miller
gave her flour. Afterwards it did not hurt,
so for a while she made chapatis. *Tasleen,*
said her friends, *Tasleen, do come out with us.*

They were in a coy near the swing. It's like
a field. Sometimes we planted melons, spinach,
marrow, and there was a well. She sat on the swing.
They pushed her till she shouted *Stop the swing,*
then she was sick. Tasleen told them to find
help. She made blood beneath the mango tree.

Her mother held her down. She thought something
was burning her stomach. We paint our hands.
We visit. We take each other money.
Outside, the children played Jack-with-Five-Stones.
Each day she'd carried water from the well
into the Mosque. Men washed and prayed to God.

After an hour she died. Her mother cried.
They called a Holy Man. He walked from Dina
to Jhang Chak. He saw her dead, then said
She went out at noon and the ghost took her heart.
From that day we were warned not to do this.
Baarh is a small red fruit. We guard our hearts.

Comprehensive

Tutumantu is like hopscotch, Kwani-kwani is like hide-and-seek.
When my sister came back to Africa she could only speak
English. Sometimes we fought in bed because she didn't know
what I was saying. I like Africa better than England.
My mother says You will like it when we get our own house.
We talk a lot about the things we used to do
in Africa and then we are happy.

Wayne. Fourteen. Games are for kids. I support
the National Front. Paki-bashing and pulling girls'
knickers down. Dad's got his own mini-cab. We watch
the video. I Spit on Your Grave. Brilliant.
I don't suppose I'll get a job. It's all them
coming over here to work. Arsenal.

Masjid at 6 o'clock. School at 8. There was
a friendly shop selling rice. They ground it at home
to make the evening nan. Families face Mecca.
There was much more room to play than here in London.
We played in an old village. It is empty now.
We got a plane to Heathrow. People wrote to us
that everything was easy here.

It's boring. Get engaged. Probably work in Safeways
worst luck. I haven't lost it yet because I want
respect. Marlon Frederic's nice but he's a bit dark.
I like Madness. The lead singer's dead good.
My mum is bad with her nerves. She won't
let me do nothing. Michelle. It's just boring.

Ejaz. They put some sausages on my plate.
As I was going to put one in my mouth
a Moslem boy jumped on me and pulled.
The plate dropped on the floor and broke. He asked me in Urdu
if I was a Moslem. I said Yes. You shouldn't be eating this.
It's a pig's meat. So we became friends.

My sister went out with one. There was murder.
I'd like to be mates, but they're different from us.
Some of them wear turbans in class. You can't help
taking the piss. I'm going in the Army.
No choice really. When I get married
I might emigrate. A girl who can cook
with long legs. Australia sounds all right.

Some of my family are named after the Moghul emperors.
Aurangzeb, Jehangir, Batur, Humayun. I was born
thirteen years ago in Jhelum. This is a hard school.
A man came in with a milk crate. The teacher told us
to drink our milk. I didn't understand what she was saying,
so I didn't go to get any milk. I have hope and am ambitious.
At first I felt as if I was dreaming, but I wasn't.
Everything I saw was true.

Alphabet for Auden

When the words have gone away
there is nothing left to say.

Unformed thought can never be,
what you feel is what you see,
write it down and set it free
on printed pages, © Me.
I love, you love, so does he –
long live English Poetry.
Four o'clock is time for tea,
I'll be Mother, who'll be me?

Murmur, underneath your breath,
incantations to the deaf.

Here we go again. Goody.
Art can't alter History.

Praise the language, treasure each
well-earned phrase your labours reach.

In hotels you sit and sigh,
crafting lines where others cry,

puzzled why it doesn't pay
shoving couplets round all day.
There is vodka on a tray.
Up your nose the hairs are grey.

When the words done gone it's hell
having nothing left to tell.

Pummel, punch, fondle, knead them
back again to life. Read them

when you doubt yourself and when
you doubt their function, read again.

Verse can say *I told you so*
but cannot sway the status quo

one inch. Now you get lonely,
Baby want love and love only.

In the mirror you see you.
Love you always, darling. True.

When the words have wandered far
poets patronise the bar,

understanding less and less.
Truth is anybody's guess
and Time's a clock, five of three,
mix another G and T.

Set 'em up, Joe, make that two.
Wallace Stevens thought in blue.

Words drown in a drunken sea,
dumb, they clutch at memory.

Pissed you have a double view,
something else to trouble you.

Inspiration clears the decks –
if all else fails, write of sex.

Every other word's a lie,
ain't no rainbow in the sky.

Some get lucky, die in bed,
one word stubbed in the ashtray. *Dead.*

Head of English

Today we have a poet in the class.
A real live poet with a published book.
Notice the inkstained fingers girls. Perhaps
we're going to witness verse hot from the press.
Who knows. Please show your appreciation
by clapping. Not too loud. Now

sit up straight and listen. Remember
the lesson on assonance, for not all poems,
sadly, rhyme these days. Still. Never mind.
Whispering's, as always, out of bounds –
but do feel free to raise some questions.
After all, we're paying forty pounds.

Those of you with English Second Language
see me after break. We're fortunate
to have this person in our midst.
Season of mists and so on and so forth.
I've written quite a bit of poetry myself,
am doing Kipling with the Lower Fourth.

Right. That's enough from me. On with the Muse.
Open a window at the back. We don't
want winds of change about the place.
Take notes, but don't write reams. Just an essay
on the poet's themes. Fine. Off we go.
Convince us that there's something we don't know.

Well. Really. Run along now girls. I'm sure
that gave an insight to an outside view.
Applause will do. Thank you
very much for coming here today. Lunch
in the hall? Do hang about. Unfortunately
I have to dash. Tracey will show you out.

Lizzie, Six

What are you doing?
I'm watching the moon.
I'll give you the moon
when I get up there.

Where are you going?
To play in the fields.
I'll give you fields,
bend over that chair.

What are you thinking?
I'm thinking of love.
I'll give you love
when I've climbed this stair.

Where are you hiding?
Deep in the wood.
I'll give you wood
when your bottom's bare.

Why are you crying?
I'm afraid of the dark.
I'll give you the dark
and I do not care.

Ash Wednesday, 1984

In St Austin's and Sacré Coeur the accents of ignorance
sing out. The Catholic's spanking wains are marked
by a bigot's thumbprint dipped in burnt black palm.
Dead language rises up and does them harm.

I remember this. The giving up of gobstoppers
for Lent, the weekly invention of venial sin
in a dusty box. Once, in pale blue dresses,
we kissed petals for the Bishop's feet.

Stafford's guilty sinners slobbered at their beads, beneath
the purple-shrouded plaster saints. We were Scottish,
moved down there for work, and every Sunday
I was leathered up the road to Church.

Get to Communion and none of your cheek.
We'll put the fear of God in your bones.
Swallow the Eucharist, humble and meek.
St Stephen was martyred with stones.

It makes me sick. My soul is not a vest
spattered with wee black marks. Miracles and shamrocks
and transubstantiation are all my ass.
For Christ's sake, do not send your kids to Mass.

Education for Leisure

Today I am going to kill something. Anything.
I have had enough of being ignored and today
I am going to play God. It is an ordinary day,
a sort of grey with boredom stirring in the streets.

I squash a fly against the window with my thumb.
We did that at school. Shakespeare. It was in
another language and now the fly is in another language.
I breathe out talent on the glass to write my name.

I am a genius. I could be anything at all, with half
the chance. But today I am going to change the world.
Something's world. The cat avoids me. The cat
knows I am a genius and has hidden itself.

I pour the goldfish down the bog. I pull the chain.
I see that it is good. The budgie is panicking.
Once a fortnight, I walk the two miles into town
for signing on. They don't appreciate my autograph.

There is nothing left to kill. I dial the radio
and tell the man he's talking to a superstar.
He cuts me off. I get our bread-knife and go out.
The pavements glitter suddenly. I touch your arm.

I Remember Me

There are not enough faces. Your own gapes back
at you on someone else, but paler, then the moment
when you see the next one and forget yourself.

It must be dreams that make us different, must be
private cells inside a common skull.
One has the other's look and has another memory.

Despair stares out from tube-trains at itself
running on the platform for the closing door. Everyone
you meet is telling wordless barefaced truths.

Sometimes the crowd yields one you put a name to,
snapping fiction into fact. Mostly your lover passes
in the rain and does not know you when you speak

This Shape

derived from a poem by Jean Genet

This shape is a rose, protect it, it's pure.
Preserve it. Already the evening unfolds you
before me. Naked, entwined, standing
in a sheet against a wall. This shape.

My lips tremble on its delicate brim
and dare to gather the drops which fall.
Your milk swells my throat to the neck of a dove.
O stay. Rose with pearl petals, remain.

Thorny sea-fruits tear my skin. Your image
at night's end. Fingertips of smoke break surface.
My tongue thrusts, drinks at the rose's edge.
My heart uncertain. Golden hair, ghostly nape.

Destroy this anchor to impossible living, vomiting
on a sea of bile. Harnessed to your body
I move through a vast world without goodness
where you come to me only in sleep.

I roll on the ocean with you vaguely above,
working the axles, twisting through your storms.
Faraway and angry. Wanting the sky
to thread the horizon with a cloth of my stitching.

How can I sleep with this flesh that uncurls the sea?
Beautiful story of love. A village child
adores the sentry wandering on the beach.
My amber hand draws in a boy of iron.

Sleeper, your body. This shape, extraordinary.
Creamy almond, star, o curled up child.
A tingling stir of blood in the blue departure
of evening. A naked foot sounding on the grass.

Saying Something

Things assume your shape; discarded clothes, a damp shroud
in the bathroom, vacant hands. This is not fiction. This is
the plain and warm material of love. My heart assumes it.

We wake. Our private language starts the day. We make
familiar movements through the house. The dreams we have
no phrases for slip through our fingers into smoke.

I dreamed I was not with you. Wandering in a city
where you did not live, I stared at strangers, searching
for a word to make them you. I woke beside you.

Sweetheart, I say. Pedestrian daylight terms scratch
darker surfaces. Your absence leaves me with the ghost
of love; half-warm coffee cups or sheets, the gentlest kiss.

Walking home, I see you turning on the lights. I come in
from outside calling your name, saying something.

Jealous as Hell

Blind black shark swim in me,
move to possess. Slow stupid shape
grin in sea, suck inky on suspicions.
Swim grin suck, it clot my heart.

Big fish brooding in the water.
Bright bird buoyant in the sky.

Tail-shudder thrust wounded, it
ugly from imaginary pains. Bones
of contention rot in gut. Mouth open
shut open shut open. Hateshark coming.

Big fish smoulder for the slaughter.
Clever wings fly small bird high.

Evilbreath lurk at base of spine,
seethe sightless from heart to mind.
Devilteeth, sack of greed, reasonless.
It will kill. Swim grin suck.

Bird skim surface of the ocean.
Fish churn clumsy in the sea.

It wait in the gurgling dark.
Bad shark. Blue belly blubber
wanting bird. Sick with lust
it flick its great tail, it flick.

Freedom bird glide in its own motion.
Shark need nothing to be free.

It watch you every move.

Terza Rima SW19

Over this Common a kestrel treads air
till the earth says *mouse* or *vole*. Far below
two lovers walking by the pond seem unaware.

She feeds the ducks. He wants her, tells her so
as she half-smiles and stands slightly apart.
He loves me, loves me not with each deft throw.

It could last a year, she thinks, possibly two
and then crumble like stale bread. The kestrel flies
across the sun as he swears his love is true

and, darling, forever. Suddenly the earth cries
Now and death drops from above like a stone.
A couple turn and see a strange bird rise.

Into the sky a kestrel climbs alone
and later she might write or he may phone.

Naming Parts

A body has been discussed between them.
The woman wears a bruise
upon her arm. Do not wear your heart
upon your sleeve, he cautions, knowing
which part of whom has caused the injury.
Underneath the lamplight you teach me new games
with a wicked pack of cards. I am
the Jack of Diamonds and, for this trick only,
you my Queen. Beware the Ace of Spades.

Her heart is broken and he fears his liver
will explode. Outside the world whimpers
and rumours bite like gnats in bloodless ears.
You have placed my small hand on your large penis.
This is an erection. This is the life. This
is another fine mess. Perhaps soup will comfort them.
To have only soup against such sorrow.
I cannot bear alone and watch
my hands reach sadly for the telephone.

Once someone asked if she was hurting him
and once a wonderful lass destroyed him
with a kiss. You've given me the benefit of your doubt.
We forgive them nothing. I want
a better part than this. He shuffles the pack
and tells her to wait. She thinks of the loved body
talked of like weather. She's putting the ingredients
into the soup he likes. It's true or none of it's true.
Someone is cared for who is past caring. Somewhere.

Till Our Face

Whispers weave webs amongst thighs. I open
like the reddest fruit. Between the rapid spaces
of the rain the world sweats seas and damp
strings tremble for a perfect sound.

A bow tugs catgut. Something inside me
steps on a highwire where you search crimson
for a silver thread. A rose glows beneath
the drift of pine needles. I bite your lip, lost.

Come further in, where eyes stare inward
at the skull as the roof of the brain
takes flight. Your mouth laps petals till our face
is a flower soaked in its own scent.

The planets abandon us.

Lovebirds

I wait for your step.
A jay on the cherry tree
    trembles the blossom.

I name you *my love*
and the gulls fly above us
    calling to the air.

Our two pale bodies
move in the late light, slowly
    as doves do, breathing.

And then you are gone.
A night-owl mourns in darkness
    for the moon's last phase.

Where We Came In

old lovers die hard, as in the restaurant
we pass the bread between us like a symbol
of betrayal. One of you tonight.
The habits are the same, small intimacies
flaring up across the table. They've placed
a candle in the middle over which
we carefully avoid our history.

How do you sleep? Something corny
like Our Song pipes out. I know
you're still too mean to pay the bill.
Our new loves sit beside us guardedly,
outside the private jokes. I think
of all the tediousness of loss but, yes,
I'm happy now. Yes. Happy. Now.

Darling, whatever it was that covered
such an ordinary form with light
has long since gone. It is a candle
shapes the memory. Perhaps the wine.
I see our gestures endlessly repeated as
you turn to yours the way you used
to turn to me. I turn to mine. And

Free Will

The country in her heart babbled a language
she couldn't explain. When she had found the money
she paid them to take something away from her.
Whatever it was she did not permit it a name.

It was nothing yet she found herself grieving nothing.
Beyond reason her body mourned, though the mind
counselled like a doctor who had heard it all before.
When words insisted they were silenced with a cigarette.

Dreams were a nightmare. Things she did not like
to think about persisted in being thought.
They were in her blood, bobbing like flotsam;
as sleep retreated they were strewn across her face.

Once, when small, she sliced a worm in half,
gazing as it twinned beneath the knife.
What she parted would not die despite
the cut, remained inside her all her life.

Alliance

What she has retained of herself is a hidden grip
working her face like a glove-puppet. She smiles
at his bullying, this Englishman who talks scathingly
of *Frogs* in front of his French wife.

She is word-perfect. Over the years he has inflated
with best bitter till she has no room. *Je t'aime*
isn't in it. One morning she awoke to a foreigner
lying beside her and her heart slammed shut.

The youngest lives at home. She stays up late
to feed what keeps her with the father. England
ruined him and holds her hostage in the garden,
thinking of her sons and what they've cost.

Or dreaming in another language with a different name
about a holiday next year. He staggers in half-pissed
and plonks his weight down on her life, hates her
for whatever reason she no longer lets him near.

A Clear Note

1 AGATHA

Eight children to feed, I worked as a nurse
tending the dying. Four kids to each breast.
You can see from the photographs
my long auburn hair.

Kiss me goodnight – me weeping in our bed.
The scunner would turn away cold, back rigid,
but come home from work and take me on the floor
with his boots on and his blue eyes shut.

Moll, all my life I wanted the fields of Ireland only
and a man to delight in me
who'd never be finished with kisses and say
Look at the moon. My darling. The moon.

Instead, a move across the water
to Glasgow and long years of loathing
with the devil I'd married. I felt love freeze
to a fine splinter in my heart.

Again and again throwing life from my loins
like a spider with enough rope
spinning and wringing its own neck. And he
wouldn't so much as hold me after the act.

It won't be over till one of us is dead.
Out there in the streets there's a corpse
walking round in a good suit and a trilby.
Don't bury him on top of me. Please.

I had a voice once, but it's broken
and cannot recall the unspoken words
I tried to whisper in his closed ear.
Look at the moon. My darling. The moon.

Who'd have thought to die alone on the telephone
wheezing at strangers? The snowqueen's heart
stopping forever and melting as it stopped.
Once I was glorious with a new frock and high hopes.

Is it mad to dream then? What a price
to pay. But when hair bled colour
and the starved body began eating itself,
I had forgotten how to dream.

What laughs, Moll, for you and me
to swim in impossible seas. You've a daughter
yourself now to talk through the night.
I was famous for my hats. Remember.

Workmen whistled as I stepped out,
although I ignored them. I had pride. Remember
my fine hair and my smart stride
in the park with the eight of you spruced.

Please. From behind silence I ask
for an epitaph of light. Let some imagine.
Bernadette, little grandchild, one day
you must tell them I wanted the moon. *Yes.*

2 MOLL

Some hurts pass, pet, but others
lurk on. They turn up
like old photos and catch at the throat
somehow. I'm forty-nine in May.

Her death haunts me, almost
as I haunted her womb and you mine.
A presence inside me which will neither grow
nor diminish. What can a woman do?

The job pays well, but more than that
there's the freedom. Your father's against it.
He loves me as much now as he did
twenty-five years ago. More.

Sometimes I think I'll walk out the door
and keep right on walking. But then
there's the dinner to cook. I take her flowers
every year and talk to the tombstone.

You were a wild wain, with an answer
for everything. Near killed me containing you.
Boys are different. I can read you
like a book, like the back of my hand.

They call me Madcap Moll. I'd love to leap
on a bike and ride to the seaside
alone. There's something out there
that's passing me by. Are you following me?

I've been drained since twenty, but not empty
yet. I roam inside myself, have
such visions you'd not credit. The best times
are daydreams with a cigarette.

There was that night, drunk, I told you
*Never have kids. Give birth to yourself
I wish I had.* And your Dad, looking daggers
stormed off to bed. Laugh? I cried.

I can't fly out to stay with you alone,
there'd be fights for a month.
He broods on what I'd get up to
given half the chance. Men!

Hardest to bear is knowing my own strength.
Does that sound strange? Yet four daft sons
and a husband handle me like gold leaf.
Me, with a black hole of resources.

Over and over again as a child
you'd be at me to sing
The stars at night are big and bright.
Aye. So still they are.

Here's me blethering on. What laughs,
Bernadette, for us to swim in impossible seas
under the moon. Let's away, my darling,
for a good long walk. And I'll tell you a secret.

3 Bernadette

The day her mother died, my mother
was on holiday. I travelled to the seaside
with bad news. She slumped over the table,
spilling wine across the telegram.

Someone burnt the diary she wrote. It was
a catalogue of hatred and it was all
she had to leave. Extracts were whispered
at the wake and then it was forgotten.

Her mouth was set as though she was angry.
Kiss me goodnight. My mother went in.
She saw him bend over the coffin to kiss her
and half-thought the corpse had flinched.

I can't remember much. Perhaps the smell
of my granny mingling with hers
in a gossipy bed. Them giggling. One sang
Hang down your head Tom Dooley in the dark.

Or assuming a virtuous expression
so they'd let you stay up late. Listening
as language placed its little markers
where the secrets were.

They buried him on top within the month.
*I don't want that bastard
rotting above me for all eternity.*
What does it matter, they said, now she's dead?

Can't see the moon now, Moll.
Listen. The hopes of your thousand mothers
sing with a clear note inside you.
Away, while you can, and travel the world.

I can almost hear her saying it now.
W'ho will remember me? Bleak decades of silence
and lovelessness placing her years away
from the things that seem natural to us.

For we swim with ease in all
possible seas and do not forget them.
It's spring again and just about now
my Granny would be buying a new hat.

And I have hair like hers. My mother
is setting off for work. An aeroplane
climbs up above her house. She imagines me
seeing it from my window later on.

As I imagine the simplest thing. The dreams
of women which will harm no one.
April in the graveyard sees new flowers
pushing out from the old earth.

The daylight disappears. Against the night
a plane's lights come from somewhere else. For Moll
the life goes streaming back in tune.
For Agatha, from Bernadette, the moon.

Words of Absolution

She clings to life by a rosary,
ninety years old. Who made you?
God made me. Pearl died a bairn
and him blacklisted. Listen
to the patterns of your prayers
down the years. What is Purgatory?

The guilt and stain of Original Sin.
Except the Virgin. Never a drink
or tobacco and the legs opened only
for childbirth. Forgive me. With her
they pass the parcel. Don't let the music
stop and me holding it. What do you mean
by the resurrection of the body?

Blessed art thou among women even if
we put you in a home. Only the silent motion
of lips and the fingering of decades.
How do we show that we love God?
Never a slack shilling, but good broth
always on the table. Which are the fasting days?
Mary Wallace, what are the days of abstinence?

Chrism, ash, holy water, beads
waiting for the end of nothing. Granny,
I have committed the Sin of Sodom.
How are we to love one another?
What are the four last things
to be ever remembered? I go to my reward.
Chastity. Piety. Modesty. Longanimity.
How should you finish the day? After
your night prayers what should you do?

Debt

He was all night sleepless over money.
Impossible scenarios danced in the dark
as though he was drunk. The woman
stirred, a soft spoon, and what had emerged
from them dreamed in the next room, safe.
He left himself and drew a gun he didn't own.

He won the pools; pearls for her and ponies
for the kids. The damp bedroom was an ocean liner
till the woman farted, drifted on, away from him.
Despair formed a useless prayer and worry an ulcer.
He bargained with something he could not believe in
for something he could not have. *Sir* . . .

Through the wallpaper men in suits appeared.
They wanted the video, wanted the furniture.
They wanted the children. Sweat soured in nylon sheets
as his heartbeat panicked, trying to get out.
There was nothing he would not do. There was
nothing to do but run the mind's mad films.

Dear Sir . . . his ghost typed on. He remembered
waiting for her, years ago, on pay-day
with a bar of fruit-and-nut. Somehow consoled
he reached out, found her, and then slept.
Add this. Take that away. The long night leaked
cold light into the house. A letter came.

You Jane

At night I fart a Guinness smell against the wife
who snuggles up to me after I've given her one
after the Dog and Fox. It's all muscle. You can punch
my gut and wait forever till I flinch. Try it.
Man of the house. Master in my own home. Solid.

Look at that bicep. Dinner on the table
and a clean shirt, but I respect her point of view.
She's borne me two in eight years, knows
when to button it. Although she's run a bit to fat
she still bends over of a weekend in suspenders.

This is the life. Australia next year and bugger
the mother-in-law. Just feel those thighs.
Karate keeps me like granite. Strength of an ox.
I can cope with the ale no problem. Pints
with the lads, a laugh, then home to her.

She says Did you dream, love? I never
dream. Sleep is as black as a good jar.
I wake half-conscious with a hard-on, shove it in.
She don't complain. When I feel, I feel here
where the purple vein in my neck throbs.

Whoever She Was

They see me always as a flickering figure
on a shilling screen. Not real. My hands,
still wet, sprout wooden pegs. I smell the apples
burning as I hang the washing out.
Mummy, say the little voices of the ghosts
of children on the telephone. Mummy.

A row of paper dollies, cleaning wounds
or boiling eggs for soldiers. The chant
of magic words repeatedly. I do not know.
Perhaps tomorrow. If we're very good.
The film is on a loop. Six silly ladies
torn in half by baby fists. When they
think of me, I'm bending over them at night,
to kiss. Perfume. Rustle of silk. Sleep tight.

Where does it hurt? A scrap of echo clings
to the bramble bush. My maiden name
sounds wrong. This was the playroom.
I turn it over on a clumsy tongue. Again.
These are the photographs. Making masks
from turnips in the candlelight. In case they come.

Whoever she was, forever their wide eyes watch her
as she shapes a church and steeple in the air.
She cannot be myself and yet I have a box
of dusty presents to confirm that she was here.
You remember the little things. Telling stories
or pretending to be strong. Mummy's never wrong.
*You open your dead eyes to look in the mirror
which they are holding to your mouth.*

Human Interest

Fifteen years minimum, banged up inside
for what took thirty seconds to complete.
She turned away. I stabbed. I felt this heat
burn through my skull until reason had died.

I'd slogged my guts out for her, but she lied
when I knew different. She used to meet
some prick after work. She stank of deceit.

I loved her. When I accused her, she cried
and denied it. Straight up, she tore me apart.
On the Monday, I found the other bloke
had bought her a chain with a silver heart.

When I think about her now, I near choke
with grief. My baby. She wasn't a tart
or nothing. I wouldn't harm a fly, no joke.

Dreaming of Somewhere Else

Those strange stone birds are smashed
on heroin. It's like the ballroom
of the frigging Titanic up here. Our friend
says nothing will happen there, ever; drinks
steadily as mortgaged dust piles up.
His cat is off its cake. *Know what I mean like?*

Long dark streets of black eternal rain
leading to nowhere. *Paris of the North this.*
Everyone's had everyone else, at least
twice. Lethal cocktails brim with revelation
and gossip. I am here to tell you
that the Cathedrals are lucky to be alive.

Behave yourself. The glass shattered, pierced
just above his eye. Laugh? He was in
stitches. Even the river is too pissed
to go anywhere; it stares upwards at stars
reflecting a hungover moon for doomed lovers.
Et in Arcadia Ego and in the Philharmonic.

Nerves of steel you need in this game
as the wind screams up from the Pier Head
dragging desolation, memory; as the orchestra
plays on for the last dancers bouncing off the walls.
Somewhere else another universe takes light years
to be seen even though it went out already. *You wha'?*

Before You Jump

for Mister Berryman

Tell us what these tough words have done
to you.

      I demand Love and Attention now
with my little fists, with the muscles
of a poem. *These songs
are not meant to be understood, you understand.
They are meant only to terrify & comfort.*

Let light come daily where I grapple with
my tiny tasks. The golden beehive
brims with honey as the bees collapse.
That much for little sweetness, yet they
fondle sculpture like a pound of flesh.
Eloi Eloi lama sabachthani.
And who shall love properly?

                        You must
or we die. Walk through the churchyard
past the crocuses. They won't last long.
My guardian angel has abandoned me but soon
we'll fly upon the curve of earth.
A miracle is all I ask. Not much.
The red wet mouth cries out that jealousy
was ruin of them all. Save me.

Or manage with a flab of language
breaking back for fitness. And alone. If in the evening
someone wanders in with open arms
we will be blessed. If one says Yes.
I mean always what I say. Listen.
Do you mean what you say?

In slow motion he is falling, spinning
down forever. Pray for us now.
Unless there was one voice. Faithfulness.
Unless that were possible. Patience.
There must be only me. For this
I'll give myself, even my breath.
But say we are not lost. Darling.
A man crimson with need and getting nothing.

The tongue licks in and out and Look
what I can do. Fame and Money better never
than too late. Let this cup pass me by.
They're killing me; the images, the sounds
of what is in this world. You turn away
repeatedly. You always turn away.

From jewels and garbage I have fashioned
marvellous machines, but am of little matter
in the end. No more to say. I disbelieve
in everything whilst nothing speaks.
Climb down from there and come into the warm.
Forever come into the warm. Unless there was
one voice. Unless I thought it possible there was.

A Provincial Party, 1956

A chemical inside you secretes the ingredients of fear.
Is it fear? You know for sure you feel
uneasy on that black, plastic sofa, even though
the ice melts in a long tumbler behind red triangles.
You don't find it sexy, your first blue movie
in a stranger's flat, but you watch it anyway.

Embarrassment crackles like three petticoats. You never
imagined, married two years and all. A woman
cackles a joke you don't understand, but you laugh anyway.
On one stocking, you have halted a ladder
with clear varnish. There are things going on
on the screen which would turn your Mam to salt.

Suddenly, the whole room is breathing. Someone hums
Magic Moments and then desists, moist lips apart.
Two men in the film are up to no good. *Christ.*
You could die with the shame. The chrome ashtray
is filled with fag-ends, lipstick-rimmed. Your suspenders
pinch you spitefully, like kids nipping spoilsports.

You daren't look, but something is happening
on the Cyril Lord. Part of you tells yourself it's only
shaving-cream. You and him do it with the light off.
This will give him ideas. It *is* fear. You nudge and nudge
till your husband squirms away from you and smiles
at the young, male host with film-star eyes.

Dear Norman

I have turned the newspaper boy into a diver
for pearls. I can do this. In my night
there is no moon, and if it happens that I speak
of stars it's by mistake. Or if it happens
that I mention these things, it's by design.

His body is brown, breaking through waves. Such white teeth.
Beneath the water he searches for the perfect shell.
He does not know that, as he posts the *Mirror*
through the door, he is equal with dolphins.
I shall name him Pablo, because I can.

Pablo laughs and shakes the seaweed from his hair.
Translucent on his palm a pearl appears. He is reminded.
Cuerpo de mujer, blancas Colinas, muslos blancos.
I find this difficult, and then again easy,
as I watch him push his bike off in the rain.

As I watch him push his bike off in the rain
I trace his name upon the window-pane.
There is little to communicate, but I have re-arranged
the order of the words. Pablo says You want for me
to dive again? I want for you to dive.

Tomorrow I shall deal with the dustman.

Talent

This is the word *tightrope*. Now imagine
a man, inching across it in the space
between our thoughts. He holds our breath.

There is no word *net*.

You want him to fall, don't you?
I guessed as much; he teeters but succeeds.
The word *applause* is written all over him.

$

A one a two a one two three four –
boogie woogie chou chou cha cha chatta
noogie. Woogie wop a loo bop a wop
bim bam. Da doo ron a doo ron oo wop a
sha na? Na na hey hey doo wah did.
Urn, didy ay didy shala lala lala lala,
boogie woogie choo choo cha cha bop.
(A woogie wop a loo bam) yeah yeah yeah.

Liverpool Echo

Pat Hodges kissed you once, although quite shy,
in sixty-two. Small crowds in Matthew Street
endure rain for the echo of a beat,
as if nostalgia means you did not die.

Inside phone-booths loveless ladies cry
on Merseyside. Their faces show defeat.
An ancient jukebox blares out Ain't She Sweet
in Liverpool, which cannot say goodbye.

Here everybody has an anecdote
of how they met you, were the best of mates.
The seagulls circle round a ferry-boat

out on the river, where it's getting late.
Like litter on the water, people float
outside the Cavern in the rain. And wait.

Back Desk

I am Franz Schubert of Dresden. It was not easy.
Quite soon I realised my prowess on the violin
was mediocre, but we had to eat.
The piece I wrote (The Bee, you may remember it)
paid for that winter's clothing, little else.
The children danced in their new clogs
till the strings snapped on the highest note.
I saw him once in Heidelberg, the other Franz.
He was older than I, seemed younger.
Smaller than I, looked taller.

Standing Female Nude

Six hours like this for a few francs.
Belly nipple arse in the window light,
he drains the colour from me. Further to the right,
Madame. And do try to be still.
I shall be represented analytically and hung
in great museums. The bourgeoisie will coo
at such an image of a river-whore. They call it Art.

Maybe. He is concerned with volume, space.
I with the next meal. You're getting thin,
Madame, this is not good. My breasts hang
slightly low, the studio is cold. In the tea-leaves
I can see the Queen of England gazing
on my shape. Magnificent, she murmurs
moving on. It makes me laugh. His name

is Georges. They tell me he's a genius.
There are times he does not concentrate
and stiffens for my warmth.
He possesses me on canvas as he dips the brush
repeatedly into the paint. Little man,
you've not the money for the arts I sell.
Both poor, we make our living how we can.

I ask him Why do you do this? Because
I have to. There's no choice. Don't talk.
My smile confuses him. These artists
take themselves too seriously. At night I fill myself
with wine and dance around the bars. When it's finished
he shows me proudly, lights a cigarette. I say
Twelve francs and get my shawl. It does not look like me.

Poem in Oils

What I have learnt I have learnt from the air,
from infinite varieties of light. Muted colours
alter gradually as clouds stir shape, till purple rain
or violet thunderstorm shudders in the corner of my eye.

Here, on this other coast, the motifs multiply.
I hesitate before the love the waves bear
to the earth. Is this what I see?
No, but this is the process of seeing.

Believe me, soundless shadows fall from trees
like brushstrokes. A painter stands
upon a cliff and turns doubt into certainty where,
far below, the ocean fills itself with sky.

I was here to do this. And was curious.

Oppenheim's Cup and Saucer

She asked me to luncheon in fur. Far from
the loud laughter of men, our secret life stirred.

I remember her eyes, the slim rope of her spine.
This is your cup, she whispered, and this mine.

We drank the sweet hot liquid and talked dirty.
As she undressed me, her breasts were a mirror

and there were mirrors in the bed. She said Place
your legs around my neck, that's right. Yes.

Ink on Paper

COMPOSITION 1

The heart is placid. The wireless makes
a slow movement to shape the invisible.
On the table, apples imitate an old motif;
beyond them, through the window, gulls applaud
the trees. Something has happened. Clouds
move away, superior and bored. A cigarette
fumes in a brown clay ashtray, ignored.

COMPOSITION 2

A dark red armchair with no one in it
waits patiently. Empty wet wellingtons
warm ghost-legs at the gas fire. There is
the sound of a woman's voice crying
on the other side of the door and the smell
of onions frying. Beneath the chair, an umbrella
half-exists. Behind the curtains, glass, rain.

COMPOSITION 3

This bowl of fruit obstinately refuses
to speak the language. Pink vain peaches
remain aloof in late light. The grapefruit
will only be yellow as long as anyone looks.
In the other bowl, two goldfish try harder.
Unwatched, the man watches the cat, watching.
An orange is more still than the near-silence.

Woman Seated in the Underground, 1941

after the drawing by Henry Moore

I forget. I have looked at the other faces and found
no memory, no love. *Christ, she's a rum one.*
Their laughter fills the tunnel, but it does not
comfort me. There was a bang and then
I was running with the rest through smoke. Thick, grey
smoke has covered thirty years at least.
I know I am pregnant, but I do not know my name.

Now they are singing. *Underneath the lantern
by the barrack gate.* But waiting for whom?
Did I? I have no wedding ring, no handbag, nothing.
I want a fag. I have either lost my ring or I am
a loose woman. No. Someone has loved me. Someone
is looking for me even now. I live somewhere.
I sing the word *darling* and it yields nothing.

Nothing. A child is crying. Mine doesn't show yet.
Baby. My hands mime the memory of knitting.
Purl. Plain. I know how to do these things, yet my mind
has unravelled into thin threads that lead nowhere.
In a moment, I shall stand up and scream until
somebody helps me. The skies were filled with sirens, planes,
fire, bombs, and I lost myself in the crowd. Dear God.

War Photographer

In his darkroom he is finally alone
with spools of suffering set out in ordered rows.
The only light is red and softly glows,
as though this were a church and he
a priest preparing to intone a Mass.
Belfast. Beirut. Phnom Penh. All flesh is grass.

He has a job to do. Solutions slop in trays
beneath his hands which did not tremble then
though seem to now. Rural England. Home again
to ordinary pain which simple weather can dispel,
to fields which don't explode beneath the feet
of running children in a nightmare heat.

Something is happening. A stranger's features
faintly start to twist before his eyes,
a half-formed ghost. He remembers the cries
of this man's wife, how he sought approval
without words to do what someone must
and how the blood stained into foreign dust.

A hundred agonies in black-and-white
from which his editor will pick out five or six
for Sunday's supplement. The reader's eyeballs prick
with tears between the bath and pre-lunch beers.
From the aeroplane he stares impassively at where
he earns his living and they do not care.

What Price?

These were his diaries. Through the writing we may find
the man and whether he has been misjudged.
Admit it, even now, most people secretly resent
the Jews. We have all evening to peruse
the truth. Outside the window summer blossom falls.

It takes me back. I always saw some sense
in what he tried to do. This country should be strong.
I'll put some Wagner on the gramophone
then we can settle down. On nights like this
it makes one glad to be alive. *My own Lili Marlene.*

Of course, one had to fight. I had a wife.
But somewhere here I think you'll find
that he'd have joined with us. More wine?
I know the Sons of David died, some say atrociously,
but that's all past. The roses are in bloom.

Look at the way we claimed the islands back.
My grandchildren are young and pink
and make me proud. She has the right idea.
These journals will be his chance to explain,
I'm certainly convinced that they are real.

Not that he didn't make mistakes, but we can learn
from him. See by the larch tree how the sun goes down.
And notice all the interest from newspapers, so soon!
I admit that it was hell to be a Jew, but how much
do you think they'll fetch? One million? Two?

Missile

The cat is itself.
Let us consider the cauliflower,
it means no harm.
Grass is grass grows grass.
Spider spins spider. Is a rose.
Everything's only itself. Grows.

Except you, Daddy.

Birds are simple.
Wings flap fly being birds.
Feathers in the sky saying bird.
Flickers in the sea saying fish.
Bird fish stone chant name,
we show no difference, we're the same.

Except you, Daddy.

Daffodil yellow with flower
stains light. Light leaks from sun
till night. Artichoke and mushroom
shift cycle till stop. Damp loam
humming at the moon. Eyes water
at the little onions. See.

Except you, Daddy.

Oranges and lemons singing singing
buttercups and daisies. Bang.
Will ye no come back again?
My true love. Bang. Two turtle doves.

Bang. The cat is spider is grass
is roses is bird fish bang.

Bang. Bang.
Except you, Daddy.

Poker in the Falklands with Henry & Jim

We three play poker whilst outside *the real world*
shrinks to a joker. So. Someone
deals me a queen, face up, and the bets roll.
I keep a straight face up my sleeve and peep
at the ace in the hole. Opposite me

the bearded poet raises on two kings. *In my country
we do this.* But my country sends giant
underwater tanks to massacre and I have
another queen. The queens are in love
with each other and spurn kings, diamonds
or not. A quiet man coughs and deals. Wheels

within wheels within worlds without words.
I get a second ace and raise
my eyebrows imperceptibly. A submarine drones on
amongst dolphins. Fifty and raise you fifty
for *the final card*. The cat is nervous as

Henry tells me any second the room could explode
and we would not know. Jim has three jacks
but I have three queens, two aces and a full house.
Perhaps any moment my full house might explode
though I will not know. Remember
one of us is just about to win. God.
God this is an awful game.

Borrowed Memory

He remembers running to the nets, in early summer,
in his cricket whites. Then there's a blur
until he's at high tea, with Harry Wharton and the rest,
in Study No. 5. What larks they had, what fun
the long terms were.

                She remembers skating on the pond
and how she laughed when Jo and Laurie slipped
upon the ice. A Christmas tree. Sitting by the fire
whilst sipping hot rum punch. But sleepy,
so the picture's not quite clear.

                        Or was it
at a midnight feast? A bite of sardine sandwich,
then of cake until you felt quite ill. He's positive
he won the rugger prize, can see the fellows' faces
as they cheered him on.

                    On their shelves
the honour of the school has gathered dust.
These fictions are as much a part of them
as fact, for if you said *Are you quite sure
of this?* they would insist.

                  As, watching demonstrations
on the box, they see themselves in shelters by the candlelight,
with tons of tuck to see them through. Fair Play Bob
and Good Egg Sue have nursed their fantasies for years.
And they will make them true.

Shooting Stars

After I no longer speak they break our fingers
to salvage my wedding ring. Rebecca Rachel Ruth
Aaron Emmanuel David, stars on all our brows
beneath the gaze of men with guns. Mourn for the daughters,

upright as statues, brave. You would not look at me.
You waited for the bullet. Fell. I say Remember.
Remember these appalling days which make the world
forever bad. One saw I was alive. Loosened

his belt. My bowels opened in a ragged gape of fear.
Between the gap of corpses I could see a child.
The soldiers laughed. Only a matter of days separate
this from acts of torture now. They shot her in the eye.

How would you prepare to die, on a perfect April evening
with young men gossiping and smoking by the graves?
My bare feet felt the earth and urine trickled
down my legs until I heard the click. Not yet. A trick.

After immense suffering someone takes tea on the lawn.
After the terrible moans a boy washes his uniform.
After the history lesson children run to their toys the world
turns in its sleep the spades shovel soil Sara Ezra . . .

Sister, if seas part us do you not consider me?
Tell them I sang the ancient psalms at dusk
inside the wire and strong men wept. Turn thee
unto me with mercy, for I am desolate and lost.

The B Movie

At a preview of That Hagen Story *in 1947, when actor Ronald Reagan became the first person on screen to say 'I love you, will you marry me?' to the nineteen-year-old Shirley Temple, there was such a cry of 'Oh, no!' from the invited audience that the scene was cut out when the film was released.*

Lap dissolve. You make a man speak crap dialogue,
one day he'll make you eat your words. OK?
Let's go for a take. Where's the rest of me? *'Oh, no!'*

Things are different now. He's got star billing,
star wars, applause. Takes her in his arms.
I'm talking about a *real* weepie. Freeze frame. *'Oh, no!'*

On his say-so, the train wipes out the heroine
and there ain't no final reel. How do you like that?
My fellow Americans, we got five minutes. *'Oh, no!'*

Classic. He holds the onion to water such sorrow.
We need a Kleenex the size of Russia here, no kidding.
Have that kid's tail any time he wants to. *Yup.*

The Dolphins

World is what you swim in, or dance, it is simple.
We are in our element but we are not free.
Outside this world you cannot breathe for long.
The other has my shape. The other's movement
forms my thoughts. And also mine. There is a man
and there are hoops. There is a constant flowing guilt.

We have found no truth in these waters,
no explanations tremble on our flesh.
We were blessed and now we are not blessed.
After travelling such space for days we began
to translate. It was the same space. It is
the same space always and above it is the man.

And now we are no longer blessed, for the world
will not deepen to dream in. The other knows
and out of love reflects me for myself.
We see our silver skin flash by like memory
of somewhere else. There is a coloured ball
we have to balance till the man has disappeared.

The moon has disappeared. We circle well-worn grooves
of water on a single note. Music of loss forever
from the other's heart which turns my own to stone.
There is a plastic toy. There is no hope. We sink
to the limits of this pool until the whistle blows.
There is a man and our mind knows we will die here.

Someone Else's Daughter

Scratching at the air *(There's nothing there)*
she is snowing constantly, coming to bits, she chips
at her smooth, white arms with needles. Her kitten laps
at a glass of cold blood and stares reproachfully
straight to the centre of her pinned blue eyes.

Beneath the skin, small volcanoes sigh and draw in fire.
She covers them with make-up, itches, slopes out.
Herpes and hepatitis set off on their journey
from the mind to elsewhere. No Surrender.
Cunt and liver erupt as the thin hand shoplifts.

On the wall of the waiting-room a snake eats itself,
tail first. This is your last chance. *I know.*
Why do you do this? *I don't know.* She smokes
a trembling chain of cancer cells. She devours everything.
She drains the listener. She is eating herself tail first.

One day there will be nothing left for those
who love her. She will shrink to a childhood snapshot
as someone else's daughter moves into the squat.
She will shrink to an earlier memory. A child
gobbling so many Easter eggs she was sick for a week.

A Healthy Meal

The gourmet tastes the secret dreams of cows
tossed lightly in garlic. Behind the green door, swish
of oxtails languish on an earthen dish. Here are
wishbones and pinkies; fingerbowls will absolve guilt.

Capped teeth chatter to a kidney or at the breast
of something which once flew. These hearts knew
no love and on their beds of saffron rice they lie
beyond reproach. What is the claret like? Blood.

On table six, the language of tongues is braised
in armagnac. The woman chewing suckling pig
must sleep with her husband later. Leg,
saddle and breast bleat against pure white cloth.

Alter *calf* to *veal* in four attempts. This is
the power of words; knife, tripe, lights, charcuterie.
A fat man orders his *rare* and a fine sweat
bastes his face. There are napkins to wipe the evidence

and sauces to gag the groans of abattoirs. The menu
lists the recent dead in French, from which they order
offal, poultry, fish. Meat flops in the jowls. Belch.
Death moves in the bowels. You are what you eat.

And Then What

Then with their hands they would break bread
wave choke phone thump thread

Then with their tired hands slump
at a table holding their head

Then with glad hands hold other hands
or stroke brief flesh in a kind bed

Then with their hands on the shovel
they would bury their dead.

Letters from Deadmen

Beneath the earth a perfect femur glows. I recall
a little pain and then a century of dust. Observe my anniversary,
place purple violets tenderly before the urn. You must.
No one can hear the mulching of the heart, which thrummed
with blood or drummed with love. Perhaps, by now,
your sadness will be less. Unless you still remember me.

I flung silver pigeons to grey air with secret messages
for men I had not met. Do they ever mention me
at work and was there weeping in the crematorium?
Dear wife, dear child, I hope you leave my room
exactly as it was. The pipe, the wireless and, of course,
the cricket photographs. They say we rest in peace.

Ash or loam. Scattered or slowly nagged by worms. I lie
above my parents in the family plot and I fit neatly
in a metal cask in ever-loving memory of myself.
*They parted his garments, casting lots upon them
what every man should take.* A crate of stout.
Small talk above the salmon sandwiches. Insurance men.

But here you cannot think. The voice-box imitates
the skeletons of leaves. Words snail imperceptibly and soundless
in the soil. Dear love, remember me. Give me biography
beyond these simple dates. Were there psalms and hired limousines?
All this eternally before my final breath and may
this find you as it leaves me here. Eventually.

The stars are filming us for no one.

Practising Being Dead

Your own ghost, you stand in dark rain
and light aches out from the windows
to lie in pools at your feet. This is the place.
Those are the big oak doors. Behind them
a waxed floor stretches away, backwards
down a corridor of years. The trees sigh.
You are both watching and remembering. Neither.

Inside, the past is the scent of candles the moment
they go out. You saw her, ancient and yellow,
laid out inside that alcove at the stairhead,
a broken string of water on her brow.
For weeks the game was Practising Being Dead,
hands in the praying position, eyes closed, lips
pressed to the colour of sellotape over the breath.

It is accidental and unbearable to recall that time,
neither bitter nor sweet but gone, the future
already lost as you open door after door, each one
peeling back a sepia room empty of promise.
This evening the sky has not enough moon
to give you a shadow. Nobody hears
your footsteps walking away along the gravel drive.

Dies Natalis

When I was cat, my mistress tossed me sweetmeats
from her couch. Even the soldiers were deferential –
she thought me sacred – I saw my sleek ghost
arch in their breastplates and I purred

my one eternal note beneath the shadow of pyramids.
The world then was measured by fine wires
which had their roots in my cat brain, trembled
for knowledge. She stroked my black pelt, singing

her different, frantic notes into my ear.
These were meanings I could not decipher. Later,
my vain, furred tongue erased a bowl of milk,
then I slept and fed on river rats . . .

She would throw pebbles at the soil, searching
with long, gold nails for logic in chaos;
or bathe at night in the moon's pool,
dissolving its light into wobbling pearls.

I was there, my collar of jewels and eyes shining,
my small heart impartial. Even now, at my spine's base,
the memory of a tail stirs idly, defining that night.
Cool breeze. Eucalyptus. Map of stars above

which told us nothing, randomly scattered like pebbles.
The man who feared me came at dawn, fought her
until she moaned into stillness, her ringed hand
with its pattern of death, palm up near my face.

*

Then a breath of sea air after blank decades,
my wings applauding this new shape. Far below,
the waves envied the sky, straining for blueness,
muttering in syllables of fish. I trod air, laughing,

what space was salt was safe. A speck became a ship,
filling its white sails like gulping lungs. Food swam.
I swooped, pincered the world in my beak, then soared
across the sun. The great whales lamented the past

wet years away, sending their bleak songs back
and forth between themselves. I hovered, listening,
as water slowly quenched fire. My cross on the surface
followed, marking where I was in the middle of nowhere . . .

Six days later found me circling the ship. Men's voices
came over the side in scraps. I warned patiently
in my private language, weighed down with loneliness.
Even the wind had dropped. The sea stood still,

flicked out its sharks, and the timber wheezed.
I could only be bird, as the wheel of the day turned slowly
between sun and moon. When night fell, it was stale,
unbearably quiet, holding the breath of the dead.

The egg was in my gut, nursing its own deaths
in a delicate shell. I remember its round weight
persistently pressing; opening my bowel onto the deck
near a young sailor, the harsh sound my cry made then.

*

But when I loved, I thought that was all I had done.
It was very ordinary, an ordinary place, the river
filthy, and with no sunset to speak of. She spoke
in a local accent, laughing at mine, kissed

with her tongue. This changed me. Christ, sweetheart,
marry me, I'll go mad. A dog barked. She ran off,
teasing, and back down the path came Happen you will . . .
Afterwards, because she asked, I told her my prospects,

branded her white neck. She promised herself
in exchange for a diamond ring. The sluggish water
shrugged past as we did it again. We whispered
false vows which would ruin our lives . . .

I cannot recall more pain. There were things one could buy
to please her, but she kept herself apart, spitefully
guarding the password. My body repelled her. Sweat.
Sinew. All that had to be hunched away in thin sheets.

We loathed in the same dull air till silver presents came,
our two hands clasping one knife to cut a stale cake. One day,
the letter. Surgery. When the treatment did not work,
she died. I cried over the wishbone body, wondering

what was familiar, watching myself from a long way off.
I carried the remains in an urn to the allotment,
trying to remember the feel of her, but it was years,
years, and what blew back in my face was grey ash, dust.

*

Now hushed voices say I have my mother's look.
Once again, there is light. The same light. I talk
to myself in shapes, though something is constantly changing
the world, rearranging the face which stares at mine.

Most of the time I am hungry, sucking on dry air
till it gives in, turning milky and warm. Sleep
is dreamless, but when I awake I have more
to contemplate. They are trying to label me,

translate me into the right word. My small sounds
bring a bitter finger to my mouth, a taste
which cannot help or comfort me. I recall
and release in a sigh the journey here . . .

The man and woman are different colours and I
am both of them. These strangers own me,
pass me between them chanting my new name. They wrap
and unwrap me, a surprise they want to have again,

mouthing their tickly love to my smooth, dark flesh.
The days are mosaic, telling a story for the years
to come. I suck my thumb. New skin thickens
on my skull, to keep the moments I have lived before

locked in. I will lose my memory, learn words
which barely stretch to cover what remains unsaid. Mantras
of consolation come from those who keep my portrait
in their eyes. And when they disappear, I cry.

Sanctuary

This morning you are not incurable, not yet, can walk
with your disease inside you, at its centre
your small pearl of hope, along the entrance path
where tall, cool pillars hold the sky. Ahead,
the archway, white, benevolent; calm doctors
who will dress you in clean robes. Now you cry
tears you have not wept for years. Relief.

Already, being here, you half believe, arriving
in Reception, acquiescent, giving your old clothes
up to the flames, giving your name. Thank you,
yes, yes, the anxious words like worry beads.
You will do as you are told, anything, accept
that the waters are holy, work wonders;
for a perfect fleshy shell exchange a golden ear.

You're sick. This placid world of thoughtful space,
philosophy, design, has taken you in. Forget.
Forget how you came here, what suffering
you endured to wait in the Circular Cure Centre
for a nurse, your heart reciting its own small number.
I want to be well, recall this treatment miles away,
pass pain on the street like a stranger. Please.

In the Library your shaking hand takes up a book,
thumbs miracles. These men were saved, prescriptions
scrawled upon their dreams. You read of venom,
oil, cream, a rooster's blood. Later your shadow
precedes you into the Chamber of Dreams. You'll dream
about yourself, chant your therapy as dawn arrives
with light for the blind stone eyes of statues.

Breathe in. Out. In. Sometimes you wake in darkness,
holding your own hand as if you will stay forever.
Think again. The months flew, that year in the Sanctuary
when you were cured. Remember a fool's face
pulling a tongue in a mirror, your dedication
carved in the Temple of Tributes. Its blatant lie
blushed on marble, one sunset as you died elsewhere.

An Old Atheist Places
His Last Bet

Ace in the hole; ten, jack, queen on the baize.
As far as I can see, you've got nothing, mate.
My old eyes are tired and it's getting late,
I have as many chips left as days.

Outside this window, a willow tree sways
in the evening breeze. Deal the cards. I wait
for a king as shadows lengthen; hesitate,
call the last bet. I think again, then raise.

Silence. I leave my card face down and stare
at the empty room. It is turning in space
slowly, sadly, and there is nothing there . . .

and opposite me, the dealer's vacant place
piled high with chips. We gamblers do not care,
win or lose. I turn the card, turn my poker face.

Strange Language in Night Fog

Not only the dark,
but a sudden mist also,
made where they walked an alien place.

Beasts moaned from nowhere,
the cows the moon would have,
and, to their left, the pond
had drowned itself.

They stopped,
wobbling on straight lines,
and watched the Common
playing hide-and-seek behind the fog.

A bush nipped out,
then disappeared again;
a tree stepped backwards.
Even their own hands
waved at their faces, teasing.

But it was a strange language,
spoken only yards away,
which turned the night into a dream;

although they told themselves
there must be a word for home,
if they only knew it.

I Live Here Now

I live here now, the place where the pond
was a doll's mirror and the trees were bits of twig.
I invented it, that wee dog barking
at the postman (an old soldier with one arm, still)
and the path of small grey pebbles
in the avenue of flowers. Tall daisies, buttercups.

It nearly got a prize, balanced on topsoil,
carried up to the Big Tent where grown-ups peered
over the rim of the world. *Highly Recommended.*
Being grown yourself was half a dream, warm breath
clouding the ruby tomatoes, a sudden
flash of sixpence on the bright green grass.

Come in. Take the window-seat. The clouds
are cotton wool on pipe-cleaners, cunningly placed,
which never rain. In the distance
you can see Pincushion Hill. That's me, waving,
at the top. I live here now
and sometimes wave back, over the fields, the years.

Homesick

When we love, when we tell ourselves we do,
we are pining for first love, somewhen,
before we thought of wanting it. When we rearrange
the rooms we end up living in, we are looking
for first light, the arrangement of light,

that time, before we knew to call it light.
Or talk of music, when we say
we cannot talk of it, but play again
C major, A flat minor, we are straining
for first sound, what we heard once,
then, in lost chords, wordless languages.

What country do we come from? This one?
The one where the sun burns
when we have night? The one
the moon chills; elsewhere, possible?

Why is our love imperfect,
music only echo of itself,
the light wrong?

We scratch in dust with sticks,
dying of homesickness
for when, where, what.

The Dummy

Balancing me with your hand up my back, listening
to the voice you gave me croaking for truth, you keep
me at it. Your lips don't move, but your eyes look
desperate as hell. Ask me something difficult.

Maybe we could sing together? Just teach me
the right words, I learn fast. Don't stare like that.
I'll start where you leave off. I can't tell you
anything if you don't throw me a cue line. We're dying

a death right here. Can you dance? No. I don't suppose
you'd be doing this if you could dance. Right? Why do you
keep me in that black box? I can ask questions too,
you know. I can see that worries you. Tough.

So funny things happen to everyone on the way to most places.
Come on. You can do getter than that, can't you?

Model Village

See the cows placed just so on the green hill.
Cows say *Moo*. The sheep look like little clouds,
don't they? Sheep say *Baa*. Grass is green
and the pillar-box is red. Wouldn't it be strange
if grass were red? This is the graveyard
where the villagers bury their dead. Miss Maiden
lives opposite in her cottage. She has a cat.
The cat says *Miaow.* What does Miss Maiden say?

*I poisoned her but no one knows. Mother, I said,
drink your tea. Arsenic. Four sugars. He waited
years for me, but she had more patience. One day,
he didn't come back. I looked in the mirror,
saw her grey hair, her lips of reproach. I found
the idea in a paperback. I loved him, you see,
who never so much as laid a finger. Perhaps now
you've learnt your lesson, she said, pouring
another cup. Yes, Mother, yes. Drink it all up.*

The white fence around the farmyard
looks as though it's smiling. The hens are tidying
the yard. Hens say *Cluck* and give us eggs. Pigs
are pink and give us sausages. *Grunt*, they say.
Wouldn't it be strange if hens laid sausages?
Hee-haw, says the donkey. The farmhouse
is yellow and shines brightly in the sun. Notice
the horse. Horses say *Neigh*. What does the Farmer say?

*To tell the truth, it haunts me. I'm a simple man,
not given to fancy. The flock was ahead of me,
the dog doing his job like a good 'un. Then
I saw it. Even the animals stiffened in fright. Look,
I understand the earth, treat death and birth
the same. A fistful of soil tells me plainly
what I need to know. You plant, you grow, you reap.
But since then, sleep has been difficult. When I shovel
deep down, I'm searching for something. Digging, desperately.*

There's the church and there's the steeple.
Open the door and there are the people. Pigeons
roost in the church roof. Pigeons say *Coo*.
The church bells say *Ding-dong*, calling
the faithful to worship. What God says
can be read in the Bible. See the postman's dog
waiting patiently outside church. *Woof*, he says.
Amen, say the congregation. What does Vicar say?

*Now they have all gone, I shall dress up
as a choirboy. I have shaved my legs. How smooth
they look. Smooth, pink knees. If I am not good,
I shall deserve punishment. Perhaps the choirmistress
will catch me smoking behind the organ. A good boy
would own up. I am naughty. I can feel
the naughtiness under my smock. Smooth, pink naughtiness.
The choirmistress shall wear boots and put me
over her lap. I tremble and dissolve into childhood.*

Quack, say the ducks on the village pond. Did you
see the frog? Frogs say *Croak*. The village-folk shop
at the butcher's, the baker's, the candlestick maker's.
The Grocer has a parrot. Parrots say *Pretty Polly*
and *Who's a pretty boy then?* The Vicar is nervous
of parrots, isn't he? Miss Maiden is nervous
of Vicar and the Farmer is nervous of everything.
The library clock says *Tick-tock*. What does the Librarian say?

Ssssh. I've seen them come and go over the years,
my ears tuned for every whisper. This place
is a refuge, the volumes breathing calmly
on their still shelves. I glide between them
like a doctor on his rounds, know their cases. Tomes
do no harm, here I'm safe. Outside is chaos,
lives with no sense of plot. Behind each front door
lurks truth, danger. I peddle fiction. Believe
you me, the books in everyone's head are stranger . . .

The Brink of Shrieks

for S.B.

Don't ask me how, but I've fetched up
living with him. You can laugh. It's no joke
from where I'm sitting. Up to the back teeth.

That *walk*. You feel ashamed going out. So-and-so's
method of perambulation, he calls it. My arse.
Thank God for plastic hips. He'll be queuing.

And the *language*. What can you say? Nothing.
Those wee stones make me want to brain him,
so they do. They're only the tip of the iceberg.

Time who stopped? says I. Ash-grey vests,
you try cleaning them. Heartbreaking. Too many nights
lying in yon ditch, counting. God's truth, I *boil*.

See him, he's not uttered a peep in weeks.
And me? I'm on the brink of shrieks.

Recognition

Things get away from one.
I've let myself go, I know.
Children? I've had three
and don't even know them.

I strain to remember a time
when my body felt lighter.
Years. My face is swollen
with regrets. I put powder on,

but it flakes off. I love him,
through habit, but the proof
has evaporated. He gets upset.
I tried to do all the essentials

on one trip. Foolish, yes,
but I was weepy all morning.
Quiche. A blond boy swung me up
in his arms and promised the earth.

You see, this came back to me
as I stood on the scales.
I wept. Shallots. In the window,
creamy ladies held a pose

which left me clogged and old.
The waste. I'd forgotten my purse,
fumbled; the shopgirl gaped at me,
compassionless. Claret. I blushed.

Cheese. Kleenex. *It did happen.*
I lay in my slip on wet grass,
laughing. Years. I had to rush out,
blind in a hot flush, and bumped

into an anxious, dowdy matron
who touched the cold mirror
and stared at me. Stared
and said I'm sorry sorry sorry.

Absolutely

Thank you. Yes please. After you. Don't mind
my asking this, but is politeness strange?
Don't mention it. What do you think yourself?

The politeness of strangers worries me,
like surgical gloves. Irrational, I know.
Nasties in childhood or the woodshed.

How very interesting. Magritte opened the door
to a journalist, politely bowed him in, then
booted him up the arse right across the room.

And How Are We Today?

The little people in the radio are picking on me
again. It is sunny, but they are going to make it
rain. I do not like their voices, they have voices
like cold tea with skin on. I go O O O.

The flowers are plastic. There is all dust
on the petals. I go Ugh. Real flowers die,
but at least they are a comfort to us all.
I know them by name, listen. Rose. Tulip. Lily.

I live inside someone else's head. He hears me
with his stethoscope, so it is no use
sneaking home at five o'clock to his nice house
because I am in his ear going Breathe Breathe.

I might take my eye out and swallow it
to bring some attention to myself. Winston did.
His name was in the paper. For the time being
I make noises to annoy them and then I go BASTARDS.

Psychopath

I run my metal comb through the D.A. and pose
my reflection between dummies in the window at Burton's.
Lamp light. Jimmy Dean. All over town, ducking and diving,
my shoes scud sparks against the night. She is in the canal.
Let me make myself crystal. With a good-looking girl crackling
in four petticoats, you feel like a king. She rode past me
on a wooden horse, laughing, and the air sang *Johnny,
Remember Me*. I turned the world faster, flash.

I don't talk much. I swing up beside them and do it
with my eyes. Brando. She was clean. I could smell her.
I thought, Here we go, old son. The fairground spun round us
and she blushed like candyfloss. You can woo them
with goldfish and coconuts, whispers in the Tunnel of Love.
When I zip up the leather, I'm in a new skin, I touch it
and love myself, sighing *Some little lady's going to get lucky
tonight*. My breath wipes me from the looking-glass.

We move from place to place. We leave on the last morning
with the scent of local girls on our fingers. They wear
our lovebites on their necks. I know what women want,
a handrail to Venus. She said *Please* and *Thank you*
to the toffee-apple, teddy-bear. I thought I was on, no error.
She squealed on the dodgems, clinging to my leather sleeve.
I took a swig of whisky from the flask and frenched it
down her throat. *No*, she said, *Don't*, like they always do.

Dirty Alice flicked my dick out when I was twelve.
She jeered. I nicked a quid and took her to the spinney.
I remember the wasps, the sun blazing as I pulled
her knickers down. I touched her and I went hard,
but she grabbed my hand and used that, moaning . . .
She told me her name on the towpath, holding the fish
in a small sack of water. We walked away from the lights.
She'd come too far with me now. She looked back, once.

A town like this would kill me. A gypsy read my palm.
She saw fame. I could be anything with my looks,
my luck, my brains. I bought a guitar and blew a smoke ring
at the moon. Elvis nothing. *I'm not that type*, she said.
Too late. I eased her down by the dull canal
and talked sexy. Useless. She stared at the goldfish, silent.
I grabbed the plastic bag. She cried as it gasped and wriggled
on the grass and here we are. A dog craps by a lamp post.

Mama, straight up, I hope you rot in hell. The old man
sloped off, sharpish. I saw her through the kitchen window.
The sky slammed down on my school cap, chicken licken.
Lady, Sweetheart, Princess I say now, but I never stay.
My sandwiches were near her thigh, then the Rent Man
lit her cigarette and I ran, ran . . . She is in the canal.
These streets are quiet, as if the town has held its breath
to watch the Wheel go round above the dreary homes.

No, don't. Imagine. One thump did it, then I was on her,
giving her everything I had. Jack the Lad, Ladies' Man.
Easier to say Yes. Easier to stay a child, wide-eyed
at the top of the helter-skelter. You get one chance in this life
and if you screw it you're done for, uncle, no mistake.
She lost a tooth. I picked her up, dead slim, and slid her in.
A girl like that should have a paid-up solitaire and high hopes,
but she asked for it. A right-well knackered outragement.

My reflection sucks a sour Woodbine and buys me a drink. Here's
looking at you. Deep down I'm talented. She found out. Don't mess
with me, angel, I'm no nutter. Over in the corner, a dead ringer
for Ruth Ellis smears a farewell kiss on the lip of a gin-and-lime.
The barman calls Time. Bang in the centre of my skull,
there's a strange coolness. I could almost fly. Tomorrow
will find me elsewhere, with a loss of memory. Drink up son,
the world's your fucking oyster. Awopbopaloobop alopbimbam.

Every Good Boy

I put this breve down, knowing in my head
the sound it makes before I play a note.
C sharp is D flat, changing if I place it here,
or here, or there. Listen. I mostly use a minor key.

These days, the world lacks harmony. The inner cities
riot in my inner ear. *Discord*, say the critics,
but that is what I hear; even in this quiet room
where I deploy blatant consecutive fifths, a hooligan.

That time I was mugged, I came back here
and sat for hours in silence. I have only ever wanted
to compose. The world strikes me and I make
my sound. I make no claim to greatness.

If they were caught, I would like half an hour
together, to show how this phrase, here, excites;
how the smash of broken glass is turned
into a new motif. I would like to share that with them.

Yes, Officer

It was about the time of day you mention, yes.
I remember noticing the quality of light
beyond the bridge. I lit a cigarette.

I saw some birds. I knew the words for them
and their collective noun. A skein of geese. This cell
is further away from anywhere I've ever been. Perhaps.

I was in love. *For God's sake, don't.*
Fear is the first taste of blood in a dry mouth.
I have no alibi. Yes, I used to have a beard.

No, no. I wouldn't use that phrase. The more you ask
the less I have to say. There was a woman crying
on the towpath, dressed in grey. *Please.* Sir.

Without my own language, I am a blind man
in the wrong house. Here come the fists, the boots.
I curl in a corner, uttering empty vowels until

they have their truth. That is my full name.
With my good arm I sign a forgery. Yes, Officer,
I did. I did and these, your words, admit it.

Statement

It happened like this. I shall never forget. Da
was drunk again, came in from the yard
with his clenched face like a big fist, leaving
the back door open . . . that low moon, full
and dangerous, at the end of the close. *Jesus Christ*,
he said, *I'd be better dead*, picked up the old clock
from the mantelpiece and flung it on the fire.

It burned till morning came. He kept her up
all night, shouting the bad bits over again
till she put her head in her hands and wept.
Her apron was a map of Ireland. He jabbed
his finger to the North, bruising her breast, yelled
There! There! God's truth, she tried to kiss him,
though Tom's near 21 and that was the last time.

Then she starts . . . *In the warfare against the devil,
the world, and the flesh, on whom must we depend?* . . .
and he's ripped the floorboard up. No chance. Her face
was at the window when they got him, watching him
dance for the Queen's men, sweating blood
doing it. I came running down, said *Mammy,
Mammy,* and she turned with her arms like the crucifix.

Money Talks

I am the authentic language of suffering. My cold, gold eye
does not blink. Mister, you want nice time? No problem.
I say *Screw You*. I buy and sell the world. I got
Midas touch, turn bread to hard cash. My million tills
sing through the night, my shining mad machines.
I stink and accumulate. Do you fancy me, lady? Really?

See me pass through the eye of a needle! Whoopee,
I cut Time dead with my sleek facelift. I travel
faster than $-sound. Don't give me away; after all, no one
can eat me. Honey, I'm a jealous God, $-stammering
my one commandment on the calculator. *Love me.*
Under your fingernails I smile up with my black grin.

Don't let my oily manner bother you, Sir, I'll get you
a taxi, get you a limousine. I know a place
where it's raining dollar bills. I got any currency
you want, women and gigolos, metal tuxedos. The party
is one long gold-toothed scream. Have a good day. I am
the big bombs, sighing in their thick lead sheaths OK.

Selling Manhattan

All yours, Injun, twenty-four bucks' worth of glass beads,
gaudy cloth. I got myself a bargain. I brandish
fire-arms and fire-water. Praise the Lord.
Now get your red ass out of here.

I wonder if the ground has anything to say.
You have made me drunk, drowned out
the world's slow truth with rapid lies.
But today I hear again and plainly see. Wherever
you have touched the earth, the earth is sore.

I wonder if the spirit of the water has anything
to say. That you will poison it. That you
can no more own the rivers and the grass than own
the air. I sing with true love for the land;
dawn chant, the song of sunset, starlight psalm.

Trust your dreams. No good will come of this.
My heart is on the ground, as when my loved one
fell back in my arms and died. I have learned
the solemn laws of joy and sorrow, in the distance
between morning's frost and firefly's flash at night.

Man who fears death, how many acres do you need
to lengthen your shadow under the endless sky?
Last time, this moment, now, a boy feels his freedom
vanish, like the salmon going mysteriously
out to sea. Loss holds the silence of great stones.

I will live in the ghost of grasshopper and buffalo.

The evening trembles and is sad.
A little shadow runs across the grass
and disappears into the darkening pines.

Politico

Corner of Thistle Street, two slack shillings jangled
in his pocket. Wee Frank. Politico. A word in the right
got things moving. *A free beer for they dockers
and the guns will come through in the morning. No bother.*

Bread rolls and Heavy came up the rope to the window
where he and McShane were making a stand. *Someone
sent up a megaphone, for Christ's sake.* Occupation.
Aye. And the soldiers below just biding their time.

Blacklisted. Bar L. *That scunner, Churchill.* The Clyde
where men cheered theirselves out of work as champagne
butted a new ship. Spikes at the back of the toilet seat.
Alls I'm doing is fighting for wur dignity. Away.

*Smoke-filled rooms? Wait till I tell you . . . Listen,
I'm ten years dead and turning in my urn. Socialism?
These days?* There's the tree that never grew. *Och,
a shower of shites.* There's the bird that never flew.

Scraps

That Thursday, it seemed they were part of the rain,
a drizzling chain,
men and women, colourless,
stretching down Renshaw Street.

This was a B movie,
grainy black-and-white,
with *Buddy, Can You Spare a Dime*
thin on the soundtrack.

Breeze from the river
scuffed litter round their shoes,
one scrap an old pound note
no one could spend.

A cat pissed on the steps of Renshaw Hall.

Scraps. Scraps. Scraps of language
mashed in a scum
above the sluggish drains.

There's nothing down for us.
Enough to make you be a bloody copper.
What's the time?

UB40. Giro.
Words had died a death.
DHSS.

Under the dripping phone wires
under the slumping clouds
a stunted man went down the line.
Help on a rusty harmonica
snagged by the wind.

And overhead
the seagulls
calling their bleak farewells to the old ships.
Nowhere to go, nothing to do
but circle the city's black grooves,
repeating its past like a scratched LP.

Nobody's famous
here and now.
The cracks in the cathedral widen.
Kids chase dragons through the drab estates,
accomplished fire-eaters.

All My Loving. Three feet from the ground
his faced peered up.
You must be joking, pal.
Everybody's breath fumed in the air.

Cats and dogs.
The line moved on.

A woman threw a silver shilling at a dwarf.

Stealing

The most unusual thing I ever stole? A snowman.
Midnight. He looked magnificent; a tall, white mute
beneath the winter moon. I wanted him, a mate
with a mind as cold as the slice of ice
within my own brain. I started with the head.

Better off dead than giving in, not taking
what you want. He weighed a ton; his torso,
frozen stiff, hugged to my chest, a fierce chill
piercing my gut. Part of the thrill was knowing
that children would cry in the morning. Life's tough.

Sometimes I steal things I don't need. I joy-ride cars
to nowhere, break into houses just to have a look.
I'm a mucky ghost, leave a mess, maybe pinch a camera.
I watch my gloved hand twisting the doorknob.
A stranger's bedroom. Mirrors. I sigh like this – *Aah*.

It took some time. Reassembled in the yard,
he didn't look the same. I took a run
and booted him. Again. Again. My breath ripped out
in rags. It seems daft now. Then I was standing
alone amongst lumps of snow, sick of the world.

Boredom. Mostly I'm so bored I could eat myself.
One time, I stole a guitar and thought I might
learn to play. I nicked a bust of Shakespeare once,
flogged it, but the snowman was strangest.
You don't understand a word I'm saying, do you?

Translation

All writing is garbage – Artaud

She wore gloves, red to the elbow, sipped
at a dry martini, dry-eyed, said *I have come
to confess. Do you want my love?* The old cathedral
exploded into bells, scattering gulls at the sky
like confetti. But no wedding. Then? The hunchback
swung on the one-armed bandit, slack eyes following
bright uneatable fruit, cranking *Bugger bugger bugger*
from stale breath. Later she held a dun root
on a scarlet palm, real satin, her lover's eyes
dark as a bell-tower, mouth bruising O O on the night.
When he pushed into her it was the gambler, crippled,
she invented. Lick me from the navel outwards
darkly in damp circles tell me strange half-truths
from your strange mind babe babe baby.

Colours by Someone Else

Sweetheart, this evening your smell is all around
down by the fishing-boats, the sky trembling

above the pier. Your tears have dried on my palms.
Darling, we should never have done that.

You made me your own, painted my face
into smithereens. Who can say where my tongue

has been in your dark boudoir? Soft heelprints
on my shoulder, sound of the hummingbird breathing its last.

Regret is in the air. Dante Gabriel Rossetti
saved his poems from her worms. Long hours

turning the rain to whisky. Weeping spectacles.
The landlord sees me mime Sinatra at the bar.

Sweetheart, are you listening? Pay heed
for I am insane on the underground, burning

the crossword with my eyes. I owe money
to a bowler hat, keep a brick from London Bridge

under the bed. We are drowning twice nightly
in rivers of silk. This is the Year of the Tiger.

Hush. There is no end to my love for you, for I
have eaten the owl's egg, endured the sharpening of spoons.

When you see me in my uniform, act unconcerned.
The pin and pomegranate will suffice to show

the workings of my mind. I am up to my eyes
in onions. Sweetheart. Undress and read this.

Three Paintings

1 The One-Eyed Flautist Plays for the Prince

Minims have one eye, crotchets, breves . . . quavers wink
with a quick wit. My one eye sees this, my good eye
can shape the invisible from inked-in rosaries.
For the glory of God's blind angels, liquid pearls.

So. You find me difficult. Your gaze drops
to the floor, you fumble awkwardly. I pause, staring,
notice your mistress, Highness, edge from the scene,
though her own ghost rustles on my darker side.

Stuff your discomfiture. I cover my flute's six eyes
till they fill with dreams beyond this brief audition.
I am only a moment away from bliss, the note
which almost bestows a kiss you cannot imagine.

As for the rest, call it unfortunate. Her punishment
was worse, whose sweet face then is locked forever
in my inner eye. I would suffer as much today
to see her see me whole. Now let me play.

2 *The Virgin Punishing the Infant*

He spoke early. Not the *goo goo goo* of infancy,
but *I am God*. Joseph kept away, carving himself
a silent Pinocchio out in the workshed. He said
he was a simple man and hadn't dreamed of this.

She grew anxious in that second year, would stare
at stars saying *Gabriel? Gabriel?* Your guess.
The village gossiped in the sun. The child was solitary,
his wide and solemn eyes could fill your head.

After he walked, our normal children crawled. Our wives
were first resentful, then superior. Mary's child
would bring her sorrow . . . better far to have a son
who gurgled nonsense at your breast. *Googoo. Googoo.*

But I am God. We heard him through the window,
heard the smacks which made us peep. What we saw
was commonplace enough. But afterwards, we wondered
why the infant did not cry. And why the Mother did.

3 *Jane Avril Dancing*

What you staring at? Buy me a bleeding drink! Jane Avril
yelled in rough red French for more wine, her mind
in a pool on the table. She had seen better days.

Me, I thought her lovely still. I am a man susceptible
to beauty. Sometimes she sang to her own reflection.
Some love song. Even her dress seemed grubbily sad.

. . . sweetest lips, I want to taste you,
something la la la embrace you . . .

But I had my own problems, that winter of absinthe,
impotence, Paris empty and the bitch off with Dufy.
I loved her almost as much as she thought I did.

Jane was a pale motif on darker shades, and I
a shadow of my former self, when she returned.
She gave me a flower and whispered *Love me. Darling.*

What is joy? I keep the petals. She promised everything
that afternoon, though what I remember now is the look
which only she could throw and *la la la* Jane Avril, dancing.

Mouth, with Soap

She didn't shit, she *soiled* or *had a soil*
and didn't piss, *passed water.* Saturday night,
when the neighbours were fucking, she *submitted
to intercourse* and, though she didn't sweat cobs then,
later she *perspired.* Jesus wept. Bloody Nora. *Language!*

She was a deadly assassin as far as
words went. Slit-eyed, thin-lipped, she
bleached and boiled the world. No Fs or Cs,
Ps and Qs minded, oh aye. She did not bleed,
had *Women's Trouble* locked in the small room, mutely.

In the beginning was The Word and, close behind,
The Censor, clacking a wooden tongue. Watch out
for the tight vocabulary of living death. *Wash out
your mouth with soap.* She hoovered on Sundays, always,
a constant drizzle in her heart; below it *The Big C*, growing.

Big Sue and *Now, Voyager*

Her face is a perfect miniature on wide, smooth flesh,
a tiny fossil in a slab of stone. Most evenings
Big Sue is Bette Davis. Alone. The curtains drawn.
The TV set an empty head which has the same
recurring dream. Mushrooms taste of kisses. Sherry trifle
is a honeymoon. *Be honest. Who'd love me?*

Paul Henreid. He lights two cigarettes and, gently,
puts one in her mouth. The little flat in Tooting
is a floating ship. Violins. Big Sue drawing deeply
on a chocolate stick. *Now, Voyager depart. Much,
much for thee is yet in store.* Her eyes are wider,
bright. The previous video unspools the sea.

This is where she lives, the wrong side of the glass
in black-and-white. To press the rewind,
replay, is to know perfection. Certainty. The soundtrack
drowns out daytime echoes. *Size of her. Great cow.*
Love is never distanced into memory, persists
unchanged. Oscar-winners looking at the sky.

Why wish for the moon? Outside the window night falls,
slender women rush to meet their dates. Men whistle
on the dark blue streets at shapes they want
or, in the pubs, light cigarettes for two. Big Sue
unwraps a Mars Bar, crying at her favourite scene.
The bit where Bette Davis says *We have the stars.*

All Days Lost Days

Living
in and out of the past,
inexplicably
so many things have died
in me.

In and out like a tide,
each tear
holds a tiny hologram.
Even this early
I am full of years.

Here are the little gravestones
where memory
stands in the wild grass,
watching the future
arrive in a line of big black cars.

All days
lost days, in and out of themselves
between dreaming
and dreaming again and half-
remembering.

Foreign

Imagine living in a strange, dark city for twenty years.
There are some dismal dwellings on the east side
and one of them is yours. On the landing, you hear
your foreign accent echo down the stairs. You think
in a language of your own and talk in theirs.

Then you are writing home. The voice in your head
recites the letter in a local dialect; behind that
is the sound of your mother singing to you,
all that time ago, and now you do not know
why your eyes are watering and what's the word for this.

You use the public transport. Work. Sleep. Imagine one night
you saw a name for yourself sprayed in red
against a brick wall. A hate name. Red like blood.
It is snowing on the streets, under the neon lights,
as if this place were coming to bits before your eyes.

And in the delicatessen, from time to time, the coins
in your palm will not translate. Inarticulate,
because this is not home, you point at fruit. Imagine
that one of you says *Me not know what these people mean.
It like they only go to bed and dream.* Imagine that.

Postcards

It was a courtship of postcards
which linked the love in London
to the love in Lancashire, franking-machines
pressing their ink kisses
over her name.

She was adored
by the sender of Renoir's summer women,
Grimshaw's rainy streets,
the Clouseau fan against the Beumb.
I miss you, L.

Some days the weather
had been moved to tears
by landscape,
like the view from Heptonstall,
blurring the words.

My Darling . . . when . . .

Or she laughed at the moustache
upon the Mona Lisa,
kept Mae West a week
upon the mantelpiece
asking her up.

A white card
with A Hole to See the Sky Through,
nothing else, arrived
and, mirror-written on the back,
.THGINOT EM ENOHP

Three words in a thought bubble
from Chairman Mao
reiterated Ronald Reagan's words
once more with feeling. Even
Thatcher loved her.

O'Keeffe. Picasso. Donald McGill.
The last one
was a photograph of Rodin's Kiss
without a stamp
and wishing she were here.

Correspondents

When you come on Thursday, bring me a letter. We have
the language of stuffed birds, teacups. We don't have
the language of bodies. My husband will be here.
I shall inquire after your wife, stirring his cup
with a thin spoon and my hand shall not tremble.
Give me the letter as I take your hat. Mention
the cold weather. My skin burns at the sight of you.

We skim the surface, gossip. I baked this cake and you
eat it. Words come from nowhere, drift off
like the smoke from his pipe. Beneath my dress, my breasts
swell for your lips, belly churns to be stilled
by your brown hands. This secret life is Gulliver,
held down by strings of pleasantries. I ache. Later
your letter flares up in the heat and is gone.

Dearest Beloved, pretend I am with you . . . I read
your dark words and do to myself things
you can only imagine. I hardly know myself.
Your soft, white body in my arms . . . When we part,
you kiss my hand, bow from the waist, all passion
patiently restrained. *Your servant, Ma'am.* Now you write
wild phrases of love. The words blur as I cry out once.

Next time we meet, in drawing-room or garden,
passing our letters cautiously between us, our eyes
fixed carefully on legal love, think of me here
on my marriage-bed an hour after you've left.
I have called your name over and over in my head
at the point your fiction brings me to. I have kissed
your sweet name on the paper as I knelt by the fire.

Telegrams

URGENT WHEN WE MEET COMPLETE STRANGERS DEAR STOP
THOUGH I COUNT THE HOURS TILL YOU ARE NEAR STOP
WILL EXPLAIN LATER DATE TILL THEN CANT WAIT STOP C

COMPLETELY FOGGED WHAT DO YOU MEAN BABY? STOP
CANT WE SLOPE OFF TO MY PLACE MAYBE? STOP
NOT POSS ACT NOT MET WITH RAISON DETRE STOP B

FOR GODS SAKE JUST TRUST ME SWEETHEART STOP
HATCH IT HURTS ME TOO WHEN WERE APART STOP
SHIT WILL HIT FAN UNLESS STICK TO PLAN STOP C

SHIT? FAN? TRUST? WHATS GOING ON HONEY? STOP
IF THIS IS A JOKE IT ISNT FUNNY STOP
INSIST ON TRUTH LOVE YOU BUT STRUTH! STOP B

YES I KNOW DARLING I LOVE YOU TOO STOP
TRY TO SEE PREDIC FROM MY POINT OF VIEW STOP
IF YOU DONT PLAY BALL I WONT COME AT ALL STOP C

PLEASE REPLY LAST TELEGRAM STOP
HAVE YOU FORGOTTEN THAT NIGHT IN MATLOCK? C

NO WAS TRYING TO TEACH YOU LESSON PET STOP
ALSO BECAUSE OF THESE AM IN DEBT STOP
TRUST WHEN NEXT MEET WILL PASSIONATELY GREET STOP B

NO NO NO NO GET IT THROUGH YOUR THICK HEAD STOP
IF SEEN WITH YOU AM AS GOOD AS DEAD STOP
THE WIFE WILL GUESS WEVE BEEN HAVING SEX STOP C

SO YOURE MARRIED? HA! I MIGHT HAVE GUESSED STOP
THOUGHT IT ODD YOU WORE STRING VEST STOP
AS SOON AS I MET YOU I WENT OVER THE TOP
NOW DO ME A FAVOUR PLEASE PLEASE STOP STOP B

Telephoning Home

I hear your voice saying *Hello* in that guarded way
you have, as if you fear bad news, imagine you
standing in our dark hall, waiting, as my silver coin
jams in the slot and frantic bleeps repeat themselves
along the line until your end goes slack. The wet platform
stretches away from me towards the South and home.

I try again, dial the nine numbers you wrote once
on a postcard. The stranger waiting outside stares
through the glass that isn't there, a sad portrait
someone abandoned. I close my eyes . . . *Hello?* . . . see myself
later this evening, two hundred miles and two hours nearer
where I want to be. *I love you.* This is me speaking.

Space, Space

1 Searching for Moons

There is something to be said but I, for one,
forget. That star went out more years ago
than we can count. Its ghosts see dinosaurs.

The brain says *No* to the Universe, *Prove it*,
but the heart is susceptible, pining for a look,
a kind word. Some are brought to their knees,

pleading in dead language at a deaf ear. Spaceships
float in nothing in the dark, searching for moons
to worship with their fish eyes. It must be love.

2 Astronomer

In love with space, stares up
as breath smokes signals into night.
Light years, loneliness, dark waves

lapping moons. From there sees absences,
gone worlds; from here perceives
new galaxies where nowhere is.

Lovesick

I found an apple.
A red and shining apple.
I took its photograph.

I hid the apple in the attic.
I opened the skylight
and the sun said *Ah!*

At night, I checked that it was safe,
under the giggling stars,
the sly moon. My cool apple.

Whatever you are calling about,
I am not interested.
Go away. You with the big teeth.

Strange Place

I watch you undress by household candlelight.
We are having an early night. On the wireless
news from other countries half distracts me.

Each small movement makes a longer shadow
on the wall. I lie here quietly as garments fall.
A faint voice talks of weather somewhere else.

But we are here and now, listening to nothing blindly,
where there is no news or weather. Love, later,
I will feel homesick for this strange place.

Only Dreaming

A ghost loves you, has got inside you in the dark.
Whose face does he wear? He changes his features
all night whilst you tell yourself you're dreaming,
only dreaming, but he puts his tongue in your mouth.
Yes, you say in your sleep to nothing, *Darling.*
He wears a dead face, a woman's face, you fold
into yourself and feel her breasts, talk gibberish.

You tell no one of this unfaithfulness in the small hours.
The ghost is devoted, stares into your eyes behind the lids.
This is the real thing. He has turned your face
to the pillow, mouth open, breathing his warm breath
for him. Name him. Say it. Come on, c'mon.
Your hands grasp him, pass straight through, wake you
touching yourself, crying aloud into the room. Abandoned.

By Heart

I made myself imagine that I didn't love you,
that your face was ordinary to me. This was in our house
when you were out, secret, guessing what such difference

would be like, never to have known your touch,
your taste. Then I went out and passed the places
where we'd go, without you there, pretending that I could.

Making believe I could, I tried to blot out longing,
or regret, when someone looked like you, head down,
laughing, running away from me behind a veil of rain.

So it was strange to see you, just ahead of me,
as I trailed up the hill, thinking how I can't unlearn
the words I've got by heart, or dream your name away,

and shouting it, involuntarily, three times, until
you turned and smiled. Love makes buildings home
and out of dreary weather, sometimes, rainbows come.

Warming Her Pearls

Next to my own skin, her pearls. My mistress
bids me wear them, warm them, until evening
when I'll brush her hair. At six, I place them
round her cool, white throat. All day I think of her,

resting in the Yellow Room, contemplating silk
or taffeta, which gown tonight? She fans herself
whilst I work willingly, my slow heat entering
each pearl. Slack on my neck, her rope.

She's beautiful. I dream about her
in my attic bed; picture her dancing
with tall men, puzzled by my faint, persistent scent
beneath her French perfume, her milky stones.

I dust her shoulders with a rabbit's foot,
watch the soft blush seep through her skin
like an indolent sigh. In her looking-glass
my red lips part as though I want to speak.

Full moon. Her carriage brings her home. I see
her every movement in my head. . . . Undressing,
taking off her jewels, her slim hand reaching
for the case, slipping naked into bed, the way

she always does. . . . And I lie here awake,
knowing the pearls are cooling even now
in the room where my mistress sleeps. All night
I feel their absence and I burn.

Deportation

They have not been kind here. Now I must leave,
the words I've learned for supplication,
gratitude, will go unused. Love is a look
in the eyes in any language, but not here,
not this year. They have not been welcoming.

I used to think the world was where we lived
in space, one country shining in big dark.
I saw a photograph when I was small.

Now I am *Alien*. Where I come from there are few jobs,
the young are sullen and do not dream. My lover
bears our child and I was to work here, find
a home. In twenty years we would say This is you
when you were a baby, when the plum tree was a shoot . . .

We will tire each other out, making our homes
in one another's arms. We are not strong enough.

They are polite, recite official jargon endlessly.
Form F. Room 12. Box 6. I have felt less small
below mountains disappearing into cloud
than entering the Building of Exile. Hearse taxis
crawl the drizzling streets towards the terminal.

I am no one special. An ocean parts me from my love.

Go back. She will embrace me, ask what it was like.
Return. One thing – there was a space to write
the colour of her eyes. They have an apple here,
a bitter-sweet, which matches them exactly. Dearest,
without you I am nowhere. It was cold.

Plainsong

Stop. Along this path, in phrases of light,
trees sing their leaves. No Midas touch
has turned the wood to gold, late in the year
when you pass by, suddenly sad, straining
to remember something you're sure you knew.

Listening. The words you have for things die
in your heart, but grasses are plainsong,
patiently chanting the circles you cannot repeat
or understand. This is your homeland,
Lost One, Stranger who speaks with tears.

It is almost impossible to be here and yet
you kneel, no one's child, absolved by late sun
through the branches of a wood, distantly
the evening bell reminding you, *Home, Home,
Home,* and the stone in your palm telling the time.

Miles Away

I want you and you are not here. I pause
in this garden, breathing the colour thought is
before language into still air. Even your name
is a pale ghost and, though I exhale it again
and again, it will not stay with me. Tonight
I make you up, imagine you, your movements clearer
than the words I have you say you said before.

Wherever you are now, inside my head you fix me
with a look, standing here while cool late light
dissolves into the earth. I have got your mouth wrong,
but still it smiles. I hold you closer, miles away,
inventing love, until the calls of nightjars
interrupt and turn what was to come, was certain,
into memory. The stars are filming us for no one.

Nothing is Silent.

nothing is not Silent.

Originally

We came from our own country in a red room
which fell through the fields, our mother singing
our father's name to the turn of the wheels.
My brothers cried, one of them bawling *Home,
Home*, as the miles rushed back to the city,
the street, the house, the vacant rooms
where we didn't live any more. I stared
at the eyes of a blind toy, holding its paw.

All childhood is an emigration. Some are slow,
leaving you standing, resigned, up an avenue
where no one you know stays. Others are sudden.
Your accent wrong. Corners, which seem familiar,
leading to unimagined, pebble-dashed estates, big boys
eating worms and shouting words you don't understand.
My parents' anxiety stirred like a loose tooth
in my head. *I want our own country*, I said.

But then you forget, or don't recall, or change,
and, seeing your brother swallow a slug, feel only
a skelf of shame. I remember my tongue
shedding its skin like a snake, my voice
in the classroom sounding just like the rest. Do I only think
I lost a river, culture, speech, sense of first space
and the right place? Now, *Where do you come from?*
strangers ask. *Originally?* And I hesitate.

In Mrs Tilscher's Class

You could travel up the Blue Nile
with your finger, tracing the route
while Mrs Tilscher chanted the scenery.
Tana. Ethiopia. Khartoum. Aswân.
That for an hour, then a skittle of milk
and the chalky Pyramids rubbed into dust.
A window opened with a long pole.
The laugh of a bell swung by a running child.

This was better than home. Enthralling books.
The classroom glowed like a sweet shop.
Sugar paper. Coloured shapes. Brady and Hindley
faded, like the faint, uneasy smudge of a mistake.
Mrs Tilscher loved you. Some mornings, you found
she'd left a good gold star by your name.
The scent of a pencil slowly, carefully, shaved.
A xylophone's nonsense heard from another form.

Over the Easter term, the inky tadpoles changed
from commas into exclamation marks. Three frogs
hopped in the playground, freed by a dunce,
followed by a line of kids, jumping and croaking
away from the lunch queue. A rough boy
told you how you were born. You kicked him, but stared
at your parents, appalled, when you got back home.

That feverish July, the air tasted of electricity.
A tangible alarm made you always untidy, hot,
fractious under the heavy, sexy sky. You asked her
how you were born and Mrs Tilscher smiled,
then turned away. Reports were handed out.
You ran through the gates, impatient to be grown,
as the sky split open into a thunderstorm.

Sit at Peace

When they gave you them to shell and you sat
on the back-doorstep, opening the small green envelopes
with your thumb, minding the queues of peas, you were
sitting at peace. *Sit at peace, sit at peace*, all summer.

When Muriel Purdy, embryonic cop, thwacked the back
of your knees with a bamboo-cane, mouth open, soundless
in a cave of pain, you ran to your house,
a greeting wain, to be kept in and told once again.

Nip was a dog. Fluff was a cat. They sat at peace
on a coloured-in mat, so why couldn't you? Sometimes
your questions were stray snipes over no-man's-land,
bringing sharp hands and the order you had to obey. *Sit –*

At – Peace! Jigsaws you couldn't do or dull stamps
you didn't want to collect arrived with the frost.
You would rather stand with your nose to the window, clouding
the strange blue view with your restless breath.

But the day you fell from the Parachute Tree, they came
from nowhere running, carried you in to a quiet room
you were glad of. A long still afternoon, dreamlike.
A voice saying *peace, sit at peace, sit at peace*.

Hometown

In that town there was a different time,
a handful of years like old-fashioned sweets
you can't find anymore. I lived there.

What am I wearing as I pine for the future,
alone, down by the river by the Brine Baths
longing to get out? But I only threw a stone

at the face in the water and went home,
while behind me my features vanished,
trembled, reappeared, though I could not see.

Those streets, the gloomy shortcut by the church,
the triangle from school to home to the high field –
below which all roads sped away and led away –

and back again. Wherever I went then, I was
still there; fretting for something else, someone else,
somewhere else. Or else, I thought, I shall die.

And so I shall. Decades ahead of this, both of me,
then and now, pass each other like ghosts
in the empty market-place, where I imagine myself

to be older and away, or remember myself
younger, not loving this tuneless, flat bell
marking the time. Or moved to tears by its same sound.

Translating the English, 1989

'. . . and much of the poetry, alas, is lost in translation . . .'

Welcome to my country! We have here Edwina Currie
and the *Sun* newspaper. Much excitement.
Also the weather has been most improving
even in February. Daffodils. (Wordsworth. Up North.) If you like
Shakespeare or even Opera we have too the Black Market.
For two hundred quids we are talking Les Miserables,
nods being as good as winks. Don't eat the eggs.
Wheel-clamp. Dogs. Vagrants. A tour of our wonderful
capital city is not to be missed. The Fergie,
The Princess Di and the football hooligan, truly you will
like it here, Squire. Also we can be talking crack, smack
and Carling Black Label if we are so inclined. Don't
drink the H_2O. All very proud we now have
a green Prime Minister. What colour yours? Binbags.
You will be knowing of Charles Dickens and Terry Wogan
and Scotland. All this can be arranged for cash no questions.
Ireland not on. Fish and chips and the Official Secrets Act
second to none. Here we go. We are liking
a smashing good time like estate agents and Neighbours,
also Brookside for we are allowed four Channels.
How many you have? Last night of Proms. Andrew
Lloyd-Webber. Jeffrey Archer. Plenty culture you will be agreeing.
Also history and buildings. The Houses of Lords. Docklands.
Many thrills and high interest rates for own good. Muggers.
Much lead in petrol. Filth. Rule Britannia and child abuse.
Electronic tagging, Boss, ten pints and plenty rape. Queen Mum.
Channel Tunnel. You get here fast no problem to my country
my country my country welcome welcome welcome.

Mrs Skinner, North Street

Milk bottles. Light through net. No post. Cat,
come here by the window, settle down. Morning
in this street awakes unwashed; a stale wind
breathing litter, last night's godlessness. This place
is hellbound in a handcart, Cat, you mark
her words. Strumpet. Slut. A different man
for every child; a byword for disgrace.

Her dentures grin at her, gargling water
on the mantelpiece. The days are gone
for smiling, wearing them to chatter down the road.
Good morning. Morning. Lovely day. Over the years
she's suffered loss, bereavement, loneliness.
A terrace of strangers. An old ghost
mouthing curses behind a cloudy, nylon veil.

Scrounger. Workshy. Cat, where is the world
she married, was carried into up a scrubbed stone step?
The young louts roam the neighbourhood.
Breaking of glass. Chants. Sour abuse of aerosols.
That social worker called her *xenophobic*. When he left
she looked the word up. Fear, morbid dislike, of strangers.
Outside, the rain pours down relentlessly.

People scurry for shelter. How many hours
has she sat here, Cat, filled with bitterness
and knowing they'll none of them come?
Not till the day the smell is noticed.
Not till the day you're starving, Cat, and begin
to lick at the corpse. She twitches the curtain
as the Asian man next door runs through the rain.

Too Bad

It was winter. Wilson had just said
we should have one in The Dog. So we did,
running through the blue wet streets
with our heads down, laughing, to get there,
down doubles in front of our drenched reflections.
The barmaid caught my eye in the mirror. Beautiful.

We had a job to do, but not till closing-time,
hard men knocking back the brandy, each of us
wearing revenge like a badge on his heart. Hatred
dresses in cheap anonymous suits, the kind
with an inside pocket for a small gun. *Good Health*.
I smiled at her. Warm rain, like blood, ran down my back.

I remembered my first time, my trembling hand
and Big Frank Connell hissing *Get a grip*.
Tonight, professional, I walked with the boys
along a filthy alley to the other pub, the one
where it happened, the one where the man
was putting on his coat, ready for home.

Home. Two weeks in a safe house and I'd be there,
glad of familiar accents and my dull wife.
He came out of a side door, clutching a carry-out.
Simple. Afterwards, Wilson was singing *dada da da
Tom Someone, hang down your head and cry*.
Too bad. I fancied that barmaid all right.

Weasel Words

*It was explained to Sir Robert Armstrong that
'weasel words' are 'words empty of meaning, like an
egg which has had its contents sucked out by a weasel'.*

Let me repeat that we Weasels mean no harm.
You may have read that we are vicious hunters,
but this is absolutely not the case. Pure bias
on the part of your Natural History Book. *Hear, hear.*

We are long, slim-bodied carnivores with exceptionally
short legs and we have never denied this.
Furthermore, anyone here today could put a Weasel
down his trouser-leg and nothing would happen. *Weasel laughter.*

Which is more than can be said for the Ferrets opposite.
You can trust a Weasel, let me continue, a Weasel
does not break the spinal cord of its victim with one bite.
Weasel cheers. Our brown fur coats turn white in winter.

And as for eggs, here is a whole egg. It looks like an egg.
It is an egg. *Slurp.* An egg. *Slurp.* A whole egg. *Slurp . . . Slurp . . .*

Poet for Our Times

I write the headlines for a Daily Paper.
It's just a knack one's born with all-right-Squire.
You do not have to be an educator,
just bang the words down like they're screaming *Fire!*
CECIL-KEAYS ROW SHOCK TELLS EYETIE WAITER.
ENGLAND FAN CALLS WHINGEING FROG A LIAR.

Cheers. Thing is, you've got to grab attention
with just one phrase as punters rush on by.
I've made mistakes too numerous to mention,
so now we print the buggers inches high.
TOP MP PANTIE ROMP INCREASES TENSION.
RENT BOY: ROCK STAR PAID ME WELL TO LIE.

I like to think that I'm a sort of poet
for our times. My shout. Know what I mean?
I've got a special talent and I show it
in punchy haikus featuring the Queen.
DIPLOMAT IN BED WITH SERBO-CROAT.
EASTENDERS' BONKING SHOCK IS WELL-OBSCENE.

Of course, these days, there's not the sense of panic
you got a few years back. What with the box
et cet. I wish I'd been around when the Titanic
sank. To headline that, mate, would've been the tops.
SEE PAGE 3 TODAY GENTS THEY'RE GIGANTIC.
KINNOCK-BASHER MAGGIE PULLS OUT STOPS.

And, yes, I have a dream – make that a scotch, ta –
that kids will know my headlines off by heart.
IMMIGRANTS FLOOD IN CLAIMS HEATHROW WATCHER.
GREEN PARTY WOMAN IS A NIGHTCLUB TART.
The poems of the decade . . . *Stuff 'em! Gotcha!*
The instant tits and bottom line of art.

Job Creation

for Ian McMillan

They have shipped Gulliver up north.
He lies at the edge of the town,
sleeping.
His snores are thunder in the night.

Round here, we reckon they have drugged him
or we dream he is a landscape
which might drag itself up and walk.

Here are ropes, they said.
Tie him down.
We will pay you.
Tie Gulliver down with these ropes.

I slaved all day at his left knee,
until the sun went down
behind it
and clouds gathered on his eyes

and darkness settled on his shoulders
like a job.

Making Money

Turnover. Profit. Readies. Cash. Loot. Dough. Income. Stash.
Dosh. Bread. Finance. Brass. I give my tongue over
to money; the taste of warm rust in a chipped mug
of tap-water. Drink some yourself. Consider
an Indian man in Delhi, Salaamat the *niyariwallah*,
who squats by an open drain for hours, sifting shit
for the price of a chapati. More than that. His hands
in crumbling gloves of crap pray at the drains
for the pearls in slime his grandfather swore he found.

Megabucks. Wages. Interest. Wealth. I sniff and snuffle
for a whiff of pelf; the stench of an abattoir blown
by a stale wind over the fields. Roll up a fiver,
snort. Meet Kim. Kim will give you the works,
her own worst enema, suck you, lick you, squeal
red weals to your whip, be nun, nurse, nanny,
nymph on a credit card. Don't worry.
Kim's only in it for the money. Lucre. Tin. Dibs.

I put my ear to brass lips; a small fire's whisper
close to a forest. Listen. His cellular telephone
rings in the Bull's car. Golden hello. Big deal. Now get this
straight. *Making a living is making a killing these days.*
Jobbers and brokers buzz. He paints out a landscape
by number. The Bull. Seriously rich. Nasty. One of us.

Salary. Boodle. Oof. Blunt. Shekels. Lolly. Gelt. Funds.
I wallow in coin, naked; the scary caress of a fake hand
on my flesh. Get stuck in. Bergama. The boys from the bazaar
hide on the target-range, watching the soldiers fire. Between bursts,

they rush for the spent shells, cart them away for scrap.
Here is the catch. Some shells don't explode. Ahmat
runs over grass, lucky for six months, so far. So
bomb-collectors die young. But the money's good.

Palmgrease. Smackers. Greenbacks. Wads. I widen my eyes
at a fortune; a set of knives on black cloth, shining,
utterly beautiful. Weep. The economy booms
like cannon, far out at sea on a lone ship. We leave
our places of work, tired, in the shortening hours, in the time
of night our town could be anywhere, and some of us pause
in the square, where a clown makes money swallowing fire.

Talent Contest

At the end of the pier, an open-air theatre, a crowd
who have paid to come in, wooden slats, the sea slopping out
like beer in a cracked plastic cup, one scrunched cloud
like a boarding-house towel, grey. You're a contestant.

Take my advice, leave now. Head for the Gaiety Bar
or the rifle-range. Better still, slink to a seat, knot your handkerchief
over your head and watch. The spoon-player has no chance.
Farmyard Noises takes out his teeth. Ambitious. In for the lot.

Why do you sneer? A cheap song sung badly
pleases the crowd. The tap-dancer spreads out his arms
and grins, a man tortured. Beware the ventriloquist,
the dark horse, whose thrown voice juggles the truth.

You don't want to hear this. *Poweran moneyan fame* you say to yourself
like a blessing, then you're into the act. Make 'em laugh. A seagull
shrieks at you out of the blue. Make 'em cry. A baby
sobs and sobs in a pram at the end of a row.

Applause. A show of hands from plonkers with day-jobs. Cheers.
You're kind to the yodeller later, sneaky and modest, not letting on
you thought it a piece of piss. Talent. A doubt like faraway thunder
threatens to ruin the day, that it's squandered on this.

Ape

There is a male silverback on the calendar.
Behind him the jungle is defocused,
except in one corner, where trees gargle the sun.

After you have numbered the days, you tear off
the page. His eyes hold your eyes
as you crumple a forest in your fist.

The Legend

Some say it was seven tons of meat in a thick black hide
you could build a boat from, stayed close to the river
on the flipside of the sun where the giant forests were.

Had shy, old eyes. You'd need both those hands for one.
Maybe. Walked in placid herds under a jungly, sweating roof
just breathing; a dry electric wind you could hear a mile off.

Huge feet. Some say if it rained you could fish in a footprint,
fruit fell when it passed. It moved, food happened, simple.
You think of a warm, inky cave and you got its mouth all right.

You dream up a yard of sandpaper, damp, you're talking tongue.
Eat? Its own weight in a week. And water. Some say
the sweat steamed from its back in small grey clouds.

But big. Enormous. Spine like the mast on a galleon.
Ears like sails gasping for a wind. You picture
a rope you could hang a man from, you're seeing its tail.

Tusks like banisters. I almost believe myself. Can you
drum up a roar as wide as a continent, a deep hot note
that bellowed out and belonged to the melting air? You got it.

But people have always lied! You know some say it had a trunk
like a soft telescope, that it looked up along it at the sky
and balanced a bright, gone star on the end, and it died.

Descendants

Most of us worked the Lancashire vineyards all year and a few
                                                   freak redheads died.
We were well-nuked. Knackered. The gaffers gave us
                                         a bonus
in Burgdy and Claray. Big fucking deal, we thought, we'd been
                                            robbing them blind
for months. Drink enough of it, you can juggle with snakes,
                                             no sweat.

Some nights, me and Sarah went down to the ocean
                                         with a few flasks
and a groundsheet and we'd have it off three or four times
                                               in a night
that barely got dark. For hours, you could hear the dolphins
                                                 rearing up
as if they were after something. Strange bastards. I like
                                           dolphins.

Anyway. She's soft, Sarah. She can read. Big green moon
                                       and her with a book
of *poetry* her Gran had. Nuke me. Nice words, right enough,
                                             and I love the girl,
but I'd had plenty. *Winter*, I goes, *Spring, Autumn, Summer,*
                                             don't give me
that crap, Sarah, and I flung the book over the white sand,
                                             into the waves,

beyond the dolphins. Click-click. Sad. I hate the
                                       bastard past, see,
I'd piss on an ancestor as soon as trace one. *What*
                                       fucking seasons

I says to her, *just look at us now*. So we looked.
                              At each other.
At the trembling unsafe sky. And she started, didn't she,
                                                  to cry.
Tears over her lovely blotchy purple face. It got to me.

We Remember Your Childhood Well

Nobody hurt you. Nobody turned off the light and argued
with somebody else all night. The bad man on the moors
was only a movie you saw. Nobody locked the door.

Your questions were answered fully. No. That didn't occur.
You couldn't sing anyway, cared less. The moment's a blur, a *Film Fun*
laughing itself to death in the coal fire. Anyone's guess.

Nobody forced you. You wanted to go that day. Begged. You chose
the dress. Here are the pictures, look at you. Look at us all,
smiling and waving, younger. The whole thing is inside your head.

What you recall are impressions; we have the facts. We called the tune.
The secret police of your childhood were older and wiser than you, bigger
than you. Call back the sound of their voices. Boom. Boom. Boom.

Nobody sent you away. That was an extra holiday, with people
you seemed to like. They were firm, there was nothing to fear.
There was none but yourself to blame if it ended in tears.

What does it matter now? No, no, nobody left the skidmarks of sin
on your soul and laid you wide open for Hell. You were loved.
Always. We did what was best. We remember your childhood well.

The Act of Imagination

*Under the Act, the following things may be
prosecuted for appalling the Imagination.*

Ten More Years.
A dog playing Beethoven's 'Moonlight Sonata'.
President Quayle.

The pyjamas of Tax Inspectors.
The Beef Tapeworm (*Taenia Saginata*).
British Rail.

Picking someone else's nose.
The Repatriation Charter.
Gaol.

The men. The Crucifix. The nails.

The sound of the neighbours having sex.
The Hanging Lobby.
The Bomb.

Glow-in-the-dark Durex.
A Hubby.
Bedtime with Nancy and Ron.

The sweet smell of success.
A camel's jobby.
On

and on. And on. And on.

Eating the weakest survivor.
A small hard lump.
Drinking meths.

Going as Lady Godiva.
A parachute jump.
One breast.

Homeless and down to a fiver.
A hump.
Bad breath.

Here is a space to fill in things you suggest.

Death.

Somewhere Someone's Eyes

What if there had been a painter – he was drunk – *equal
to Picasso, who filled his canvases for years,
destroyed them all, and died?* It was the old one
about the tree, the empty wood, the unheard moan
of a great oak falling unobserved. We thought
we'd humour him. *Or a composer, whose scores
were never played — who also died — nor ever found?*

Because I remember this, a cool room flares
with the heat of a winter's fire, briefly. His face
glowed red-brown when he spoke to the flames.
I recollect it more than well, smell malt. *What
happens to the lost?* The shadow his mind made legless
lurched against the wall, glass raised. He cursed,
demanded an answer from the dog. All night it snowed.

Somewhere . . . he said, but we'd had enough, began
to joke and get half-screwed ourselves. *Somewhere someone's . . .*
Outside, the trees shifted under their soft burdens,
or I imagine so. Our footsteps disappeared. It was easy
to laugh in that snug house, talk nonsense
half the night, drink. Across the white fields somewhere
someone's eyes blazed as they burned words in their mouth.

Liar

She made things up: for example, that she was really
a man. After she'd taken off her cotton floral
day-frock she was him alright, in her head,
dressed in that heavy herringbone from Oxfam.
He was called Susan actually. The eyes in the mirror
knew that, but she could stare them out.

Of course, a job; of course, a humdrum city flat;
of course, the usual friends. Lover? Sometimes.
She lived like you do, a dozen slack rope-ends
in each dream hand, tugging uselessly on memory
or hope. Frayed. She told stories. *I lived
in Moscow once . . . I nearly drowned . . .* Rotten.

Lightning struck me and I'm here to tell . . . Liar.
Hyperbole, falsehood, fiction, fib were pebbles tossed
at the evening's flat pool; her bright eyes
fixed on the ripples. No one believed her.
Our secret films are private affairs, watched
behind the eyes. She spoke in subtitles. Not on.

From bad to worse. The ambulance whinged all the way
to the park where she played with the stolen child.
You know the rest. The man in the long white wig
who found her sadly confused. The top psychiatrist
who studied her in gaol, then went back home and did
what he does every night to the Princess of Wales.

Boy

I liked being small. When I'm on my own
I'm small. I put my pyjamas on
and hum to myself. I like doing that.

What I don't like is being large, you know,
grown-up. Just like that. Whoosh. Hairy.
I think of myself as a boy. Safe slippers.

The world is terror. Small you can go *As I
lay down my head to sleep, I pray* . . . I remember
my three wishes sucked up a chimney of flame.

I can do it though. There was an older woman
who gave me a bath. She was joking, of course,
but I wasn't. I said *Mummy* to her. Off-guard.

Now it's a question of getting the wording right
for the Lonely Hearts verse. There must be someone
out there who's kind to boys. Even if they grew.

Eley's Bullet

Out walking in the fields, Eley found a bullet
with his name on it. Pheasants korred
and whirred at the sound of gunfire.
Eley's dog began to whine. England
was turning brown at the edges. Autumn. Rime
in the air. A cool bullet in his palm.

Eley went home. He put the tiny missile
in a matchbox and put that next to a pistol
in the drawer of his old desk. His dog
sat at his feet by the coal fire as he drank
a large whisky, then another one, but this
was usual. Eley went up the stairs to his bath.

He was in love with a woman in the town. The water
was just right, slid over his skin as he gave out
a long low satisfied moan into the steam.
His telephone began to ring and Eley cursed,
then dripped along the hall. She was in a call-box.
She'd lied all afternoon and tonight she was free.

The woman was married. Eley laughed aloud
with apprehension and delight, the world
expanded as he thought of her, his dog
trembled under his hand. Eley knelt,
he hugged the dog till it barked. Outside, the wind
knew something was on and nudged at the clouds.

They lay in each other's arms, as if what they had done
together had broken the pair of them. The woman
was half-asleep and Eley was telling himself

how he would spend a wish, if he could have only one
for the whole of his life. His fingers counted
the beads of her back as he talked in the dark.

At ten, Eley came into the bedroom with drinks.
She was combing her hair at the mirror. His eyes
seemed to hurt at the sight. She told him sorry,
but this was the last time. She tried to smile.
He stared, then said her words himself, the way
he'd spoken Latin as a boy. Dead language.

By midnight the moon was over the house, full
and lethal, and Eley alone. He went to his desk
with a bottle and started to write. Upstairs,
the dog sniffed at the tepid bed. Eley held
his head in his hands and wanted to cry,
but *Beloved* he wrote and *forever* and *why*.

Some men have no luck. Eley knew he'd as well
send her his ear as mail these stale words,
although he could taste her still. Nearby, a bullet
was there for the right moment and the right man.
He got out his gun, slowly, not even thinking,
and loaded it. Now he would choose. He paused.

He could finish the booze, sleep without dreams
with the morning to face, the loss of her
sore as the sunlight; or open his mouth
for a gun with his name on its bullet to roar
in his brains. Thunder or silence. Eley wished to God
he'd never loved. And then the frightened whimper of a dog.

Following Francis

*Watch me. I start with a low whistle, twist it,
pitch it higher and thinner till the kestrel treads air.
There! I have a genius for this, which I offer
to God. Do they say I am crazy, brother?*

Yes, they say that. My own wife said it. *Dropping everything
and following that fool! You want to be covered
in birdshit? You make me sick.* I left anyway,
hurried to the woods to meet him. Francis. Francis.
We had nothing. Later, I wept in his arms like a boy;
his hands were a woman's, plucking my tears off, tasting them.

We are animals, he said.

I am more practical. He fumbles with two sticks
hoping for fire; swears, laughs, cups glow-worms
in his palm while I start up a flame. Some nights
we've company, local accents in the dusk. He sees
my jealousy flare beneath dark trees. He knows.
I know he knows. When he looks at me, he thinks

I cannot tame this.

This evening, Francis preaches to the birds. If he is crazy,
what does that make me? I close my eyes. Tell my children
we move north tomorrow, away from here where the world
sings through cool grass, water, air, a saint's voice.
Tell them that what I am doing I do from choice.

He holds a fist to the sky and a hawk swoops down.

Survivor

For some time now, at the curve of my mind,
I have longed to embrace my brother, my sister, myself,
when we were seven years old. It is making me ill.

Also my first love, who was fifteen, Leeds, I know
it is thirty years, but when I remember him now
I can feel his wet, young face in my hands, melting
snow, my empty hands. This is bereavement.

Or I spend the weekend in bed, dozing, lounging
in the past. Why has this happened? I mime
the gone years where I lived. I want them back.

My lover rises and plunges above me, not knowing
I have hidden myself in my heart, where I rock
and weep for what has been stolen, lost. Please.
It is like an earthquake and no one to tell.

An Afternoon with Rhiannon

The night before, our host had pointed out the Building
Larkin feared. *He was right*, I said, suddenly cold
and wanting home; cold later, too, in bed, listening
to wind and rain whip in to the lonely, misplaced town.

But lunchtime brought a clip of spring; a gold man mounted
on a prancing golden horse en route to the pier-head rendezvous
where your mother set you down. We watched you bumble
after pigeons, squeal as sun and air and Humber spun you around.

Around and around. Then you shouted *Boat!*, pointing
at nothing, *Boat!*, an empty river, a boatless blue painting
you haven't begun yet. A small child's daylight
is a safer place than a poet's slow, appalling, ticking night;

a place where you say, in a voice so new it shines, *I like
buildings!* The older people look, the shy town smiles.

Losers

Con-artists, barefaced liars, clocks shuffle the hours slowly.
Remember the hands you were dealt, the full-house of love,
the ace-high you bluffed on. Never again. Each day
is a new game, sucker, with mornings and midnights
raked in by the dealer. Did you think you could keep those cards?

Imagination is memory. We are the fools who dwell in time
outside of time. One saves up for a lifelong dream, another
spends all she has on a summer decades ago. The clocks
click like chips in a casino, piled to a wobbly tower. An hour
fills up with rain. An hour runs down a gutter into a drain.

Where do you live? In a kiss in a darkened cricket pavilion
after the war? Banker? In the scent, from nowhere, of apples
seconds before she arrived? Poet? You don't live here
and now. Where? In the day your mother didn't come home? Priest?
In the chalky air of the classroom, still? Doctor? Assassin? Whore?

Look at the time. There will be more but there is always less.
Place your bets. Mostly we do not notice our latest loss
under the rigged clocks. Remember the night we won! The times
it hurts are when we grab the moment for ourselves, nearly –
the corniest sunset, taste of a lover's tears, a fistful of snow –

and the bankrupt feeling we have as it disappears.

M-M-Memory

Scooping spilt, soft, broken oil
with a silver spoon
from a flagstone floor
into a clay bowl –

the dull scrape of the spoon
on the cool stone,
lukewarm drops in the bowl –

m-m-memory.

Kneel there,
words like fossils
trapped in the roof of the mouth,
forgotten, half-forgotten, half-
recalled, the tongue dreaming
it can trace their shape.

Names, ghosts, m-memory.

Through the high window of the hall
clouds obfuscate the sun
and you sit, exhaling grey smoke
into a purpling, religious light
trying to remember everything

perfectly
in time and space
where you cannot.

Those unstrung beads of oil
seem precious now, now
that the light has changed.

Père Lachaise

Along the ruined avenues the long gone lie
under the old stones. For 10 francs, a map unravels
the crumbling paths which lead to the late great.
A silent town. A vast, perplexing pause.

The living come, murmuring with fresh flowers, their maps
fluttering like white flags in the slight breeze.
April. Beginning of spring. Lilies for Oscar,
one red rose for Colette. Remembrance. Do not forget.

Turn left for Seurat, Chopin, Proust, and Gertrude Stein
with nothing more to say. Below the breathing trees
a thousand lost talents dream into dust; decay
into largely familiar names for a stranger's bouquet.

Forever dead. Say these words and let their meaning
dizzy you like the scent of innumerable petals
here in Père Lachaise. The sad tourists stand
by the graves, reciting the titles of poems, paintings, songs,

things which have brought them here for the afternoon.
We thread our way through the cemetery, misquoting
or humming quietly and almost comforted.
Two young men embrace near Piaf's tomb.

Funeral

Say milky cocoa we'd say,
you had the accent for it,
drunk you sometimes would. *Milky*

cocoa. Preston. We'd all
laugh. *Milky cocoa*. Drunk,
drunk. You laughed, saying it.

From all over the city
mourners swarmed, a demo against
death, into the cemetery.

You asked for nothing.
Three gravediggers, two minutes
of silence in the wind. Black

cars took us back. Serious
drinking. Awkward ghosts
getting the ale in. All afternoon

we said your name, repeated
the prayers of anecdotes,
bereaved and drunk

enough to think you might arrive,
say milky cocoa . . . Milky
cocoa, until we knew you'd gone.

Dream of a Lost Friend

You were dead, but we met, dreaming,
before you had died. Your name, twice,
then you turned, pale, unwell. *My dear,
my dear, must this be?* A public building
where I've never been, and, on the wall,
an AIDS poster. Your white lips. *Help me.*

We embraced, standing in a long corridor
which harboured a fierce pain neither of us felt yet.
The words you spoke were frenzied prayers
to Chemistry; or you laughed, a child-man's laugh,
innocent, hysterical, out of your skull. *It's only
a dream*, I heard myself saying, *only a bad dream.*

Some of our best friends nurture a virus, an idle,
charmed, purposeful enemy, and it dreams
they are dead already. In fashionable restaurants,
over the crudités, the healthy imagine a time
when all these careful moments will be dreamed
and dreamed again. *You look well. How do you feel?*

Then, as I slept, you backed away from me, crying
and offering a series of dates for lunch, waving.
I missed your funeral, I said, knowing you couldn't hear
at the end of the corridor, thumbs up, acting.
Where there's life . . . Awake, alive, for months I think of you
almost hopeful in a bad dream where you were long dead.

Like This

When you die in the city where everyone was young,
at the end of the dark, drunken years that kept you there,
old friends walk up through the wild streets
to the alehouse, whose watery, yellow lights
are a faint, hopeless beacon in the night,
and, nearer now to you, they get in the rounds,
the solemn, slow, ceremonial rounds which soften their tongues
to speak brief epitaphs of love, regret; meanwhile,
you lie in an ice-cold drawer, two postal codes away,
without recall or recourse, although you had both,
although you are not yet old, although a woman is crying
in the big house on the park where they carried you out
for the last time, where you were told how it would end,
how it would be like this unless, unless. And it is.

Who Loves You

I worry about you travelling in those mystical machines.
Every day people fall from the clouds, dead.
Breathe in and out and in and out easy.
Safety, safely, safe home.

Your photograph is in the fridge, smiles when the light comes on.
All the time people are burnt in the public places.
Rest where the cool trees drop to a gentle shade.
Safety, safely, safe home.

Don't lie down on the sands where the hole in the sky is.
Too many people being gnawed to shreds.
Send me your voice however it comes across oceans.
Safety, safely, safe home.

The loveless men and homeless boys are out there and angry.
Nightly people end their lives in the shortcut.
Walk in the light, steadily hurry towards me.
Safety, safely, safe home. (Who loves you?)
Safety, safely, safe home.

Two Small Poems of Desire

1

The little sounds I make against your skin
don't mean anything. They make me
an animal learning vowels; not that I know
I do this, but I hear them
floating away over your shoulders, sticking
to the ceiling. *Aa Ee Iy Oh Uu.*

Are they sounds of surprise
at the strange ghosts your nakedness makes
moving above me in how much light
a net can catch?

Who cares. Sometimes language virtuously used
is language badly used. It's tough
and difficult and true to say
I love you when you do these things to me.

2

The way I prefer to play you back
is naked in the cool lawn of those green sheets,
just afterwards,
and saying *What secret am I?*

I am brought up sharp in a busy street,
staring inwards as you put down your drink
and touch me again. *How does it feel?*

It feels like tiny gardens
growing in the palms of the hands,
invisible,
sweet, if they had a scent.

Girlfriends

derived from Verlaine

That hot September night, we slept in a single bed,
naked, and on our frail bodies the sweat
cooled and renewed itself. I reached out my arms
and you, hands on my breasts, kissed me. Evening of amber.

Our nightgowns lay on the floor where you fell to your knees
and became ferocious, pressed your head to my stomach,
your mouth to the red gold, the pink shadows; except
I did not see it like this at the time, but arched

my back and squeezed water from the sultry air
with my fists. Also I remember hearing, clearly
but distantly, a siren some streets away – *de*

da de da de da – which mingled with my own
absurd cries, so that I looked up, even then,
to see my fingers counting themselves, dancing.

A Shilling for the Sea

You get a shilling if you see it first.
You take your lover to a bar nearby, late evening,
spend it all night and still have change. If,

if it were me, if it were you, we'd drink up
and leave; screw on the beach, with my bare arse
soaked by the night-tide's waves, your face moving
between mine and that gambler's throw of stars.

Then we'd dress and go back to the bar, order
the same again, and who's this whispering filthy suggestions
into my ear? *My tongue in the sea slow salt wet . . .*

Yes. All for a shilling, if you play that game.

Hard to Say

I asked him to give me an image for Love, something I could see,
or imagine seeing, or something that, because of the word
for its smell, would make me remember, something possible
to hear. *Don't just say love*, I said, *love, love, I love you.*

On the way home, I thought of our love and how, lately,
I too have grown lazy in expressing it, snuggling up to you
in bed, idly murmuring those tired clichés without even thinking.
My words have been grubby confetti, faded, tacky, blown far

from the wedding feast. And so it was, with a sudden shock of love,
like a peacock flashing wide its hundred eyes, or a boy's voice
flinging top G to the roof of an empty church, or a bottle
of French perfume knocked off the shelf, spilling into the steamy bath,

I wanted you. After the wine, the flowers I brought you drowned
in the darkening light. As we slept, we breathed their scent all night.

The Kissing Gate

After I've spoken to you, I walk out to the gate
at the edge of the field, watch a bird make a nonsense
of the air, and wish. This is not my landscape,
though I feel at home here, in a way, in a light
that rolls a dreg of memory around itself, spills it.
You'll not see it now. The bird. Me at the gate. Call it
a yellowy light. There it goes, into the grass, green,

greener, going. Love holds words to itself, repeats them
till they're smooth, sit silent on the tongue
like a small stone you sucked once, for some reason,
on a beach. I tell myself the things you'd like to do to me
if you were here, where there's no one to see for miles,
where I sense myself grow lighter and heavier, dizzy, solid,
and a bird swoops down, down, the light follows it.

Words, Wide Night

Somewhere on the other side of this wide night
and the distance between us, I am thinking of you.
The room is turning slowly away from the moon.

This is pleasurable. Or shall I cross that out and say
it is sad? In one of the tenses I singing
an impossible song of desire that you cannot hear.

La lala la. See? I close my eyes and imagine
the dark hills I would have to cross
to reach you. For I am in love with you and this

is what it is like or what it is like in words.

The *Darling* Letters

Some keep them in shoeboxes away from the light,
sore memories blinking out as the lid lifts,
their own recklessness written all over them. *My own . . .*
Private jokes, no longer comprehended, pull their punchlines,
fall flat in the gaps between endearments. *What
are you wearing?*

                Don't ever change.
They start with Darling; end in recriminations,
absence, sense of loss. Even now, the fist's bud flowers
into trembling, the fingers trace each line and see
the future then. *Always . . .* Nobody burns them,
the *Darling* letters, stiff in their cardboard coffins.

Babykins . . . We all had strange names
which make us blush, as though we'd murdered
someone under an alias, long ago. *I'll die
without you. Die.* Once in a while, alone,
we take them out to read again, the heart thudding
like a spade on buried bones.

Away from Home

Somewhere someone will always be leaving open
a curtain, as you pass up the dark mild street,
uncertain, on your way to the lodgings.

You put down your case, and a blurred longing
sharpens like a headache. A woman carries
a steamy bowl into the room – a red room –

talking to no one, the pleasant and yawning man
who comes in behind her and kisses her palms.
Miles away, you go on, strumming the privet.

*

The train unzips the landscape, sheds fields
and hedges. On the outskirts of a town, the first houses
deal you their bright cards. The Queen of Hearts. A kitchen.

A suburban king counting his money. Jacks.
Behind the back-to-backs, a bruised industrial sky
blackens, and fills with cooking smells, and rains.

Treacherous puddles lead to the Railway Hotel. *No bar
till 7 pm*. At the first drink, a haunted jukebox
switches itself on, reminds you, reminds you, reminds you.

*

Anonymous night. Something wrong. The bedside lamp
absent. Different air. Against the hazarded wall
a door starts faintly to be drawn.

You mime your way ineptly to a switch,
turn to a single room with shower,
an empty flask, a half-drunk glass of wine.

Calm yourself. By dawn you will have slept again
and gone. You have a ticket for the plane.
Check it. The flight number. Your home address. Your name.

*

Urinous broken phone booths lead you
from street to back street, to this last one
which stands at the edge of a demolition site.

Unbelievably, it works. With a sense of luxury
you light a cigarette. There is time yet.
Your fingers press the numbers, almost sensually.

Tomorrow you return. Below the flyover
the sparkling merging motorways glamorise
the night. The telephone is ringing in your house.

November

How they can ruin a day, the funeral cars proceeding
over the edge of the Common, while fat black crows
leer and jeer in gangs. A parliament all right.

Suddenly the hour is less pleasant than it first appeared
to take a walk and post a harmless, optimistic letter.
Face up to it. It is far too hot for November

and far too late for more than the corpse stopped
at a red light near the Post Office, where you pause
wishing you could make some kind of gesture

like the old woman who crosses herself as the hearse moves on.

The Literature Act

My poem will be a fantasy about living in a high-rise flat,
on the edge of a dirty industrial town, as the lawful wife of a yob
who spent the morning demonstrating in the market square
for the benefit of the gutter press. This was against a book
of which he violently disapproves and which was written by some cunt
who is a blasphemer or a lesbian or whose filth is being studied
in our local schools as part of some pisspot exam, the bastard.
I feel a thrill of fear as I imagine frying his evening meal
and keeping his children quiet as he shouts at the News. Later
he will thrash in the bed, like a fish out of water, not censoring
the words and pictures in his head. I would like my poem
to be given to such a man by the Police. Should he resist
I would like him to be taken to court; where the Jury,
the Judge, will compel him to learn it by heart. Every word.

River

At the turn of the river the language changes,
a different babble, even a different name
for the same river. Water crosses the border,
translates itself, but words stumble, fall back,
and there, nailed to a tree, is proof. A sign

in new language brash on a tree. A bird,
not seen before, singing on a branch. A woman
on the path by the river, repeating a strange sound
to clue the bird's song and ask for its name, after.
She kneels for a red flower, picks it, later
will press it carefully between the pages of a book.

What would it mean to you if you could be
with her there, dangling your own hands in the water
where blue and silver fish dart away over stone,
stoon, stein, like the meanings of things, vanish?
She feels she is somewhere else, intensely, simply because
of words; sings loudly in nonsense, smiling, smiling.

If you were really there what would you write on a postcard,
or on the sand, near where the river runs into the sea?

The Way My Mother Speaks

I say her phrases to myself
in my head
or under the shallows of my breath,
restful shapes moving.
The day and ever. The day and ever.

The train this slow evening
goes down England
browsing for the right sky,
too blue swapped for a cool grey.
For miles I have been saying
What like is it
the way I say things when I think.
Nothing is silent. Nothing is not silent.
What like is it.

Only tonight
I am happy and sad
like a child
who stood at the end of summer
and dipped a net
in a green, erotic pond. *The day
and ever. The day and ever.*
I am homesick, free, in love
with the way my mother speaks.

In Your Mind

The other country, is it anticipated or half-remembered?
Its language is muffled by the rain which falls all afternoon
one autumn in England, and in your mind
you put aside your work and head for the airport
with a credit card and a warm coat you will leave
on the plane. The past fades like newsprint in the sun.

You know people there. Their faces are photographs
on the wrong side of your eyes. A beautiful boy
in the bar on the harbour serves you a drink – what? –
asks you if men could possibly land on the moon.
A moon like an orange drawn by a child. No.
Never. You watch it peel itself into the sea.

Sleep. The rasp of carpentry wakes you. On the wall,
a painting lost for thirty years renders the room yours.
Of course. You go to your job, right at the old hotel, left,
then left again. You love this job. Apt sounds
mark the passing of the hours. Seagulls. Bells. A flute
practising scales. You swap a coin for a fish on the way home.

Then suddenly you are lost but not lost, dawdling
on the blue bridge, watching six swans vanish
under your feet. The certainty of place turns on the lights
all over town, turns up the scent on the air. For a moment
you are there, in the other country, knowing its name.
And then a desk. A newspaper. A window. English rain.

Someone calls a child's name as though they named their loss.

The Captain of the 1964
Top of the Form Team

Do Wah Diddy Diddy, Baby Love, Oh Pretty Woman
were in the Top Ten that month, October, and the Beatles
were everywhere else. I can give you the B-side
of the Supremes one. Hang on. *Come See About Me?*
I lived in a kind of fizzing hope. Gargling
with Vimto. The clever smell of my satchel. Convent girls.
I pulled my hair forward with a steel comb that I blew
like Mick, my lips numb as a two-hour snog.

No snags. The Nile rises in April. Blue and White.
The humming-bird's song is made by its wings, which beat
so fast that they blur in flight. I knew the capitals,
the Kings and Queens, the dates. In class, the white sleeve
of my shirt saluted again and again. *Sir! . . . Correct.*
Later, I whooped at the side of my bike, a cowboy,
mounted it running in one jump. I sped down Dyke Hill,
no hands, famous, learning, *dominus domine dominum.*

Dave Dee Dozy . . . Try me. Come on. My mother kept my
    mascot Gonk
on the TV set for a year. And the photograph. I look
so brainy you'd think I'd just had a bath. The blazer.
The badge. The tie. The first chord of *A Hard Day's Night*
loud in my head. I ran to the Spinney in my prize shoes,
up Churchill Way, up Nelson Drive, over pink pavements
that girls chalked on, in a blue evening; and I stamped
the pawprints of badgers and skunks in the mud. My country.

I want it back. The captain. The one with all the answers. Bzz.
My name was in red on Lucille Green's jotter. I smiled
as wide as a child who went missing on the way home
from school. The keeny. I say to my stale wife
Six hits by Dusty Springfield. I say to my boss *A pint!*
How can we know the dancer from the dance? Nobody.
My thick kids wince. *Name the Prime Minister of Rhodesia.*
My country. *How many florins in a pound?*

Litany

The soundtrack then was a litany – *candlewick*
bedspread three piece suite display cabinet –
and stiff-haired wives balanced their red smiles,
passing the catalogue. *Pyrex*. A tiny ladder
ran up Mrs Barr's American Tan leg, sly
like a rumour. Language embarrassed them.

The terrible marriages crackled, cellophane
round polyester shirts, and then The Lounge
would seem to bristle with eyes, hard
as the bright stones in engagement rings,
and sharp hands poised over biscuits as a word
was spelled out. An embarrassing word, broken

to bits, which tensed the air like an accident.
This was the code I learnt at my mother's knee, pretending
to read, where no one had cancer, or sex, or debts,
and certainly not leukaemia, which no one could spell.
The year a mass grave of wasps bobbed in a jam-jar;
a butterfly stammered itself in my curious hands.

A boy in the playground, I said, *told me*
to fuck off; and a thrilled, malicious pause
salted my tongue like an imminent storm. Then
uproar. *I'm sorry, Mrs Barr, Mrs Hunt, Mrs Emery,*
sorry, Mrs Raine. Yes, I can summon their names.
My mother's mute shame. The taste of soap.

Nostalgia

Those early mercenaries, it made them ill –
leaving the mountains, leaving the high, fine air
to go down, down. What they got
was money, dull crude coins clenched
in the teeth; strange food, the wrong taste,
stones in the belly; and the wrong sounds,
the wrong smells, the wrong light, every breath –
wrong. They had an ache *here*, Doctor,
they pined, wept, grown men. It was killing them.

It was given a name. Hearing tell of it,
there were those who stayed put, fearful
of a sweet pain in the heart; of how it hurt,
in that heavier air, to hear
the music of home – the sad pipes – summoning,
in the dwindling light of the plains,
a particular place – where maybe you met a girl,
or searched for a yellow ball in long grass,
found it just as your mother called you in.

But the word was out. Some would never
fall in love had they not heard of love.
So the priest stood at the stile with his head
in his hands, crying at the workings of memory
through the colour of leaves, and the schoolteacher
opened a book to the scent of her youth, too late.
It was spring when one returned, with his life
in a sack on his back, to find the same street
with the same sign on the inn, the same bell
chiming the hour on the clock, and everything changed.

Stafford Afternoons

Only there, the afternoons could suddenly pause
and when I looked up from lacing my shoe
a long road held no one, the gardens were empty,
an ice-cream van chimed and dwindled away.

On the motorway bridge, I waved at windscreens,
oddly hurt by the blurred waves back, the speed.
So I let a horse in the noisy field sponge at my palm
and invented, in colour, a vivid lie for us both.

In a cul-de-sac, a strange boy threw a stone.
I crawled through a hedge into long grass
at the edge of a small wood, lonely and thrilled.
The green silence gulped once and swallowed me whole.

I knew it was dangerous. The way the trees
drew sly faces from light and shade, the wood
let out its sticky breath on the back of my neck,
and flowering nettles gathered spit in their throats.

Too late. *Touch*, said the long-haired man
who stood, legs apart, by a silver birch
with a living, purple root in his hand. The sight
made sound rush back; birds, a distant lawnmower,

his hoarse, frightful endearments as I backed away
then ran all the way home; into a game
where children scattered and shrieked
and time fell from the sky like a red ball.

Brothers

Once, I slept in a bed with these four men who share
an older face and can be made to laugh, even now,
at random quotes from the play we were in. *There's no way
in the creation of God's earth*, I say. They grin and nod.

What was possible retreats and shrinks, and in my other eyes
they shrink to an altar boy, a boy practising scales,
a boy playing tennis with a wall, a baby
crying in the night like a new sound flailing for a shape.

Occasionally, when people ask, I enjoy reciting their names.
I don't have photographs, but I like to repeat the names.
My mother chose them. I hear her life in the words,
the breeding words, the word that broke her heart.

Much in common, me, with thieves and businessmen,
fathers and UB40s. We have nothing to say of now,
but time owns us. How tall they have grown. One day
I shall pay for a box and watch them shoulder it.

Before You Were Mine

I'm ten years away from the corner you laugh on
with your pals, Maggie McGeeney and Jean Duff.
The three of you bend from the waist, holding
each other, or your knees, and shriek at the pavement.
Your polka-dot dress blows round your legs. Marilyn.

I'm not here yet. The thought of me doesn't occur
in the ballroom with the thousand eyes, the fizzy, movie tomorrows
the right walk home could bring. I knew you would dance
like that. Before you were mine, your Ma stands at the close
with a hiding for the late one. You reckon it's worth it.

The decade ahead of my loud, possessive yell was the best one, eh?
I remember my hands in those high-heeled red shoes, relics,
and now your ghost clatters toward me over George Square
till I see you, clear as scent, under the tree,
with its lights, and whose small bites on your neck, sweetheart?

Cha cha cha! You'd teach me the steps on the way home from Mass,
stamping stars from the wrong pavement. Even then
I wanted the bold girl winking in Portobello, somewhere
in Scotland, before I was born. That glamorous love lasts
where you sparkle and waltz and laugh before you were mine.

Welltread

Welltread was Head and the Head's face was a fist. Yes,
I've got him. Spelling and Punishment. A big brass bell
dumb on his desk till only he shook it, and children
ran shrieking in the locked yard. Mr Welltread. Sir.

He meant well. They all did then. The loud, inarticulate dads,
the mothers who spat on hankies and rubbed you away.
But Welltread looked like a gangster. Welltread stalked
the forms, collecting thruppenny bits in a soft black hat.

We prayed for Aberfan, vaguely reprieved. My socks dissolved,
two grey pools at my ankles, at the shock of my name
called out. The memory brings me to my feet
as a foul would. The wrong child for a trite crime.

And all I could say was No. Welltread straightened my hand
as though he could read the future there, then hurt himself
more than he hurt me. There was no cause for complaint.
There was the burn of a cane in my palm, still smouldering.

Confession

Come away into this dark cell and tell
your sins to a hidden man your guardian angel
works your conscience like a glove-puppet It
smells in here doesn't it does it smell
like a coffin how would you know C'mon
out with them sins those little maggoty things
that wriggle in the soul . . . *Bless me Father* . . .

Just how bad have you been there's no water
in hell merely to think of a wrong's as evil
as doing it . . . *For I have sinned* . . . Penance
will cleanse you like a bar of good soap so
say the words into the musty gloom aye
on your knees let's hear that wee voice
recite transgression in the manner approved . . . *Forgive me* . . .

You do well to stammer A proper respect
for eternal damnation see the flicker
of your white hands clasping each other like
Hansel and Gretel in the big black wood
cross yourself Remember the vinegar and sponge
there's light on the other side of the door . . . *Mother
of God* . . . if you can only reach it Jesus loves you.

The Good Teachers

You run round the back to be in it again.
No bigger than your thumbs, those virtuous women
size you up from the front row. Soon now,
Miss Ross will take you for double History.
You breathe on the glass, making a ghost of her, say
South Sea Bubble Defenestration of Prague.

You love Miss Pirie. So much, you are top
of her class. So much, you need two of you
to stare out from the year, serious, passionate.
The River's Tale by Rudyard Kipling by heart.
Her kind intelligent green eye. Her cruel blue one.
You are making a poem up for her in your head.

But not Miss Sheridan. Comment vous appelez.
But not Miss Appleby. Equal to the square
of the other two sides. Never Miss Webb.
Dar es Salaam. Kilimanjaro. Look. The good teachers
swish down the corridor in long, brown skirts,
snobbish and proud and clean and qualified.

And they've got your number. You roll the waistband
of your skirt over and over, all leg, all
dumb insolence, smoke-rings. You won't pass.
You could do better. But there's the wall you climb
into dancing, lovebites, marriage, the Cheltenham
and Gloucester, today. The day you'll be sorry one day.

Like Earning a Living

What's an elephant like? I say
to the slack-mouthed girl
who answers back, a trainee ventriloquist,
then smirks at Donna. She dunno.
Nor does the youth with the face.
And what would that say, fingered?
I know. Video. Big Mac. Lager. Lager.
What like's a wart-hog? Come on.

Ambition. Rage. Boredom. Spite. How
do they taste, smell, sound?
Nobody cares. Jason doesn't. Nor does his dad.
He met a poet. Didn't know it. Uungh.
What would that aftershave say
if it could think? What colour's the future?

Somewhere in England, Major-Balls,
the long afternoon empties of air, meaning, energy, point.
Kin-L. There just aren't the words for it.
Darren. Paul. Kelly. Marie. What's it like? Mike?

Like earning a living.
Earning a living like.

The Cliché Kid

I need help, Doc, and bad; I can't forget
the rustle of my father's ballgown as he bent
to say goodnight to me, his kiss, his French scent . . .

Give me a shot of something. Or the sound of Ma
and her pals up late, boozing, dealing the cards.
Big Bertha pissing out from the porch under the stars . . .

It gets worse. Chalkdust. The old schoolroom empty.
This kid so unpopular even my imaginary friend left me
for another child. I'm screwed up, Doc, jumpy . . .

Distraught in autumn, kneeling under the chestnut trees,
seeing childhood in the conkers through my tears.
Bonkers. And me so butch in my boots down the macho bars . . .

Give me a break. Don't let me pine for that first love,
that faint down on the cheeks, that easy laugh
in my ears, in my lonesome heart, the day that I had to leave . . .

Sweet Jesus, Doc, I worry I'll miss when a long time dead
the smell the smell the smell of the baby's head,
the fresh-baked grass, dammit, the new-mown bread . . .

Pluto

When I awoke
a brand new planet
had been given a name –

    this Home I'm in,
    it has the same soap suddenly;
    so, washing my hands,
    I'm thinking *Pluto Pluto Pluto*,
    thrilled,
    beside myself.

    And then I notice things;
    brown coins of age on my face the size of ha'pennies.
    An hourglass weeping the future into the past

– and I was a boy.

I cry out now in my bath,
shocked and bereaved again
by not quite seeing us all,
half-hearing my father's laugh –
without the help and support of the woman I love.

Tangerine soap.
To think of another world out there
in the dark,
unreachable,
of what it was like.

Beachcomber

If you think till it hurts
you can almost do it without getting off that chair,
scare yourself
within an inch of the heart
at the prompt of a word.
How old are you now?
This is what happens –

the child,
and not in sepia,
lives,
you can see her;
comes up the beach,
alone;
bucket and spade.
In her bucket, a starfish, seaweed,
a dozen alarming crabs
caught with string and a mussel.
Don't move.
Trow.

Go for the sound of the sea,
don't try to describe it,
get it into your head;
and then the platinum blaze of the sun as the earth
    seemed to turn away.
Now she is kneeling.

This is about something.
Harder.
The red spade
scooping a hole in the sand.
Sea-water seeping in.
The girl suddenly holding a conch, listening, sssh.
You remember that cardigan, yes?
You remember that cardigan.

But this is as close as you get.
Nearly there.
Open your eyes.
Those older, those shaking, hands cannot touch
the child
or the spade
or the sand
or the seashell on the shore;
and what
what would you have to say,
of all people,
to her
given the chance?
Exactly.

Caul

No, I don't remember the thing itself.
I remember the word.
Amnion, inner membrane, *caul*.
I'll never be drowned.

The past is the future waiting for dreams
and will find itself there.
I came in a cloak of cool luck
and smiled at the world.

Where the man asked the woman to tell
how it felt, how it looked,
and a sailor purchased my charm
to bear to the sea.

I imagine it now, a leathery sheath
the length of a palm
empty as mine, under the waves
or spoil on a beach.

I'm all that is left of then. It spools
itself out like a film
a talented friend can recall
using speech alone.

The light of a candle seen in a caul
eased from my crown that day,
when all but this living noun
was taken away.

Away and See

Away and see an ocean suck at a boiled sun
and say to someone things I'd blush even to dream.
Slip off your dress in a high room over the harbour.
Write to me soon.

New fruits sing on the flipside of night in a market
of language, light, a tune from the chapel nearby
stopping you dead, the peach in your palm respiring.
Taste it for me.

Away and see the things that words give a name to, the flight
of syllables, wingspan stretching a noun. Test words
wherever they live; listen and touch, smell, believe.
Spell them with love.

Skedaddle. Somebody chaps at the door at a year's end, hopeful.
Away and see who it is. Let in the new, the vivid,
horror and pity, passion, the stranger holding the future.
Ask him his name.

Nothing's the same as anything else. Away and see
for yourself. Walk. Fly. Take a boat till land reappears,
altered forever, ringing its bells, alive. Go on. G'on. Gon.
Away and see.

Drunk

Suddenly the rain is hilarious.
The moon wobbles in the dusk.

What a laugh. Unseen frogs
belch in the damp grass.

The strange perfumes of darkening trees.
Cheap red wine

and the whole world a mouth.
Give me a double, a kiss.

Small Female Skull

With some surprise, I balance my small female skull in my hands.
What is it like? An ocarina? Blow in its eye.
It cannot cry, holds my breath only as long as I exhale,
mildly alarmed now, into the hole where the nose was,
press my ear to its grin. A vanishing sigh.

For some time, I sit on the lavatory seat with my head
in my hands, appalled. It feels much lighter than I'd thought;
the weight of a deck of cards, a slim volume of verse,
but with something else, as though it could levitate. Disturbing.
So why do I kiss it on the brow, my warm lips to its papery bone,

and take it to the mirror to ask for a gottle of geer?
I rinse it under the tap, watch dust run away, like sand
from a swimming-cap, then dry it – firstborn – gently
with a towel. I see the scar where I fell for sheer love
down treacherous stairs, and read that shattering day like braille.

Love, I murmur to my skull, then, louder, other grand words,
shouting the hollow nouns in a white-tiled room.
Downstairs they will think I have lost my mind. No. I only weep
into these two holes here, or I'm grinning back at the joke, this is
a friend of mine. See, I hold her face in trembling, passionate hands.

Moments of Grace

I dream through a wordless, familiar place.
The small boat of the day sails into morning,
past the postman with his modest haul, the full trees
which sound like the sea, leaving my hands free
to remember. Moments of grace. *Like this*.

Shaken by first love and kissing a wall. Of course.
The dried ink on the palms then ran suddenly wet,
a glistening blue name in each fist. I sit now
in a kind of sly trance, hoping I will not feel me
breathing too close across time. A face to the name. *Gone*.

The chimes of mothers calling in children
at dusk. *Yes*. It seems we live in those staggering years
only to haunt them; the vanishing scents
and colours of infinite hours like a melting balloon
in earlier hands. The boredom since.

Memory's caged bird won't fly. These days
we are adjectives, nouns. In moments of grace
we were verbs, the secret of poems, talented.
A thin skin lies on the language. We stare
deep in the eyes of strangers, look for the doing words.

Now I smell you peeling an orange in the other room.
Now I take off my watch, let a minute unravel
in my hands, listen and look as I do so,
and mild loss opens my lips like *No*.
Passing, you kiss the back of my neck. A blessing.

First Love

Waking, with a dream of first love forming real words,
as close to my lips as lipstick, I speak your name,
after a silence of years, into the pillow, and the power
of your name brings me here to the window, naked,
to say it again to a garden shaking with light.

This was a child's love, and yet I clench my eyes
till the pictures return, unfocused at first, then
almost clear, an old film played at a slow speed.
All day I will glimpse it, in windows of changing sky,
in mirrors, my lover's eyes, wherever you are.

And later a star, long dead, here, seems precisely
the size of a tear. Tonight, a love-letter out of a dream
stammers itself in my heart. Such faithfulness.
You smile in my head on the last evening. Unseen
flowers suddenly pierce and sweeten the air.

Café Royal

He arrives too late to tell him how it will be.
Oscar is gone. Alone, he orders hock,
sips in the style of an earlier century
in glamorous mirrors under the clocks.

He would like to live then now, suddenly find
himself early, nod to Harris and Shaw;
then sit alone at a table, biding his time
till the Lord of Language stands at the door.

So tall. Breathing. He is the boy who fades away
as Oscar laughingly draws up a chair.
A hundred years on, he longs at the bar to say
Dear, I know where you're going. Don't go there.

But pays for his drink, still tasting the wine's sweet fruit,
and leaves. It matters how everyone dies,
he thinks, half-smiles at an older man in a suit
who stares at his terrible, wonderful eyes.

Crush

The older she gets,
the more she awakes
with somebody's face strewn in her head
like petals which once made a flower.

What everyone does
is sit by a desk
and stare at the view, till the time
where they live reappears. Mostly in words.

Imagine a girl
turning to see
love stand by a window, taller,
clever, anointed with sudden light.

Yes, like an angel then,
to be truthful now.
At first a secret, erotic, mute;
today a language she cannot recall.

And we're all owed joy,
sooner or later.
The trick's to remember whenever
it was, or to see it coming.

Never Go Back

In the bar where the living dead drink all day
and a jukebox reminisces in a cracked voice
there is nothing to say. You talk for hours
in agreed motifs, anecdotes shuffled and dealt
from a well-thumbed pack, snapshots. The smoky mirrors
flatter; your ghost buys a round for the parched,
old faces of the past. Never return
to the space where you left time pining till it died.

Outside, the streets tear litter in their thin hands,
a tired wind whistles through the blackened stumps of houses
at a limping dog. *God, this is an awful place*
says the friend, the alcoholic, whose head is a negative
of itself. You listen and nod, bereaved. Baby,
what you owe to this place is unpayable
in the only currency you have. So drink up. Shut up,
then get them in again. Again. And never go back.

*

The house where you were one of the brides
has cancer. It prefers to be left alone
nursing its growth and cracks, each groan and creak
accusing as you climb the stairs to the bedroom
and draw your loved body on blurred air
with the simple power of loss. All the lies
told here, and all the cries of love,
suddenly swarm in the room, sting you, disappear.

You shouldn't be here. You follow your shadow
through the house, discover that objects held
in the hands can fill a room with pain.
You lived here only to stand here now
and half-believe that you did. A small moment
of death by a window myopic with rain.
You learn this lesson hard, speechless, slamming
the front door, shaking plaster confetti from your hair.

*

A taxi implying a hearse takes you slowly,
the long way round, to the station. The driver
looks like death. The places you knew
have changed their names by neon, cheap tricks
in a theme-park with no theme. Sly sums of money
wink at you in the cab. At a red light,
you wipe a slick of cold sweat from the glass
for a drenched whore to stare you full in the face.

You pay to get out, pass the *Welcome To* sign
on the way to the barrier, an emigrant
for the last time. The train sighs
and pulls you away, rewinding the city like a film,
snapping it off at the river. You go for a drink,
released by a journey into nowhere, nowhen,
and all the way home you forget. Forget. Already
the fires and lights come on wherever you live.

Oslo

What you do. Follow the slow tram
into the night. Wear your coat with the hood.
You're foreign here. The town reveals itself
the way the one you live in never could.

Not to speak the language makes you
innocent again, invisible. But if you like
you bribe the bellboy in this grand hotel
to tell where the casino is, a blue light

over its door. You're in. A cool drink.
Your money changed. Too early yet,
at ten o'clock, for scented, smoking, silent
men to gather round and, you bet, bet and bet.

This life, you win some, lose some. Then?
You want to go home. With only a numbered key,
you take the shortcut past the palace, through
the tall Norwegian wood. For now, you're lucky –

across the world, someone loves you hard enough
to sieve a single star from this dark sky.

The Grammar of Light

Even barely enough light to find a mouth,
and bless both with a meaningless O, teaches,
spells out. The way a curtain opened at night
lets in neon, or moon, or a car's hasty glance,
and paints for a moment someone you love, pierces.

And so many mornings to learn; some
when the day is wrung from damp, grey skies
and rooms come on for breakfast
in the town you are leaving early. The way
a wasteground weeps glass tears at the end of a street.

Some fluent, showing you how the trees
in the square think in birds, telepathise. The way
the waiter balances light in his hands, the coins
in his pocket silver, and a young bell shines
in its white tower ready to tell.

Even a saucer of rain in a garden at evening
speaks to the eye. Like the little fires
from allotments, undressing in veils of mauve smoke
as you walk home under the muted lamps,
perplexed. The way the shy stars go stuttering on.

And at midnight, a candle next to the wine
slurs its soft wax, flatters. Shadows
circle the table. The way all faces blur
to dreams of themselves held in the eyes.
The flare of another match. The way everything dies.

Valentine

Not a red rose or a satin heart.

I give you an onion.
It is a moon wrapped in brown paper.
It promises light
like the careful undressing of love.

Here.
It will blind you with tears
like a lover.
It will make your reflection
a wobbling photo of grief.

I am trying to be truthful.

Not a cute card or a kissogram.

I give you an onion.
Its fierce kiss will stay on your lips,
possessive and faithful
as we are,
for as long as we are.

Take it.
Its platinum loops shrink to a wedding-ring,
if you like.
Lethal.
Its scent will cling to your fingers,
cling to your knife.

Sleeping

Under the dark warm waters of sleep
your hands part me.
I am dreaming you anyway.

Your mouth is hot fruit, wet, strange,
night-fruit I taste with my opening mouth;
my eyes closed.

You, you. Your breath flares into fervent words
which explode in my head. Then you ask, push,
for an answer.

And this is how we sleep. You're in now, hard,
demanding; so I dream more fiercely, dream
till it hurts

that this is for real, yes, I feel it.
When you hear me, you hold on tight, frantic,
as if we were drowning.

Steam

Not long ago so far, a lover and I
in a room of steam –

a sly, thirsty, silvery word – lay down,
opposite ends, and vanished.

Quite recently, if one of us sat up,
or stood, or stretched, naked,

a nude pose in soft pencil
behind tissue paper

appeared, rubbed itself out, slow,
with a smoky cloth.

Say a matter of months. This hand reaching
through the steam

to touch the real thing, shockingly there,
not a ghost at all.

Close

Lock the door. In the dark journey of our night,
two childhoods stand in the corner of the bedroom
watching the way we take each other to bits
to stare at our heart. I hear a story
told in sleep in a lost accent. You know the words.

Undress. A suitcase crammed with secrets
bursts in the wardrobe at the foot of the bed.
Dress again. Undress. You have me like a drawing,
erased, coloured in, untitled, signed by your tongue.
The name of a country written in red on my palm,

unreadable. I tell myself where I live now,
but you move in close till I shake, homeless,
further than that. A coin falls from the bedside table,
spinning its heads and tails. How the hell
can I win. How can I lose. Tell me again.

Love won't give in. It makes a hired room tremble
with the pity of bells, a cigarette smoke itself
next to a full glass of wine, time ache
into space, space, wants no more talk. Now
it has me where I want me, now you, you do.

Put out the light. Years stand outside on the street
looking up to an open window, black as our mouth
which utters its tuneless song. The ghosts of ourselves,
behind and before us, throng in a mirror, blind,
laughing and weeping. They know who we are.

Adultery

Wear dark glasses in the rain.
Regard what was unhurt
as though through a bruise.
Guilt. A sick, green tint.

New gloves, money tucked in the palms,
the handshake crackles. Hands
can do many things. Phone.
Open the wine. Wash themselves. Now

you are naked under your clothes all day,
slim with deceit. Only the once
brings you alone to your knees,
miming, more, more, older and sadder,

creative. Suck a lie with a hole in it
on the way home from a lethal, thrilling night
up against a wall, faster. Language
unpeels to a lost cry. You're a bastard.

Do it do it do it. Sweet darkness
in the afternoon; a voice in your ear
telling you how you are wanted,
which way, now. A telltale clock

wiping the hours from its face, your face
on a white sheet, gasping, radiant, yes.
Pay for it in cash, fiction, cab-fares back
to the life which crumbles like a wedding-cake.

Paranoia for lunch; too much
to drink, as a hand on your thigh
tilts the restaurant. You know all about love,
don't you. Turn on your beautiful eyes

for a stranger who's dynamite in bed, again
and again; a slow replay in the kitchen
where the slicing of innocent onions
scalds you to tears. Then, selfish autobiographical sleep

in a marital bed, the tarnished spoon of your body
stirring betrayal, your heart over-ripe at the core.
You're an expert, darling; your flowers
dumb and explicit on nobody's birthday.

So write the script – illness and debt,
a ring thrown away in a garden
no moon can heal, your own words
commuting to bile in your mouth, terror –

and all for the same thing twice. And all
for the same thing twice. You did it.
What. Didn't you. Fuck. Fuck. No. That was
the wrong verb. This is only an abstract noun.

Havisham

Beloved sweetheart bastard. Not a day since then
I haven't wished him dead. Prayed for it
so hard I've dark green pebbles for eyes,
ropes on the back of my hands I could strangle with.

Spinster. I stink and remember. Whole days
in bed cawing Nooooo at the wall; the dress
yellowing, trembling if I open the wardrobe;
the slewed mirror, full-length, her, myself, who did this

to me? Puce curses that are sounds not words.
Some nights better, the lost body over me,
my fluent tongue in its mouth in its ear
then down till I suddenly bite awake. Love's

hate behind a white veil; a red balloon bursting
in my face. Bang. I stabbed at a wedding-cake.
Give me a male corpse for a long slow honeymoon.
Don't think it's only the heart that b-b-b-breaks.

The Suicide

Small dark hours with a bitter moon buffed by the smudgy clouds
till it gleams with resentment.
I dress in a shroud. Despair
laced with a little glee.
Leave it to me.

Never never never
never enough.
The horrid smiling mouths
pout on the wallpaper. Kisses
on a collar. Lies. Blood.
My body is a blank page I will write on.

Famous.

Nobody drinks with their whole face.
I do.
Nobody's ears are confessionals.
Mine are.
Eyes in the glass like squids. Sexy.

I get out the knives. Who wants
a bloody valentine pumping its love hate love?
Utterly selfless
I lie back under the lightbulb.
Something like a cat claws from my head, spiteful.

Fuck off.
Worship.

This will kill my folks.

Stuffed

I put two yellow peepers in an owl.
Wow. I fix the grin of Crocodile.
Spiv. I sew the slither of an eel.

I jerk, kick-start, the back hooves of a mule.
Wild. I hold a red rag to a bull.
Mad. I spread the feathers of a gull.

I screw a tight snarl to a weasel.
Fierce. I stitch the flippers on a seal.
Splayed. I pierce the heartbeat of a quail.

I like her to be naked and to kneel.
Tame. My motionless, my living doll.
Mute. And afterwards I like her not to tell.

Fraud

Firstly, I changed my name
to that of a youth I knew for sure had bought it in 1940,
    Rotterdam.
Private M.
I was my own poem,
pseudonym,
rule of thumb.
What was my aim?
To change from a bum
to a billionaire. I spoke the English. Mine was a scam
involving pensions, papers, politicians in-and-out of their pram.
And I was to blame.

For what? There's a gnome
in Zürich knows more than people assume.
There's a military man, Jerusalem
way, keeping schtum.
Then there's Him –
for whom
I paid for a butch and femme
to make him come.
And all of the crème
de la crème
considered me scum.

Poverty's dumb.
Take it from me, Sonny Jim,
learn to lie in the mother-tongue of the motherfucker you want
    to charm.
They're all the same,
turning their wide blind eyes to crime.

And who gives a damn
when the keys to a second home
are pressed in his palm,
or polaroids of a Night of Shame
with a Boy on the Game
are passed his way at the A.G.M.?

So read my lips. Mo-ney. Pow-er. Fame.
And had I been asked, in my time,
in my puce and prosperous prime,
if I recalled the crumbling slum
of my Daddy's home,
if I was a shit, a sham,
if I'd done immeasurable harm,
I could have replied with a dream:
the water that night was calm
and with my enormous mouth, in bubbles and blood and phlegm,
I gargled my name.

The Biographer

Because you are dead,
I stand at your desk,
my fingers caressing the grooves in the wood
your initials made;
and I manage a quote,
echo one of your lines in the small, blue room
where an early daguerreotype shows you
excitedly staring out
from behind your face,
the thing that made you yourself
still visibly there,
like a hood and a cloak of light.
The first four words that I write are your name.

I'm a passionate man
with a big advance
who's loved your work since he was a boy;
but the night
I slept alone in your bed,
the end of a fire going out in the grate,
I came awake –
certain, had we ever met,
you wouldn't have wanted me,
or needed me,
would barely have noticed me at all.
Guilt and rage
hardened me then,
and later I felt your dislike
chilling the air
as I drifted away.
Your wallpaper green and crimson and gold.

How close can I get
to the sound of your voice
which Emma Elizabeth Hibbert described –
lively, eager and lightly-pitched,
with none of the later, bitter edge.
Cockney, a little.
In London Town,
the faces you wrote
leer and gape and plead at my feet.
Once, high on Hungerford Bridge,
a stew and tangle of rags, sniffed by a dog, stood, spoke,
spat at the shadow I cast,
at the meagre shadow I cast in my time.
I heard the faraway bells of St Paul's as I ran.

Maestro. Monster. Mummy's Boy.
My Main Man.
I write you and write you for five hard years.
I have an affair with a thespian girl –
you would have approved –
then I snivel home to my wife.
Her poems and jam.
Her forgiveness.
Her violent love.
And this is a life.
I print it out.
I print it out.
In all of your mirrors, my face;
with its smallish, its quizzical eyes,
its cheekbones, its sexy jaw,
its talentless, dustjacket smile.

The Windows

How do you earn a life going on
behind yellow windows, writing at night
the Latin names of plants for a garden,
opening the front door to a wet dog?

Those you love forgive you, clearly,
with steaming casseroles and red wine.
It's the same film down all the suburban streets,
It's A Wonderful Life. How do you learn it?

What you hear – the doorbell's familiar chime.
What you touch – the clean, warm towels.
What you see what you smell what you taste
all tangible to the stranger passing your gate.

There you are again, in a room where those early hyacinths
surely sweeten the air, and the right words wait
in the dictionaries, on the tip of the tongue you touch
in a kiss, drawing your crimson curtains now

against dark hours. And again, in a kitchen,
the window ajar, sometimes the sound of your radio
or the scent of your food, and a cat in your arms,
a child in your arms, a lover. Such vivid flowers.

Disgrace

But one day we woke to disgrace; our house
a coldness of rooms, each nursing
a thickening cyst of dust and gloom.
We had not been home in our hearts for months.

And how our words changed. Dead flies in a web.
How they stiffened and blackened. Cherished italics
suddenly sour on our tongues, obscenities
spraying themselves on the wall in my head.

Woke to your clothes like a corpse on the floor,
the small deaths of lightbulbs pining all day
in my ears, their echoes audible tears;
nothing we would not do to make it worse

and worse. Into the night with the wrong language,
waving and pointing, the shadows of hands
huge in the bedroom. Dreamed of a naked crawl
from a dead place over the other; both of us. Woke.

Woke to the absence of grace; the still-life
of a meal, untouched, wine-bottle, empty, ashtray,
full. In our sullen kitchen, the fridge
hardened its cool heart, selfish as art, hummed.

To a bowl of apples rotten to the core. Lame shoes
empty in the hall where our voices asked
for a message after the tone, the telephone
pressing its ear to distant, invisible lips.

And our garden bowing its head, vulnerable flowers
unseen in the dusk as we shouted in silhouette.
Woke to the screaming alarm, the banging door,
the house-plants trembling in their brittle soil. Total

disgrace. Up in the dark to stand at the window,
counting the years to arrive there, faithless,
unpenitent. Woke to the meaningless stars, you
and me both, lost. Inconsolable vowels from the next room.

Room

One chair to sit in,
a greasy dusk wrong side of the tracks,
and watch the lodgers' lights come on in the other rooms.

No curtains yet. A cool lightbulb
waiting for a moth. Hard silence.
The roofs of terraced houses stretch from here to how many months.

Room. One second-hand bed
to remind of a death, somewhen. Room.
Then clouds the colour of smokers' lungs. Then what.

In a cold black window, a face
takes off its glasses and stares out again.
Night now; the giftless moon and a cat pissing on a wall. £90 pw.

Mean Time

The clocks slid back an hour
and stole light from my life
as I walked through the wrong part of town,
mourning our love.

And, of course, unmendable rain
fell to the bleak streets
where I felt my heart gnaw
at all our mistakes.

If the darkening sky could lift
more than one hour from this day
there are words I would never have said
nor have heard you say.

But we will be dead, as we know,
beyond all light.
These are the shortened days
and the endless nights.

Prayer

Some days, although we cannot pray, a prayer
utters itself. So, a woman will lift
her head from the sieve of her hands and stare
at the minims sung by a tree, a sudden gift.

Some nights, although we are faithless, the truth
enters our hearts, that small familiar pain;
then a man will stand stock-still, hearing his youth
in the distant Latin chanting of a train.

Pray for us now. Grade I piano scales
console the lodger looking out across
a Midlands town. Then dusk, and someone calls
a child's name as though they named their loss.

Darkness outside. Inside, the radio's prayer –
Rockall. Malin. Dogger. Finisterre.

That shut him up.
I laughed last,
longest.

Little Red-Cap

At childhood's end, the houses petered out
into playing fields, the factory, allotments
kept, like mistresses, by kneeling married men,
the silent railway line, the hermit's caravan,
till you came at last to the edge of the woods.
It was there that I first clapped eyes on the wolf.

He stood in a clearing, reading his verse out loud
in his wolfy drawl, a paperback in his hairy paw,
red wine staining his bearded jaw. What big ears
he had! What big eyes he had! What teeth!
In the interval, I made quite sure he spotted me,
sweet sixteen, never been, babe, waif, and bought me a drink,

my first. You might ask why. Here's why. Poetry.
The wolf, I knew, would lead me deep into the woods,
away from home, to a dark tangled thorny place
lit by the eyes of owls. I crawled in his wake,
my stockings ripped to shreds, scraps of red from my blazer
snagged on twig and branch, murder clues. I lost both shoes

but got there, wolf's lair, better beware. Lesson one that night,
breath of the wolf in my ear, was the love poem.
I clung till dawn to his thrashing fur, for
what little girl doesn't dearly love a wolf?
Then I slid from between his heavy matted paws
and went in search of a living bird – white dove –

which flew, straight, from my hands to his open mouth.
One bite, dead. How nice, breakfast in bed, he said,
licking his chops. As soon as he slept, I crept to the back
of the lair, where a whole wall was crimson, gold, aglow with books.
Words, words were truly alive on the tongue, in the head,
warm, beating, frantic, winged; music and blood.

But then I was young – and it took ten years
in the woods to tell that a mushroom
stoppers the mouth of a buried corpse, that birds
are the uttered thought of trees, that a greying wolf
howls the same old song at the moon, year in, year out,
season after season, same rhyme, same reason. I took an axe

to a willow to see how it wept. I took an axe to a salmon
to see how it leapt. I took an axe to the wolf
as he slept, one chop, scrotum to throat, and saw
the glistening, virgin white of my grandmother's bones.
I filled his old belly with stones. I stitched him up.
Out of the forest I come with my flowers, singing, all alone.

Thetis

I shrank myself
to the size of a bird in the hand
of a man.
Sweet, sweet, was the small song
that I sang,
till I felt the squeeze of his fist.

Then I did this:
shouldered the cross of an albatross
up the hill of the sky.
Why? To follow a ship.
But I felt my wings
clipped by the squint of a crossbow's eye.

So I shopped for a suitable shape.
Size 8. Snake.
Big Mistake.
Coiled in my charmer's lap,
I felt the grasp of his strangler's clasp
at my nape.

Next I was roar, claw, 50 lb paw,
jungle-floored, meateater, raw,
a zebra's gore
in my lower jaw.
But my gold eye saw
the guy in the grass with the gun. Twelve-bore.

I sank through the floor of the earth
to swim in the sea.
Mermaid, me, big fish, eel, dolphin,
whale, the ocean's opera singer.
Over the waves the fisherman came
with his hook and his line and his sinker.

I changed my tune
to racoon, skunk, stoat,
to weasel, ferret, bat, mink, rat.
The taxidermist sharpened his knives.
I smelled the stink of formaldehyde.
Stuff that.

I was wind, I was gas,
I was all hot air, trailed
clouds for hair.
I scrawled my name with a hurricane,
when out of the blue
roared a fighter plane.

Then my tongue was flame
and my kisses burned,
but the groom wore asbestos.
So I changed, I learned,
turned inside out – or that's
how it felt when the child burst out.

Queen Herod

Ice in the trees.
Three Queens at the Palace gates,
dressed in furs, accented;
their several sweating, panting beasts,
laden for a long, hard trek,
following the guide and boy to the stables;
courteous, confident; oh, and with gifts
for the King and Queen of here – Herod, me –
in exchange for sunken baths, curtained beds,
fruit, the best of meat and wine,
dancers, music, talk –
as it turned out to be,
with everyone fast asleep, save me,
those vivid three –
till bitter dawn.

They were wise. Older than I.
They knew what they knew.
Once drunken Herod's head went back,
they asked to see her,
fast asleep in her crib,
my little child.
Silver and gold,
the loose change of herself,
glowed in the soft bowl of her face.
Grace, said the tallest Queen.
Strength, said the Queen with the hennaed hands.
The black Queen
made a tiny starfish of my daughter's fist,
said *Happiness*; then stared at me,
Queen to Queen, with insolent lust.

Watch, they said, *for a star in the East –*
a new star
pierced through the night like a nail.
It means he's here, alive, new-born.
Who? *Him. The Husband. Hero. Hunk.*
The Boy Next Door. The Paramour. The Je t'adore.
The Marrying Kind. Adulterer. Bigamist.
The Wolf. The Rip. The Rake. The Rat.
The Heartbreaker. The Ladykiller. Mr Right.

My baby stirred,
suckled the empty air for milk,
till I knelt
and the black Queen scooped out my breast,
the left, guiding it down
to the infant's mouth.
No man, I swore,
will make her shed one tear.
A peacock screamed outside.

Afterwards, it seemed like a dream.
The pungent camels
kneeling in the snow,
the guide's rough shout
as he clapped his leather gloves,
hawked, spat, snatched
the smoky jug of mead
from the chittering maid –
she was twelve, thirteen.
I watched each turbaned Queen
rise like a god on the back of her beast.

And splayed that night
below Herod's fusty bulk,
I saw the fierce eyes of the black Queen
flash again, felt her urgent warnings scald
my ear. *Watch for a star, a star.*
It means he's here . . .

Some swaggering lad to break her heart,
some wincing Prince to take her name away
and give a ring, a nothing, nowt in gold.
I sent for the Chief of Staff,
a mountain man
with a red scar, like a tick
to the mean stare of his eye.
Take men and horses,
knives, swords, cutlasses.
Ride East from here
and kill each mother's son.
Do it. Spare not one.

The midnight hour. The chattering stars
shivered in a nervous sky.
Orion to the South
who knew the score, who'd seen,
not seen, then seen it all before;
the yapping Dog Star at his heels.
High up in the West
a studded, diamond W.
And then, as prophesied,
blatant, brazen, buoyant in the East –
and blue –
The Boyfriend's Star.

We do our best,
we Queens, we mothers,
mothers of Queens.

We wade through blood
for our sleeping girls.
We have daggers for eyes.

Behind our lullabies,
the hooves of terrible horses
thunder and drum.

Mrs Midas

It was late September. I'd just poured a glass of wine, begun
to unwind, while the vegetables cooked. The kitchen
filled with the smell of itself, relaxed, its steamy breath
gently blanching the windows. So I opened one,
then with my fingers wiped the other's glass like a brow.
He was standing under the pear tree snapping a twig.

Now the garden was long and the visibility poor, the way
the dark of the ground seems to drink the light of the sky,
but that twig in his hand was gold. And then he plucked
a pear from a branch – we grew Fondante d'Automne –
and it sat in his palm like a light bulb. On.
I thought to myself, Is he putting fairy lights in the tree?

He came into the house. The doorknobs gleamed.
He drew the blinds. You know the mind; I thought of
the Field of the Cloth of Gold and of Miss Macready.
He sat in that chair like a king on a burnished throne.
The look on his face was strange, wild, vain. I said,
What in the name of God is going on? He started to laugh.

I served up the meal. For starters, corn on the cob.
Within seconds he was spitting out the teeth of the rich.
He toyed with his spoon, then mine, then with the knives, the forks.
He asked where was the wine. I poured with a shaking hand,
a fragrant, bone-dry white from Italy, then watched
as he picked up the glass, goblet, golden chalice, drank.

It was then that I started to scream. He sank to his knees.
After we'd both calmed down, I finished the wine
on my own, hearing him out. I made him sit
on the other side of the room and keep his hands to himself.
I locked the cat in the cellar. I moved the phone.
The toilet I didn't mind. I couldn't believe my ears:

how he'd had a wish. Look, we all have wishes; granted.
But who has wishes granted? Him. Do you know about gold?
It feeds no one; aurum, soft, untarnishable; slakes
no thirst. He tried to light a cigarette; I gazed, entranced,
as the blue flame played on its luteous stem. At least,
I said, you'll be able to give up smoking for good.

Separate beds. In fact, I put a chair against my door,
near petrified. He was below, turning the spare room
into the tomb of Tutankhamun. You see, we were passionate then,
in those halcyon days; unwrapping each other, rapidly,
like presents, fast food. But now I feared his honeyed embrace,
the kiss that would turn my lips to a work of art.

And who, when it comes to the crunch, can live
with a heart of gold? That night, I dreamt I bore
his child, its perfect ore limbs, its little tongue
like a precious latch, its amber eyes
holding their pupils like flies. My dream-milk
burned in my breasts. I woke to the streaming sun.

So he had to move out. We'd a caravan
in the wilds, in a glade of its own. I drove him up
under cover of dark. He sat in the back.
And then I came home, the woman who married the fool
who wished for gold. At first I visited, odd times,
parking the car a good way off, then walking.

You knew you were getting close. Golden trout
on the grass. One day, a hare hung from a larch,
a beautiful lemon mistake. And then his footprints,
glistening next to the river's path. He was thin,
delirious; hearing, he said, the music of Pan
from the woods. Listen. That was the last straw.

What gets me now is not the idiocy or greed
but lack of thought for me. Pure selfishness. I sold
the contents of the house and came down here.
I think of him in certain lights, dawn, late afternoon,
and once a bowl of apples stopped me dead. I miss most,
even now, his hands, his warm hands on my skin, his touch.

from Mrs Tiresias

All I know is this:
he went out for his walk a man
and came home female.

Out the back gate with his stick,
the dog;
wearing his gardening kecks,
an open-necked shirt,
and a jacket in Harris tweed I'd patched at the elbows myself.

Whistling.

He liked to hear
the first cuckoo of spring
then write to *The Times*.
I'd usually heard it
days before him
but I never let on.

I'd heard one that morning
while he was asleep;
just as I heard,
at about 6 p.m.,
a faint sneer of thunder up in the woods
and felt
a sudden heat
at the back of my knees.

He was late getting back.

I was brushing my hair at the mirror
and running a bath
when a face
swam into view
next to my own.

The eyes were the same.
But in the shocking V of the shirt were breasts.
When he uttered my name in his woman's voice I passed out.

*

Life has to go on.

I put it about that he was a twin
and this was his sister
come down to live
while he himself
was working abroad.

And at first I tried to be kind;
blow-drying his hair till he learnt to do it himself,
lending him clothes till he started to shop for his own,
sisterly, holding his soft new shape in my arms all night.

Then he started his period.

One week in bed.
Two doctors in.
Three painkillers four times a day.

And later
a letter
to the powers that be
demanding full-paid menstrual leave twelve weeks per year
I see him still,
his selfish pale face peering at the moon
through the bathroom window.
The curse, he said, *the curse.*

Don't kiss me in public,
he snapped the next day,
I don't want folk getting the wrong idea.

It got worse.

*

After the split I would glimpse him
out and about,
entering glitzy restaurants
on the arms of powerful men –
though I knew for sure
there'd be nothing of *that*
going on
if he had his way –
or on TV
telling the women out there
how, as a woman himself,
he knew how we felt.

His flirt's smile.

The one thing he never got right
was the voice.
A cling peach slithering out from its tin.

I gritted my teeth.

*

And this is my lover, I said,
the one time we met
at a glittering ball
under the lights,
among tinkling glass,
and watched the way he stared
at her violet eyes,
at the blaze of her skin,
at the slow caress of her hand on the back of my neck;
and saw him picture
her bite,
her bite at the fruit of my lips,
and hear
my red wet cry in the night
as she shook his hand
saying *How do you do*;
and I noticed then his hands, her hands,
the clash of their sparkling rings and their painted nails.

Pilate's Wife

Firstly, his hands – a woman's. Softer than mine,
with pearly nails, like shells from Galilee.
Indolent hands. Camp hands that clapped for grapes.
Their pale, mothy touch made me flinch. Pontius.

I longed for Rome, home, someone else. When the Nazarene
entered Jerusalem, my maid and I crept out,
bored stiff, disguised, and joined the frenzied crowd.
I tripped, clutched the bridle of an ass, looked up

and there he was. His face? Ugly. Talented.
He looked at me. I mean he looked at *me*. My God.
His eyes were eyes to die for. Then he was gone,
his rough men shouldering a pathway to the gates.

The night before his trial, I dreamt of him.
His brown hands touched me. Then it hurt.
Then blood. I saw that each tough palm was skewered
by a nail. I woke up, sweating, sexual, terrified.

Leave him alone. I sent a warning note, then quickly dressed.
When I arrived, the Nazarene was crowned with thorns.
The crowd was baying for Barabbas. Pilate saw me,
looked away, then carefully turned up his sleeves

and slowly washed his useless, perfumed hands.
They seized the prophet then and dragged him out,
up to the Place of Skulls. My maid knows all the rest.
Was he God? Of course not. Pilate believed he was.

Mrs Aesop

By Christ, he could bore for Purgatory. He was small,
didn't prepossess. So he tried to impress. *Dead men,
Mrs Aesop,* he'd say, *tell no tales.* Well, let me tell you now
that the bird in his hand shat on his sleeve,
never mind the two worth less in the bush. Tedious.

Going out was worst. He'd stand at our gate, look, then leap;
scour the hedgerows for a shy mouse, the fields
for a sly fox, the sky for one particular swallow
that couldn't make a summer. The jackdaw, according to him,
envied the eagle. Donkeys would, on the whole, prefer to be lions.

On one appalling evening stroll, we passed an old hare
snoozing in a ditch – he stopped and made a note –
and then, about a mile further on, a tortoise, somebody's pet,
creeping, slow as marriage, up the road. *Slow
but certain, Mrs Aesop, wins the race.* Asshole.

What race? What sour grapes? What silk purse,
sow's ear, dog in a manger, what big fish? Some days
I could barely keep awake as the story droned on
towards the moral of itself. *Action, Mrs A., speaks louder
than words.* And that's another thing, the sex

was diabolical. I gave him a fable one night
about a little cock that wouldn't crow, a razor-sharp axe
with a heart blacker than the pot that called the kettle.
I'll cut off your tail, all right, I said, *to save my face.*
That shut him up. I laughed last, longest.

Mrs Darwin

7 April 1852.

Went to the Zoo.
I said to Him –
Something about that Chimpanzee over there
 reminds me of you.

Mrs Sisyphus

That's him pushing the stone up the hill, the jerk.
I call it a stone – it's nearer the size of a kirk.
When he first started out, it just used to irk,
but now it incenses me, and him, the absolute berk.
I could do something vicious to him with a dirk.

Think of the perks, he says.
What use is a perk, I shriek,
when you haven't the time to pop open a cork
or go for so much as a walk in the park?
He's a dork.
Folk flock from miles around just to gawk.
They think it's a quirk,
a bit of a lark.
A load of auld bollocks is nearer the mark.
He might as well bark
at the moon –
that feckin' stone's no sooner up
than it's rolling back
all the way down.
And what does he say?
Mustn't shirk –
keen as a hawk,
lean as a shark –
Mustn't shirk!

But I lie alone in the dark,
feeling like Noah's wife did
when he hammered away at the Ark;
like Frau Johann Sebastian Bach.

My voice reduced to a squawk,
my smile to a twisted smirk;
while, up on the deepening murk of the hill,
he is giving one hundred per cent and more to his work.

Mrs Faust

First things first –
I married Faust.
We met as students,
shacked up, split up,
made up, hitched up,
got a mortgage on a house,
flourished academically,
BA. MA. Ph.D. No kids.
Two towelled bathrobes. Hers. His.

We worked. We saved.
We moved again.
Fast cars. A boat with sails.
A second home in Wales.
The latest toys – computers,
mobile phones. Prospered.
Moved again. Faust's face
was clever, greedy, slightly mad.
I was as bad.

I grew to love the lifestyle,
not the life.
He grew to love the kudos,
not the wife.
He went to whores.
I felt, not jealousy,
but chronic irritation.
I went to yoga, t'ai chi,
Feng Shui, therapy, colonic irrigation.

And Faust would boast
at dinner parties
of the cost
of doing deals out East.
Then take his lust
to Soho in a cab,
to say the least,
to lay the ghost,
get lost, meet panthers, feast.

He wanted more.
I came home late one winter's evening,
hadn't eaten.
Faust was upstairs in his study,
in a meeting.
I smelled cigar smoke,
hellish, oddly sexy, not allowed.
I heard Faust and the other
laugh aloud.

Next thing, the world,
as Faust said,
spread its legs.
First politics –
Safe seat. MP. Right Hon. KG.
Then banks –
offshore, abroad –
and business –
Vice-chairman. Chairman. Owner. Lord.

Enough? *Encore!*
Faust was Cardinal, Pope,
knew more than God;
flew faster than the speed of sound
around the globe,
lunched;
walked on the moon,
golfed, holed in one;
lit a fat Havana on the sun.

Then backed a hunch –
invested in smart bombs,
in harms,
Faust dealt in arms.
Faust got in deep, got out.
Bought farms,
cloned sheep,
Faust surfed the Internet
for like-minded Bo-Peep.

As for me,
I went my own sweet way,
saw Rome in a day,
spun gold from hay,
had a facelift,
had my breasts enlarged,
my buttocks tightened;
went to China, Thailand, Africa,
returned, enlightened.

Turned 40, celibate,
teetotal, vegan,
Buddhist, 41.
Went blonde,
redhead, brunette,
went native, ape,
berserk, bananas;
went on the run, alone;
went home.

Faust was in. *A word*, he said,
I spent the night being pleasured
by a virtual Helen of Troy.
Face that launched a thousand ships.
I kissed its lips.
Thing is –
I've made a pact
with Mephistopheles,
the Devil's boy.

He's on his way
to take away
what's owed,
reap what I sowed.
For all these years of
gagging for it,
going for it,
rolling in it,
I've sold my soul.

At this, I heard
a serpent's hiss,
tasted evil, knew its smell,
as scaly devil hands
poked up
right through the terracotta Tuscan tiles
at Faust's bare feet
and dragged him, oddly smirking, there and then
straight down to Hell.

Oh, well.
Faust's will
left everything –
the yacht,
the several homes,
the Lear jet, the helipad,
the loot, et cet, et cet,
the lot –
to me.

C'est la vie.
When I got ill,
it hurt like hell.
I bought a kidney
with my credit card,
then I got well.
I keep Faust's secret still –
the clever, cunning, callous bastard
didn't have a soul to sell.

Delilah

Teach me, he said –
we were lying in bed –
how to care.
I nibbled the purse of his ear.
What do you mean? Tell me more.
He sat up and reached for his beer.

I can rip out the roar
from the throat of a tiger,
or gargle with fire,
or sleep one whole night in the Minotaur's lair,
or flay the bellowing fur
from a bear,
all for a dare.
There's nothing I fear.
Put your hand here –

he guided my fingers over the scar
over his heart,
a four-medal wound from the war –
but I cannot be gentle, or loving, or tender.
I have to be strong.
What is the cure?

He fucked me again
until he was sore,
then we both took a shower.
Then he lay with his head on my lap
for a darkening hour;
his voice, for a change, a soft burr
I could just about hear.

And, yes, I was sure
that he wanted to change,
my warrior.

I was there.

So when I felt him soften and sleep,
when he started, as usual, to snore,
I let him slip and slide and sprawl, handsome and huge,
on the floor.
And before I fetched and sharpened my scissors –
snipping first at the black and biblical air –
I fastened the chain to the door.

That's the how and the why and the where.

Then with deliberate, passionate hands
I cut every lock of his hair.

Anne Hathaway

'Item I gyve unto my wief my second best bed . . .'
(from Shakespeare's will)

The bed we loved in was a spinning world
of forests, castles, torchlight, clifftops, seas
where he would dive for pearls. My lover's words
were shooting stars which fell to earth as kisses
on these lips; my body now a softer rhyme
to his, now echo, assonance; his touch
a verb dancing in the centre of a noun.
Some nights, I dreamed he'd written me, the bed
a page beneath his writer's hands. Romance
and drama played by touch, by scent, by taste.
In the other bed, the best, our guests dozed on,
dribbling their prose. My living laughing love –
I hold him in the casket of my widow's head
as he held me upon that next best bed.

Queen Kong

I remember peeping in at his skyscraper room
and seeing him fast asleep. My little man.
I'd been in Manhattan a week,
making my plans; staying at 2 quiet hotels
in the Village, where people were used to strangers
and more or less left you alone. To this day
I'm especially fond of pastrami on rye.

I digress. As you see, this island's a paradise.
He'd arrived, my man, with a documentary team
to make a film. (There's a particular toad
that lays its eggs only here.) I found him alone
in a clearing, scooped him up in my palm,
and held his wriggling, shouting life till he calmed.
For me, it was absolutely love at first sight.

I'd been so *lonely*. Long nights in the heat
of my own pelt, rumbling an animal blues.
All right, he was small, but perfectly formed
and *gorgeous*. There were things he could do
for me with the sweet finesse of those hands
that no gorilla could. I swore in my huge heart
to follow him then to the ends of the earth.

For he wouldn't stay here. He was nervous.
I'd go to his camp each night at dusk,
crouch by the delicate tents, and wait. His colleagues
always sent him out pretty quick. He'd climb
into my open hand, sit down; and then I'd gently pick
at his shirt and his trews, peel him, put
the tip of my tongue to the grape of his flesh.

Bliss. But when he'd finished his prize-winning film,
he packed his case; hopped up and down
on my heartline, miming the flight back home
to New York. *Big metal bird.* Didn't he know
I could swat his plane from these skies like a gnat?
But I let him go, my man. I watched him fly
into the sun as I thumped at my breast, distraught.

I lasted a month. I slept for a week,
then woke to binge for a fortnight. I didn't wash.
The parrots clacked their migraine chant.
The swinging monkeys whinged. Fevered, I drank
handfuls of river right by the spot where he'd bathed.
I bled when a fat, red moon rolled on the jungle roof.
And after that, I decided to get him back.

So I came to sail up the Hudson one June night,
with the New York skyline a concrete rainforest
of light; and felt, lovesick and vast, the first
glimmer of hope in weeks. I was discreet, prowled
those streets in darkness, pressing my passionate eye
to a thousand windows, each with its modest peep-show
of boredom or pain, of drama, consolation, remorse.

I found him, of course. At 3 a.m. on a Sunday,
dreaming alone in his single bed; over his lovely head
a blown-up photograph of myself. I stared for a long time
till my big brown eyes grew moist; then I padded away
through Central Park, under the stars. He was mine.
Next day, I shopped. Clothes for my man, mainly,
but one or two treats for myself from Bloomingdale's.

I picked him, like a chocolate from the top layer
of a box, one Friday night, out of his room
and let him dangle in the air betwen my finger
and my thumb in a teasing, lover's way. Then we sat
on the tip of the Empire State Building, saying farewell
to the Brooklyn Bridge, to the winking yellow cabs,
to the helicopters over the river, dragonflies.

Twelve happy years. He slept in my fur, woke early
to massage the heavy lids of my eyes. I liked that.
He liked me to gently blow on him; or scratch,
with care, the length of his back with my nail.
Then I'd ask him to play on the wooden pipes he'd made
in our first year. He'd sit, cross-legged, near my ear
for hours: his plaintive, lost tunes making me cry.

When he died, I held him all night, shaking him
like a doll, licking his face, breast, soles of his feet,
his little rod. But then, heartsore as I was, I set to work.
He would be pleased. I wear him now about my neck,
perfect, preserved, with tiny emeralds for eyes. No man
has been loved more. I'm sure that, sometimes, in his silent death,
against my massive, breathing lungs, he hears me roar.

Mrs Quasimodo

I'd loved them fervently since childhood.
Their generous bronze throats
gargling, or chanting slowly, calming me –
the village runt, name-called, stunted, lame, hare-lipped;
but bearing up, despite it all, sweet-tempered,
    good at needlework;
an ugly cliché in a field
pressing dock-leaves to her fat, stung calves
and listening to the five cool bells of evensong.
I believed that they could even make it rain.

The city suited me; my lumpy shadow
lurching on its jagged alley walls;
my small eyes black
as rained-on cobblestones.
I frightened cats.
I lived alone up seven flights,
boiled potatoes on a ring
and fried a single silver fish;
then stared across the grey lead roofs
as dusk's blue rubber rubbed them out,
and then the bells began.

I climbed the belltower steps,
out of breath and sweating anxiously, puce-faced,
and found the campanologists beneath their ropes.
They made a space for me,
telling their names,
and when it came to him
I felt a thump of confidence,
a recognition like a struck match in my head.

It was Christmas time.
When the others left,
he fucked me underneath the gaping, stricken bells
until I wept.

We wed.
He swung an epithalamium for me,
embossed it on the fragrant air.
Long, sexy chimes,
exuberant peals,
slow scales trailing up and down the smaller bells,
an angelus.
We had no honeymoon
but spent the week in bed.
And did I kiss
each part of him –
that horseshoe mouth,
that tetrahedron nose,
that squint left eye,
that right eye with its pirate wart,
the salty leather of that pig's hide throat,
and give his cock
a private name –
or not?

So more fool me.

We lived in the Cathedral grounds.
The bellringer.
The hunchback's wife.
(The Quasimodos. Have you met them? Gross.)
And got a life.
Our neighbours – sullen gargoyles, fallen angels,
    cowled saints

who raised their marble hands in greeting
as I passed along the gravel paths,
my husband's supper on a tray beneath a cloth.
But once,
one evening in the lady chapel on my own,
throughout his ringing of the seventh hour,
I kissed the cold lips of a Queen next to her King.

Something had changed,
or never been.
Soon enough
he started to find fault.
Why did I this?
How could I that?
Look at myself.
And in that summer's dregs,
I'd see him
watch the pin-up gypsy
posing with the tourists in the square;
then turn his discontented, mulish eye on me
with no more love than stone.

I should have known.

Because it's better, isn't it, to be well formed.
Better to be slim, be slight,
your slender neck quoted between two thumbs;
and beautiful, with creamy skin,
and tumbling auburn hair,
those devastating eyes;
and have each lovely foot
held in a bigger hand
and kissed;
then be watched till morning as you sleep,

so perfect, vulnerable and young
you hurt his blood.

And given sanctuary.

But not betrayed.
Not driven to an ecstasy of loathing of yourself:
banging your ugly head against a wall,
gaping in the mirror at your heavy dugs,
your thighs of lard,
your mottled upper arms;
thumping your belly –
look at it –
your wobbling gut.
You pig. You stupid cow. You fucking buffalo.
Abortion. Cripple. Spastic. Mongol. Ape.

Where did it end?
A ladder. Heavy tools. A steady hand.
And me, alone all night up there,
bent on revenge.
He had pet names for them.
Marie.
The belfry trembled when she spoke for him.
I climbed inside her with my claw-hammer,
my pliers, my saw, my clamp;
and, though it took an agonizing hour,
ripped out her brazen tongue
and let it fall.
Then Josephine,
his second-favourite bell,
kept open her astonished, golden lips
and let me in.
The bells. The bells.

I made them mute.
No more arpeggios or scales, no stretti, trills
for christenings, weddings, great occasions, happy days.
No more practising
for bellringers
on smudgy autumn nights.
No clarity of sound, divine, articulate,
to purify the air
and bow the heads of drinkers in the city bars.
No single
solemn
funeral note
to answer
grief.

I sawed and pulled and hacked.
I wanted silence back.

Get this:

When I was done,
and bloody to the wrist,
I squatted down among the murdered music of the bells
and pissed.

Medusa

A suspicion, a doubt, a jealousy
grew in my mind,
which turned the hairs on my head
    to filthy snakes,
as though my thoughts
hissed and spat on my scalp.

My bride's breath soured, stank
in the grey bags of my lungs.
I'm foul mouthed now, foul tongued,
yellow fanged.
There are bullet tears in my eyes.
Are you terrified?

Be terrified.
It's you I love,
perfect man, Greek God, my own;
but I know you'll go, betray me, stray
from home.
So better by far for me if you were stone.

I glanced at a buzzing bee,
a dull grey pebble fell
to the ground.
I glanced at a singing bird,
a handful of dusty gravel
spattered down.

I looked at a ginger cat,
a housebrick
shattered a bowl of milk.
I looked at a snuffling pig,
a boulder rolled
in a heap of shit.

I stared in the mirror.
Love gone bad
showed me a Gorgon.
I stared at a dragon.
Fire spewed
from the mouth of a mountain.

And here you come
with a shield for a heart
and a sword for a tongue
and your girls, your girls.
Wasn't I beautiful?
Wasn't I fragrant and young?

Look at me now.

The Devil's Wife

1. Dirt

The Devil was one of the men at work.
Different. Fancied himself. Looked at the girls
in the office as though they were dirt. Didn't flirt.
Didn't speak. Was sarcastic and rude if he did.
I'd stare him out, chewing my gum, insolent, dumb.
I'd lie on my bed at home, on fire for him.

I scowled and pouted and sneered. I gave
as good as I got till he asked me out. In his car
he put two fags in his mouth and lit them both.
He bit my breast. His language was foul. He entered me.
We're the same, he said, That's it. I swooned in my soul.
We drove to the woods and he made me bury a doll.

I went mad for the sex. I won't repeat what we did.
We gave up going to work. It was either the woods
or looking at playgrounds, fairgrounds. Coloured lights
in the rain. I'd walk around on my own. He tailed.
I felt like this: Tongue of stone. Two black slates
for eyes. Thumped wound of a mouth. Nobody's Mam.

2. Medusa

I flew in my chains over the wood where we'd buried
the doll. I know it was me who was there.
I know I carried the spade. I know I was covered in mud.
But I cannot remember how or when or precisely where.

Nobody liked my hair. Nobody liked how I spoke.
He held my heart in his fist and he squeezed it dry.
I gave the cameras my Medusa stare.
I heard the judge summing up. I didn't care.

I was left to rot. I was locked up, double-locked.
I know they chucked the key. It was nowt to me.
I wrote to him every day in our private code.
I thought in twelve, fifteen, we'd be out on the open road.

But life, they said, means life. Dying inside.
The Devil was evil, mad, but I was the Devil's wife
which made me worse. I howled in my cell.
If the Devil was gone then how could this be hell?

3. BIBLE

I said No not me I didn't I couldn't I wouldn't.
Can't remember no idea not in the room.
Get me a Bible honestly promise you swear.
I never not in a million years it was him.

I said Send me a lawyer a vicar a priest.
Send me a TV crew send me a journalist.
Can't remember not in the room. Send me
a shrink where's my MP send him to me.

I said Not fair not right not on not true
not like that. Didn't see didn't know didn't hear.
Maybe this maybe that not sure not certain maybe.
Can't remember no idea it was him it was him.

Can't remember no idea not in the room.
No idea can't remember not in the room.

4. Night

In the long fifty-year night,
these are the words that crawl out of the wall:
Suffer. Monster. Burn in Hell.

When morning comes,
I will finally tell.

Amen.

5. Appeal

If I'd been stoned to death
If I'd been hung by the neck
If I'd been shaved and strapped to the Chair
If an injection
If my peroxide head on the block
If my outstretched hands for the chop
If my tongue torn out at the root
If from ear to ear my throat
If a bullet a hammer a knife
If life means life means life means life

But what did I do to us all, to myself
When I was the Devil's wife?

Circe

I'm fond, nereids and nymphs, unlike some, of the pig,
of the tusker, the snout, the boar and the swine.
One way or another, all pigs have been mine –
under my thumb, the bristling, salty skin of their backs,
in my nostrils here, their yobby, porky colognes.
I'm familiar with hogs and runts, their percussion of oinks
and grunts, their squeals. I've stood with a pail of swill
at dusk, at the creaky gate of the sty,
tasting the sweaty, spicy air, the moon
like a lemon popped in the mouth of the sky.
But I want to begin with a recipe from abroad

which uses the cheek – and the tongue in cheek
at that. Lay two pig's cheeks, with the tongue,
in a dish, and strew it well over with salt
and cloves. Remember the skills of the tongue –
to lick, to lap, to loosen, lubricate, to lie
in the soft pouch of the face – and how each pig's face
was uniquely itself, as many handsome as plain,
the cowardly face, the brave, the comical, noble,
sly or wise, the cruel, the kind, but all of them,
nymphs, with those piggy eyes. Season with mace.

Well-cleaned pig's ears should be blanched, singed, tossed
in a pot, boiled, kept hot, scraped, served, garnished
with thyme. Look at that simmering lug, at that ear,
did it listen, ever, to you, to your prayers and rhymes,
to the chimes of your voice, singing and clear? Mash
the potatoes, nymph, open the beer. Now to the brains,
to the trotters, shoulders, chops, to the sweetmeats slipped
from the slit, bulging, vulnerable bag of the balls.
When the heart of a pig has hardened, dice it small.

Dice it small. I, too, once knelt on this shining shore
watching the tall ships sail from the burning sun
like myths; slipped off my dress to wade,
breast-deep, in the sea, waving and calling;
then plunged, then swam on my back, looking up
as three black ships sighed in the shallow waves.
Of course, I was younger then. And hoping for men. Now,
let us baste that sizzling pig on the spit once again.

Mrs Lazarus

I had grieved. I had wept for a night and a day
over my loss, ripped the cloth I was married in
from my breasts, howled, shrieked, clawed
at the burial stones till my hands bled, retched
his name over and over again, dead, dead.

Gone home. Gutted the place. Slept in a single cot,
widow, one empty glove, white femur
in the dust, half. Stuffed dark suits
into black bags, shuffled in a dead man's shoes,
noosed the double knot of a tie round my bare neck,

gaunt nun in the mirror, touching herself. I learnt
the Stations of Bereavement, the icon of my face
in each bleak frame; but all those months
he was going away from me, dwindling
to the shrunk size of a snapshot, going,

going. Till his name was no longer a certain spell
for his face. The last hair on his head
floated out from a book. His scent went from the house.
The will was read. See, he was vanishing
to the small zero held by the gold of my ring.

Then he was gone. Then he was legend, language;
my arm on the arm of the schoolteacher – the shock
of a man's strength under the sleeve of his coat –
along the hedgerows. But I was faithful
for as long as it took. Until he was memory.

So I could stand that evening in the field
in a shawl of fine air, healed, able
to watch the edge of the moon occur to the sky
and a hare thump from a hedge; then notice
the village men running towards me, shouting,

behind them the women and children, barking dogs,
and I knew. I knew by the sly light
on the blacksmith's face, the shrill eyes
of the barmaid, the sudden hands bearing me
into the hot tang of the crowd parting before me.

He lived. I saw the horror on his face.
I heard his mother's crazy song. I breathed
his stench; my bridegroom in his rotting shroud,
moist and dishevelled from the grave's slack chew,
croaking his cuckold name, disinherited, out of his time.

Pygmalion's Bride

Cold, I was, like snow, like ivory.
I thought *He will not touch me*,
but he did.

He kissed my stone-cool lips.
I lay still
as though I'd died.
He stayed.
He thumbed my marbled eyes.

He spoke –
blunt endearments, what he'd do and how.
His words were terrible.
My ears were sculpture,
stone-deaf, shells.
I heard the sea.
I drowned him out.
I heard him shout.

He brought me presents, polished pebbles,
little bells.
I didn't blink,
was dumb.
He brought me pearls and necklaces and rings.
He called them *girly things*.
He ran his clammy hands along my limbs.
I didn't shrink,
played statue, shtum.

He let his fingers sink into my flesh,
he squeezed, he pressed.
I would not bruise.
He looked for marks,
for purple hearts,
for inky stars, for smudgy clues.
His nails were claws.
I showed no scratch, no scrape, no scar.
He propped me up on pillows,
jawed all night.
My heart was ice, was glass.
His voice was gravel, hoarse.
He talked white black.

So I changed tack,
grew warm, like candle wax,
kissed back,
was soft, was pliable,
began to moan,
got hot, got wild,
arched, coiled, writhed,
begged for his child,
and at the climax
screamed my head off –
all an act.

And haven't seen him since.
Simple as that.

Mrs Rip Van Winkle

I sank like a stone
into the still, deep waters of late middle age,
aching from head to foot.

I took up food
and gave up exercise.
It did me good.

And while he slept
I found some hobbies for myself.
Painting. Seeing the sights I'd always dreamed about:

The Leaning Tower.
The Pyramids. The Taj Mahal.
I made a little watercolour of them all.

But what was best,
what hands-down beat the rest,
was saying a none-too-fond farewell to sex.

Until the day
I came home with this pastel of Niagara
and he was sitting up in bed rattling Viagra.

Mrs Icarus

I'm not the first or the last
to stand on a hillock,
watching the man she married
prove to the world
he's a total, utter, absolute, Grade A pillock.

Frau Freud

Ladies, for argument's sake, let us say
that I've seen my fair share of ding-a-ling, member and jock,
of todger and nudger and percy and cock, of tackle,
of three-for-a-bob, of willy and winky; in fact,
you could say, I'm as au fait with Hunt-the-Salami
as Ms M. Lewinsky – equally sick up to here
with the beef bayonet, the pork sword, the saveloy,
love-muscle, night-crawler, dong, the dick, prick,
dipstick and wick, the rammer, the slammer, the rupert,
the shlong. Don't get me wrong, I've no axe to grind
with the snake in the trousers, the wife's best friend,
the weapon, the python – I suppose what I mean is,
ladies, dear ladies, the average penis – not pretty . . .
the squint of its envious solitary eye . . . one's feeling of pity . . .

Salome

I'd done it before
(and doubtless I'll do it again,
sooner or later)
woke up with a head on the pillow beside me – whose? –
what did it matter?
Good-looking, of course, dark hair, rather matted;
the reddish beard several shades lighter;
with very deep lines round the eyes,
from pain, I'd guess, maybe laughter;
and a beautiful crimson mouth that obviously knew
how to flatter . . .
which I kissed . . .
Colder than pewter.
Strange. What was his name? Peter?

Simon? Andrew? John? I knew I'd feel better
for tea, dry toast, no butter,
so rang for the maid.
And, indeed, her innocent clatter
of cups and plates,
her clearing of clutter,
her regional patter,
were just what I needed –
hungover and wrecked as I was from a night on the batter.

Never again!
I needed to clean up my act,
get fitter,
cut out the booze and the fags and the sex.

Yes. And as for the latter,
it was time to turf out the blighter,
the beater or biter,
who'd come like a lamb to the slaughter
to Salome's bed.

In the mirror, I saw my eyes glitter.
I flung back the sticky red sheets,
and there, like I said – and ain't life a bitch –
was his head on a platter.

Eurydice

Girls, I was dead and down
in the Underworld, a shade,
a shadow of my former self, nowhen.
It was a place where language stopped,
a black full stop, a black hole
where words had to come to an end.
And end they did there,
last words,
famous or not.
It suited me down to the ground.

So imagine me there,
unavailable,
out of this world,
then picture my face in that place
of Eternal Repose,
in the one place you'd think a girl would be safe
from the kind of a man
who follows her round
writing poems,
hovers about
while she reads them,
calls her His Muse,
and once sulked for a night and a day
because she remarked on his weakness for abstract nouns.
Just picture my face
when I heard –
Ye Gods –
a familiar knock-knock-knock at Death's door.

Him.
Big O.
Larger than life.
With his lyre
and a poem to pitch, with me as the prize.

Things were different back then.
For the men, verse-wise,
Big O was the boy. Legendary.
The blurb on the back of his books claimed
that animals,
aardvark to zebra,
flocked to his side when he sang,
fish leapt in their shoals
at the sound of his voice,
even the mute, sullen stones at his feet
wept wee, silver tears.

Bollocks. (I'd done all the typing myself,
I should know.)
And given my time all over again,
rest assured that I'd rather speak for myself
than be Dearest, Beloved, Dark Lady, White Goddess,
    etc., etc.

In fact, girls, I'd rather be dead.

But the Gods are like publishers,
usually male,
and what you doubtless know of my tale
is the deal.

Orpheus strutted his stuff.

The bloodless ghosts were in tears.
Sisyphus sat on his rock for the first time in years.
Tantalus was permitted a couple of beers.
The woman in question could scarcely believe her ears.

Like it or not,
I must follow him back to our life –
Eurydice, Orpheus' wife –
to be trapped in his images, metaphors, similes,
octaves and sextets, quatrains and couplets,
elegies, limericks, villanelles,
histories, myths . . .

He'd been told that he mustn't look back
or turn round,
but walk steadily upwards,
myself right behind him,
out of the Underworld
into the upper air that for me was the past.
He'd been warned
that one look would lose me
for ever and ever.

So we walked, we walked.
Nobody talked.

Girls, forget what you've read.
It happened like this –
I did everything in my power
to make him look back.
What did I have to do, I said,
to make him see we were through?
I was dead. Deceased.
I was Resting in Peace. Passé. Late.

Past my sell-by date . . .
I stretched out my hand
to touch him once
on the back of his neck.
Please let me stay.
But already the light had saddened from purple to grey.

It was an uphill schlep
from death to life
and with every step
I willed him to turn.
I was thinking of filching the poem
out of his cloak,
when inspiration finally struck.
I stopped, thrilled.
He was a yard in front.
My voice shook when I spoke –
Orpheus, your poem's a masterpiece.
I'd love to hear it again . . .

He was smiling modestly
when he turned,
when he turned and he looked at me.

What else?
I noticed he hadn't shaved.
I waved once and was gone.

The dead are so talented.
The living walk by the edge of a vast lake
near the wise, drowned silence of the dead.

The Kray Sisters

There go the twins! geezers would say
when we walked down the frog and toad
in our Savile Row whistle and flutes, tailored
to flatter our thr'penny bits, which were big,
like our East End hearts. No one could tell us apart,
except when one twin wore glasses or shades
over two of our four mince pies. Oh, London,
London, London Town, made for a girl and her double
to swagger around; or be driven at speed
in the back of an Austin Princess, black,
up West to a club; to order up bubbly, the best,
in a bucket of ice. Garland singing that night. Nice.

Childhood. When we were God Forbids, we lived
with our grandmother – God Rest Her Soul – a tough suffragette
who'd knocked out a Grand National horse, name of
Ballytown Boy, with one punch, in front of the King,
for the cause. She was known round our manor thereafter
as Cannonball Vi. By the time we were six,
we were sat at her skirts, inhaling the juniper fumes
of her Vera Lynn; hearing the stories of Emmeline's Army
before and after the '14 war. Diamond ladies,
they were, those birds who fought for the Vote, salt
of the earth. And maybe this marked us for ever,
because of the loss of our mother, who died giving birth

to the pair of unusual us. Straight up, we knew,
even then, what we wanted to be; had, you could say,
a vocation. We wanted respect for the way
we entered a bar, or handled a car, or shrivelled
a hard-on with simply a menacing look, a threatening word
in a hairy ear, a knee in the orchestra stalls. Belles
of the balls. Queens of the Smoke. We dreamed it all,
trudging for miles, holding the hand of the past, learning
the map of the city under our feet; clocking the boozers,
back alleys, mews, the churches and bridges, the parks,
the Underground stations, the grand hotels where Vita and Violet,
pin-ups of ours, had given it wallop. We stared from Hungerford Bridge
as the lights of London tarted up the old Thames. All right,

we made our mistakes in those early years. We were soft
when we should have been hard; enrolled a few girls
in the firm who were well out of order – two of them
getting Engaged; a third sneaking back up the Mile End Road
every night to be some plonker's wife. Rule Number One –
A boyfriend's for Christmas, not just for life.
But we learned – and our twenty-first birthday saw us installed
in the first of our clubs, Ballbreakers, just off
Evering Road. The word got around and about
that any woman in trouble could come to the Krays,
no questions asked, for Protection. We'd soon earned the clout
and the dosh and respect for a move, Piccadilly way,

to a classier gaff – to the club at the heart of our legend,
Prickteasers. We admit, bang to rights, that the fruits
of feminism – fact – made us rich, feared, famous,
friends of the stars. Have a good butcher's at these –
there we for ever are in glamorous black-and-white,
assertively staring out next to Germaine, Bardot,
Twiggy and Lulu, Dusty and Yoko, Bassey, Babs,
Sandy, Diana Dors. And London was safer then
on account of us. Look at the letters we get –
*Dear Twins, them were the Good Old Days when you ruled
the streets. There was none of this mugging old ladies
or touching young girls.* We hear what's being said.

Remember us at our peak, in our prime, dressed to kill
and swaggering in to our club, stroke of twelve,
the evening we'd leaned on Sinatra to sing for free.
There was always a bit of a buzz when we entered, stopping
at favoured tables, giving a nod or a wink, buying someone
a drink, lighting a fag, lending an ear. That particular night
something electric, trembling, blue, crackled the air. Leave us both there,
spotlit, strong, at the top of our world, with Sinatra drawling *And here's
a song for the twins*, then opening her beautiful throat to take
it away. *These boots are made for walking, and that's
just what they'll do. One of these days these boots
are gonna walk all over you. Are you ready, boots?*
    Start walkin' . . .

Elvis's Twin Sister

Are you lonesome tonight? Do you miss me tonight?
Elvis is alive and she's female: Madonna

In the convent, y'all,
I tend the gardens,
watch things grow,
pray for the immortal soul
of rock 'n' roll.

They call me
Sister Presley here.
The Reverend Mother
digs the way I move my hips
just like my brother.

Gregorian chant
drifts out across the herbs,
Pascha nostrum immolatus est . . .
I wear a simple habit,
darkish hues,

a wimple with a novice-sewn
lace band, a rosary,
a chain of keys,
a pair of good and sturdy
blue suede shoes.

I think of it
as Graceland here,
a land of grace.
It puts my trademark slow lopsided smile
back on my face.

Lawdy.
I'm alive and well.
Long time since I walked
down Lonely Street
towards Heartbreak Hotel.

Pope Joan

After I learned to transubstantiate
unleavened bread
into the sacred host

and swung the burning frankincense
till blue-green snakes of smoke
coiled round the hem of my robe

and swayed through those fervent crowds,
high up in a papal chair,
blessing and blessing the air,

nearer to heaven
than cardinals, archbishops, bishops, priests,
being Vicar of Rome,

having made the Vatican my home,
like the best of men,
in nomine patris et filii et spiritus sancti amen,

but twice as virtuous as them,
I came to believe
that I did not believe a word,

so I tell you now,
daughters or brides of the Lord,
that the closest I felt

to the power of God
was the sense of a hand
lifting me, flinging me down,

lifting me, flinging me down,
as my baby pushed out
from between my legs

where I lay in the road
in my miracle,
not a man or a pope at all.

Penelope

At first, I looked along the road
hoping to see him saunter home
among the olive trees,
a whistle for the dog
who mourned him with his warm head on my knees.
Six months of this
and then I noticed that whole days had passed
without my noticing.
I sorted cloth and scissors, needle, thread,

thinking to amuse myself,
but found a lifetime's industry instead.
I sewed a girl
under a single star – cross-stitch, silver silk –
running after childhood's bouncing ball.
I chose between three greens for the grass;
a smoky pink, a shadow's grey
to show a snapdragon gargling a bee.
I threaded walnut brown for a tree,

my thimble like an acorn
pushing up through umber soil.
Beneath the shade
I wrapped a maiden in a deep embrace
with heroism's boy
and lost myself completely
in a wild embroidery of love, lust, loss, lessons learnt;
then watched him sail away
into the loose gold stitching of the sun.

And when the others came to take his place,
disturb my peace,
I played for time.
I wore a widow's face, kept my head down,
did my work by day, at night unpicked it.
I knew which hour of the dark the moon
would start to fray,
I stitched it.
Grey threads and brown

pursued my needle's leaping fish
to form a river that would never reach the sea.
I tricked it. I was picking out
the smile of a woman at the centre
of this world, self-contained, absorbed, content,
most certainly not waiting,
when I heard a far-too-late familiar tread outside the door.
I licked my scarlet thread
and aimed it surely at the middle of the needle's eye once more.

Mrs Beast

These myths going round, these legends, fairytales,
I'll put them straight; so when you stare
into my face – Helen's face, Cleopatra's,
Queen of Sheba's, Juliet's – then, deeper,
gaze into my eyes – Nefertiti's, Mona Lisa's,
Garbo's eyes – think again. The Little Mermaid slit
her shining, silver tail in two, rubbed salt
into that stinking wound, got up and walked,
in agony, in fishnet tights, stood up and smiled, waltzed,
all for a Prince, a pretty boy, a charming one
who'd dump her in the end, chuck her, throw her overboard.
I could have told her – look, love, I should know,
they're bastards when they're Princes.
What you want to do is find yourself a Beast. The sex

is better. Myself, I came to the House of the Beast
no longer a girl, knowing my own mind,
my own gold stashed in the bank,
my own black horse at the gates
ready to carry me off at one wrong word,
one false move, one dirty look.
But the Beast fell to his knees at the door
to kiss my glove with his mongrel lips – good –
showed by the tears in his bloodshot eyes
that he knew he was blessed – better –
didn't try to conceal his erection,
size of a mule's – best. And the Beast
watched me open, decant and quaff
a bottle of Château Margaux '54,
the year of my birth, before he lifted a paw.

I'll tell you more. Stripped of his muslin shirt
and his corduroys, he steamed in his pelt,
ugly as sin. He had the grunts, the groans, the yelps,
the breath of a goat. I had the language, girls.
The lady says Do this. Harder. The lady says
Do that. Faster. The lady says That's not where I meant.
At last it all made sense. The pig in my bed
was *invited*. And if his snout and trotters fouled
my damask sheets, why, then, he'd wash them. Twice.
Meantime, here was his horrid leather tongue
to scour in between my toes. Here
were his hooked and yellowy claws to pick my nose,
if I wanted that. Or to scratch my back
till it bled. Here was his bullock's head
to sing off-key all night where I couldn't hear.
Here was a bit of him like a horse, a ram,
an ape, a wolf, a dog, a donkey, dragon, dinosaur.

Need I say more? On my Poker nights, the Beast
kept out of sight. We were a hard school, tough as fuck,
all of us beautiful and rich – the Woman
who Married a Minotaur, Goldilocks, the Bride
of the Bearded Lesbian, Frau Yellow Dwarf, et Moi.
I watched those wonderful women shuffle and deal –
Five and Seven Card Stud, Sidewinder, Hold 'Em, Draw –
I watched them bet and raise and call. One night,
a head-to-head between Frau Yellow Dwarf and Bearded's Bride
was over the biggest pot I'd seen in my puff.

The Frau had the Queen of Clubs on the baize
and Bearded the Queen of Spades. Final card. Queen each.
Frau Yellow raised. Bearded raised. Goldilocks' eyes
were glued to the pot as though porridge bubbled there.
The Minotaur's wife lit a stinking cheroot. Me,
I noticed the Frau's hand shook as she placed her chips.
Bearded raised her a final time, then stared,
stared so hard you felt your dress would melt
if she blinked. I held my breath. Frau Yellow
swallowed hard, then called. Sure enough, Bearded flipped
her Aces over; diamonds, hearts, the pubic Ace of Spades.
And that was a lesson learnt by all of us –
the drop-dead gorgeous Bride of the Bearded Lesbian didn't bluff.

But behind each player stood a line of ghosts
unable to win. Eve. Ashputtel. Marilyn Monroe.
Rapunzel slashing wildly at her hair.
Bessie Smith unloved and down and out.
Bluebeard's wives, Henry VIII's, Snow White
cursing the day she left the seven dwarfs, Diana,
Princess of Wales. The sheepish Beast came in
with a tray of schnapps at the end of the game
and we stood for the toast – *Fay Wray* –
then tossed our fiery drinks to the back of our crimson throats.
Bad girls. Serious ladies. Mourning our dead.

So I was hard on the Beast, win or lose,
when I got upstairs, those tragic girls in my head,
turfing him out of bed; standing alone
on the balcony, the night so cold I could taste the stars
on the tip of my tongue. And I made a prayer –
thumbing my pearls, the tears of Mary, one by one,
like a rosary – words for the lost, the captive beautiful,
the wives, those less fortunate than we.
The moon was a hand-mirror breathed on by a Queen.
My breath was a chiffon scarf for an elegant ghost.
I turned to go back inside. Bring me the Beast for the night.
Bring me the wine-cellar key. Let the less-loving one be me.

Demeter

Where I lived – winter and hard earth.
I sat in my cold stone room
choosing tough words, granite, flint,

to break the ice. My broken heart –
I tried that, but it skimmed,
flat, over the frozen lake.

She came from a long, long way,
but I saw her at last, walking,
my daughter, my girl, across the fields,

in bare feet, bringing all spring's flowers
to her mother's house. I swear
the air softened and warmed as she moved,

the blue sky smiling, none too soon,
with the small shy mouth of a new moon.

Your soul a flame, bright in the window of your maiden name.

The Long Queen

The Long Queen couldn't die.
Young when she bowed her head
for the cold weight of the crown, she'd looked
at the second son of the earl, the foreign prince,
the heir to the duke, the lord, the baronet, the count,
then taken Time for a husband. Long live the Queen.

What was she queen of? Women, girls,
spinsters and hags, matrons, wet nurses,
witches, widows, wives, mothers of all these.
Her word of law was in their bones, in the graft
of their hands, in the wild kicks of their dancing.
No girl born who wasn't the Long Queen's always child.

Unseen, she ruled and reigned; some said
in a castle, some said in a tower in the dark heart
of a wood, some said out and about in rags, disguised,
sorting the bad from the good. She sent her explorers away
in their creaking ships and was queen of more, of all the dead
when they lived if they did so female. All hail to the Queen.

What were her laws? *Childhood*: whether a girl
awoke from the bad dream of the worst, or another
swooned into memory, bereaved, bereft, or a third one
wrote it all down like a charge-sheet, or the fourth never left,
scouring the markets and shops for her old books and toys –
no girl growing who wasn't the apple of the Long Queen's eye.

Blood: proof, in the Long Queen's colour,
royal red, of intent; the pain when a girl
first bled to be insignificant, no cause for complaint,
and this to be monthly, linked to the moon, till middle age
when the law would change. *Tears*: salt pearls, bright jewels
for the Long Queen's fingers to weigh as she counted their sorrow.

Childbirth: most to lie on the birthing beds,
push till the room screamed scarlet and children
bawled and slithered into their arms, sore flowers;
some to be godmother, aunt, teacher, teller of tall tales,
but all who were there to swear that the pain was worth it.
No mother bore daughter not named to honour the Queen.

And her pleasures were stories, true or false,
that came in the evening, drifting up on the air
to the high window she watched from, confession
or gossip, scandal or anecdote, secrets, her ear tuned
to the light music of girls, the drums of women, the faint strings
of the old. Long Queen. All her possessions for a moment of time.

The Map-Woman

A woman's skin was a map of the town
where she'd grown from a child.
When she went out, she covered it up
with a dress, with a shawl, with a hat,
with mitts or a muff, with leggings, trousers
or jeans, with an ankle-length cloak, hooded
and fingertip-sleeved. But – birthmark, tattoo –
the A-Z street-map grew, a precise second skin,
broad if she binged, thin when she slimmed,
a precis of where to end or go back or begin.

Over her breast was the heart of the town,
from the Market Square to the Picture House
by way of St Mary's Church, a triangle
of alleys and streets and walks, her veins
like shadows below the lines of the map, the river
an artery snaking north to her neck. She knew
if you crossed the bridge at her nipple, took a left
and a right, you would come to the graves,
the grey-haired teachers of English and History,
the soldier boys, the Mayors and Councillors,

the beloved mothers and wives, the nuns and priests,
their bodies fading into the earth like old print
on a page. You could sit on a wooden bench
as a wedding pair ran, ringed, from the church,
confetti skittering over the marble stones,
the big bell hammering hail from the sky, and wonder
who you would marry and how and where and when
you would die; or find yourself in the coffee house
nearby, waiting for time to start, your tiny face
trapped in the window's bottle-thick glass like a fly.

And who might you see, short-cutting through
the Grove to the Square – that line there, the edge
of a fingernail pressed on her flesh – in the rain,
leaving your empty cup, to hurry on after
calling their name? When she showered, the map
gleamed on her skin, blue-black ink from a nib.
She knew you could scoot down Greengate Street,
huddling close to the High House, the sensible shops,
the Swan Hotel, till you came to the Picture House,
sat in the musty dark watching the Beatles

run for a train or Dustin Hoffman screaming
Elaine! Elaine! Elaine! or the spacemen in 2001
floating to Strauss. She sponged, soaped, scrubbed;
the prison and hospital stamped on her back,
the park neat on her belly, her navel marking the spot
where the empty bandstand stood, the river again,
heading south, clear as an operation scar,
the war memorial facing the railway station
where trains sighed on the platforms, pining
for Glasgow, London, Liverpool. She knew

you could stand on the railway bridge, waving
goodbye to strangers who stared as you vanished
into the belching steam, tasting future time
on your lip with your tongue. She knew you could run
the back way home – there it was on her thigh –
taking the southern road then cutting off to the left,
the big houses anchored behind their calm green lawns,
the jewels of conkers falling down at your feet,
then duck and dive down Nelson and Churchill
and Kipling and Milton Way until you were home.

She didn't live there now. She lived down south,
abroad, en route, up north, on a plane or train
or boat, on the road, in hotels, in the back of cabs,
on the phone; but the map was under her stockings,
under her gloves, under the soft silk scarf at her throat,
under her chiffon veil, a delicate braille. Her left knee
marked the grid of her own estate. When she knelt
she felt her father's house pressing into the flesh,
heard in her head the looped soundtrack of then –
a tennis ball repeatedly thumping a wall,

an ice-cream van crying and hurrying on, a snarl
of children's shrieks from the overgrown land
where the houses ran out. The motorway groaned
just out of sight. She knew you could hitch
from Junction 13 and knew of a girl who had not
been seen since she did; had heard of a kid who'd run
across all six lanes for a dare before he was tossed
by a lorry into the air like a doll. But the motorway
was flowing away, was a roaring river of metal
and light, cheerio, au revoir, auf wiedersehen, ciao.

She stared in the mirror as she got dressed,
both arms raised over her head, the roads
for east and west running from shoulder
to wrist, the fuzz of woodland or countryside under
each arm. Only her face was clear, her fingers
smoothing in cream, her baby-blue eyes unsure
as they looked at themselves. But her body was certain,
an inch to the mile, knew every nook and cranny,
cul-de-sac, stile, back road, high road, low road,
one-way street of her past. There it all was, back

to front in the glass. She piled on linen, satin, silk,
leather, wool, perfume and mousse and went out.
She got in a limousine. The map perspired
under her clothes. She took a plane. The map seethed
on her flesh. She spoke in a foreign tongue.
The map translated everything back to herself.
She turned out the light and a lover's hands
caressed the map in the dark from north to south,
lost tourists wandering here and there, all fingers
and thumbs, as their map flapped in the breeze.

So one day, wondering where to go next,
she went back, drove a car for a night and a day,
till the town appeared on her left, the stale cake
of the castle crumbled up on the hill; and she hired
a room with a view and soaked in the bath.
When it grew dark, she went out, thinking
she knew the place like the back of her hand,
but something was wrong. She got lost in arcades,
in streets with new names, in precincts
and walkways, and found that what was familiar

was only facade. Back in her hotel room, she stripped
and lay on the bed. As she slept, her skin sloughed
like a snake's, the skin of her legs like stockings, silvery,
sheer, like the long gloves of the skin of her arms,
the papery camisole from her chest a perfect match
for the tissuey socks of the skin of her feet. Her sleep
peeled her, lifted a honeymoon thong from her groin,
a delicate bra of skin from her breasts, and all of it
patterned A to Z; a small cross where her parents' skulls
grinned at the dark. Her new skin showed barely a mark.

She woke and spread out the map on the floor. What
was she looking for? Her skin was her own small ghost,
a shroud to be dead in, a newspaper for old news
to be read in, gift-wrapping, litter, a suicide letter.
She left it there, dressed, checked out, got in the car.
As she drove, the town in the morning sun glittered
behind her. She ate up the miles. Her skin itched,
like a rash, like a slow burn, felt stretched, as though
it belonged to somebody else. Deep in the bone
old streets tunnelled and burrowed, hunting for home.

Beautiful

She was born from an egg,
a daughter of the gods,
divinely fair, a pearl, drop-dead
gorgeous, beautiful, a peach,
a child of grace, a stunner, in her face
the starlike sorrows of immortal eyes.
Who looked there, loved.

She won the heart
of every man she saw.
They stood in line, sighed,
knelt, beseeched *Be Mine*.
She married one,
but every other mother's son
swore to be true to her
till death, enchanted
by the perfume of her breath,
her skin's celebrity.

So when she took a lover, fled,
was nowhere to be seen,
her side of the bed unslept in, cold,
the small coin of her wedding ring
left on the bedside table like a tip,
the wardrobe empty
of the drama of her clothes,
it was War.

A thousand ships –
on every one a thousand men,
each heaving at an oar,
each with her face

before his stinging eyes,
her name tattooed
upon the muscle of his arm,
a handkerchief she'd dropped once
for his lucky charm,
each seeing her as a local girl
made good, the girl next door,
a princess with the common touch,
queen of his heart, pin-up, superstar,
the heads of every coin he'd tossed,
the smile on every note he'd bet at cards –
bragged and shoved across a thousand miles of sea.

Meanwhile, lovely she lay high up
in a foreign castle's walls, clasped
in a hero's brawn, loved and loved
and loved again, her cries
like the bird of calamity's,
drifting down to the boys at the gates
who marched now to the syllables of her name.

Beauty is fame. Some said
she turned into a cloud
and floated home,
falling there like rain, or tears,
upon her husband's face.
Some said her lover woke
to find her gone,
his sword and clothes gone too,
before they sliced a last grin in his throat.

Some swore they saw her smuggled
on a boat dressed as a boy,
rowed to a ship which slid away at dusk,
beckoned by the finger of the moon.

Some vowed that they were in the crowd
that saw her hung, stared up at her body
as it swung there on the creaking rope,
and noticed how the black silk of her dress
clung to her form, a stylish shroud.

Her maid, who loved her most,
refused to say one word
to anyone at any time or place,
would not describe
one aspect of her face
or tell one anecdote about her life and loves.

But lived alone
and kept a little bird inside a cage.

*

She never aged.
She sashayed up the river
in a golden barge,
her fit girls giggling at her jokes.
She'd tumbled from a rug at Caesar's feet,
seen him kneel to pick her up
and felt him want her as he did.
She had him gibbering in bed by twelve.

But now, she rolled her carpet on the sand,
put up her crimson tent, laid out
silver plate with grapes and honey, yoghurt,
roasted songbirds, gleaming figs, soft wines,
and soaked herself in jasmine-scented milk.
She knew her man. She knew that when
he stood that night, ten times her strength,

inside the fragrant boudoir of her tent,
and saw her wrapped in satins like a gift,
his time would slow to nothing, zilch,
until his tongue could utter in her mouth.
She reached and pulled him down
to Alexandria, the warm muddy Nile.

Tough beauty. She played with him
at dice, rolled sixes in the dust,
cleaned up, slipped her gambling hand
into his pouch and took his gold, bit it,
Caesar's head between her teeth.
He crouched with lust. On her couch,
she lay above him, painted him,
her lipstick smeared on his mouth,
her powder blushing on his stubble,
the turquoise of her eyes over his lids.
She matched him glass for glass
in drinking games: sucked lemons, licked
at salt, swallowed something from a bottle
where a dead rat floated, gargled doubles
over trebles, downed a liquid fire in one,
lit a coffee bean in something else, blew it,
gulped, tipped chasers down her throat,
pints down her neck, and held her drink
until the big man slid beneath the table, wrecked.

She watched him hunt. He killed a stag.
She hacked the heart out, held it,
dripping, in the apron of her dress.
She watched him exercise in arms.
His soldiers marched, eyes right, her way.
She let her shawl slip down to show
her shoulders, breasts, and every man

that night saw them again and prayed
her name. She waved him off to war,
then pulled on boy's clothes, crept
at dusk into his camp, his shadowed tent,
touched him, made him fuck her as a lad.
He had no choice, upped sticks,
downed tools, went back with her,
swooned on her flesh for months,
her fingers in his ears, her kiss
closing his eyes, her stories blethering
on his lips: of armies changing sides,
of cities lost forever in the sea, of snakes.

*

The camera loved her, close-up, back-lit,
adored the waxy pouting of her mouth,
her sleepy, startled gaze. She breathed
the script out in her little voice. They filmed her
famous, filmed her beautiful. Guys fell
in love, dames copied her. An athlete
licked the raindrops from her fingertips
to quench his thirst. She married him.
The US whooped.

They filmed her harder, harder, till her hair
was platinum, her teeth gems, her eyes
sapphires pressed by a banker's thumb.
She sang to camera one, gushed
at the greased-up lens, her skin investors' gold,
her fingernails mother-of-pearl, her voice
champagne to sip from her lips. A poet came,
found her wondrous to behold. She married him.
The whole world swooned.

Dumb beauty. She slept in an eye-mask, naked,
drugged, till the maid came, sponged
at her puffy face, painted the beauty on in beige,
pinks, blues. Then it was coffee, pills, booze,
Frank on the record-player, it was put on the mink,
get in the studio car. Somebody big was watching her –
white fur, mouth at the mike, under the lights. *Happy
Birthday to you. Happy Birthday, Mr President.*
The audience drooled.

They filmed on, deep, dumped what they couldn't use
on the cutting-room floor, filmed more, quiet please,
action, cut, quiet please, action, cut, quiet please,
action, cut, till she couldn't die when she died,
couldn't get older, ill, couldn't stop saying the lines
or singing the tunes. The smoking cop who watched
as they zipped her into the body-bag noticed
her strong resemblance to herself, the dark roots
of her pubic hair.

*

Dead, she's elegant bone
in mud, ankles crossed,
knees clamped, hands clasped,
empty head. You know her name.

Plain women turned in the streets
where her shadow fell, under
her spell, swore that what she wore
they'd wear, coloured their hair.

The whole town came
to wave at her on her balcony,
to stare and stare and stare.
Her face was surely a star.

Beauty is fate. They gaped
as her bones danced
in a golden dress in the arms
of her wooden prince, gawped

as she posed alone
in front of the Taj Mahal,
betrayed, beautifully pale.
The cameras gibbered away.

Act like a fucking princess –
how they loved her,
the men from the press –
Give us a smile, cunt.

And her blue eyes widened
to take it all in: the flashbulbs,
the half-mast flags, the acres of flowers,
History's stinking breath in her face.

The Diet

The diet worked like a dream. No sugar,
salt, dairy, fat, protein, starch or alcohol.
By the end of week one, she was half a stone
shy of ten and shrinking, skipping breakfast,
lunch, dinner, thinner; a fortnight in, she was
eight stone; by the end of the month, she was skin
and bone.

        She starved on, stayed in, stared in
the mirror, svelter, slimmer. The last apple
aged in the fruit bowl, untouched. The skimmed milk
soured in the fridge, unsupped. Her skeleton preened
under its tight flesh dress. She was all eyes,
all cheekbones, had guns for hips. Not a stitch
in the wardrobe fitted.

              What passed her lips? Air,
water. She was Anorexia's true daughter, a slip
of a girl, a shadow, dwindling away. One day,
the width of a stick, she started to grow smaller –
child-sized, doll-sized, the height of a thimble.
She sat at her open window and the wind
blew her away.

          Seed small, she was out and about,
looking for home. An empty beer bottle rolled
in the gutter. She crawled in, got drunk on the dregs,
started to sing, down, out, nobody's love. Tiny others
joined in. They raved all night. She woke alone,
head splitting, mouth dry, hungry and cold, and made
for the light.

   She found she could fly on the wind,
could breathe, if it rained, underwater. That night,
she went to a hotel bar that she knew and floated into
the barman's eye. She slept for hours, left at dawn
in a blink, in a wink, drifted away on a breeze.
Minute, she could suit herself from here on in, go
where she pleased.

   She stayed near people,
lay in the tent of a nostril like a germ, dwelled
in the caves of an ear. She lived in a tear, swam
clear, moved south to a mouth, kipped in the chap
of a lip. She loved flesh and blood, wallowed
in mud under fingernails, dossed in a fold of fat
on a waist.

   But when she squatted the tip of a tongue,
she was gulped, swallowed, sent down the hatch
in a river of wine, bottoms up, cheers, fetched up
in a stomach just before lunch. She crouched
in the lining, hearing the avalanche munch of food,
then it was carrots, peas, courgettes, potatoes,
gravy and meat.

   Then it was sweet. Then it was stilton,
roquefort, weisslacker-käse, gex; it was smoked salmon
with scrambled eggs, hot boiled ham, plum flan, frogs'
legs. She knew where she was all right, clambered
onto the greasy breast of a goose, opened wide, then
chomped and chewed and gorged; inside the Fat Woman now,
trying to get out.

The Woman Who Shopped

went out with a silver shilling, willing to buy, bought
an apple, red as first love's heart, bright as her eye,
had plenty of change, purchased a hat with a brim,
walked with a suitor under its shadow, ditched him;

saved up a pound, a fiver, a tenner, haggled the price
of a dancing dress down to a snip, spent the remainder
on shoes, danced from the house down the street, tapped
to the centre of town where the sales had commenced,

applied for a job for the wage and the bonus, blew it
on clothes; wanted a wedding, a wedding dress, groom,
married him, wanted a honeymoon, went on one,
looked at the gold of her ring as it flashed in the sun;

flew away home to furnish each room of the house,
shuffle his plastic with hers, deal them out in the shops
for cutlery, crockery, dishwashers, bed linen, TV sets,
three-piece suites, stereos, microwaves, telephones,

curtains and mirrors and rugs; shrugged at the cost,
then fixed up a loan, filled up the spare room with boxes
of merchandise, unopened cartons, over-stuffed bags;
went on the Internet, shopped in America, all over Europe,

tapping her credit card numbers all night, ordering
swimming pools, caravans, saunas; when they arrived,
stacked up on the lawn, she fled, took to the streets,
where the lights from the shops ran like paint in the rain,

and pressed her face to the pane of the biggest and best;
the happy shoppers were fingering silk, holding cashmere
close to their cheeks, dancing with fur; she slept there,
curled in the doorway, six shopping bags at her feet.

*

Stone cold when she woke, she was stone, was concrete
and glass, her eyes windows squinting back at the light,
her brow a domed roof, her thoughts neon, flashing on
and off, vague in the daylight. She seemed to be kneeling

or squatting, her shoulders broad and hunched, her hands
huge and part of the pavement. She looked down. Her skirts
were glass doors opening and closing, her stockings were
moving stairs, her shoes were lifts, going up, going down:

first floor for perfumery and cosmetics, ladies' accessories,
lingerie, fine jewels and watches; second for homewares,
furniture, travel goods, luggage; third floor for menswear,
shaving gear, shoes; fourth floor for books, toyland,

childrenswear, sports; fifth floor for home entertainment,
pianos, musical instruments, beauty and hair. Her ribs
were carpeted red, her lungs glittered with chandeliers
over the singing tills, her gut was the food hall, hung

with fat pink hams, crammed with cheeses, fruits, wines,
truffles and caviar. She loved her own smell, sweat and Chanel,
loved the crowds jostling and thronging her bones, loved
the credit cards swiping themselves in her blood, her breath

was gift wrapping, the whisper of tissue and string, she loved
the changing rooms of her heart, the rooftop restaurant
in her eyes, the dark basement under the lower ground floor
where juggernauts growled, unloading their heavy crates.

The sky was unwrapping itself, ripping itself into shreds.
She would have a sale and crowds would queue overnight
at her cunt, desperate for bargains. Light blazed from her now.
Birds shrieked and voided themselves in her stone hair.

Work

To feed one, she worked from home,
took in washing, ironing, sewing.
One small mouth, a soup-filled spoon,
life was a dream.

          To feed two,
she worked outside, sewed seeds, watered,
threshed, scythed, gathered barley, wheat, corn.
Twins were born. To feed four,

she grafted harder, second job in the alehouse,
food in the larder, food on the table,
she was game, able. Feeding ten
was a different kettle,

                    was factory gates
at first light, oil, metal, noise, machines.
To feed fifty, she toiled, sweated, went
on the night shift, schlepped, lifted.

For a thousand more, she built streets,
for double that, high-rise flats. Cities grew,
her brood doubled, peopled skyscrapers,
trebled. To feed more, more,

she dug underground, tunnelled,
laid down track, drove trains. Quadruple came,
multiplied, she built planes, outflew sound.
Mother to millions now,

                        she flogged TVs,
designed PCs, ripped CDs, burned DVDs.
There was no stopping her. She slogged
night and day at Internet shopping.

                                A billion named,
she trawled the seas, hoovered fish, felled trees,
grazed beef, sold cheap fast food, put in
a 90-hour week. Her offspring swelled. She fed

the world, wept rain, scattered the teeth in her head
for grain, swam her tongue in the river to spawn,
sickened, died, lay in a grave, worked, to the bone,
her fingers twenty-four seven.

Tall

Then, like a christening gift or a wish arriving
later in life, the woman had height, grew tall,
was taller daily.

          Day one saw her rising at 8 foot
bigger than any man. She knelt in the shower
as if she were praying for rain. Her clothes
would be curtains and eiderdowns, towels and rugs.

Out. Eye-high with street lamps, she took a walk
downtown. Somebody whooped. She stooped,
hands on both knees,

                and stared at his scared face,
the red heart tattooed on his small chest. He turned
and fled like a boy.

          On. A tree dangled an apple
at bite-height. She bit it. A traffic-light stuttered
on red, went out. She lit it. Personal birds
sang on her ears. She whistled.

          Further. Taller
as she went, she glanced into upper windows
in passing, saw lovers in the rented rooms
over shops, saw an old man long dead in a chair,
paused there, her breath on the glass.

She bowed herself into a bar, ordered a stiff drink.
It came on the rocks, on the house. A drunk
passed out or fainted. She pulled up a stool, sat
at the bar with her knees

                          under her chin, called
for another gin, a large one. She saw a face, high
in the mirror behind the top shelf. Herself.

Day two, she was hungover, all over, her head
in her hands in the hall, her feet at the top
of the stairs, more tall.

                She needed a turret,
found one, day three, on the edge of town, moved in,
her head in the clouds now, showering in rain.

But pilgrims came –
small women with questions and worries, men
on stilts. She was 30 foot, growing, could see for miles.

So day six, she upped sticks, horizon-bound
in seven-league boots. Local crowds swarmed
round her feet, chanting.

                  She cured no one. Grew.
The moon came closer at night, its scarred face
an old mirror. She slept outdoors, stretched
across empty fields or sand.

                    The stars trembled. Taller
was colder, aloner, no wiser. What could she see
up there? She told them what kind of weather
was heading their way –

                            dust storms over the Pyramids,
hurricanes over the USA, floods in the UK –
but by now the people were tiny

                                  and far away, and she
was taller than Jupiter, Saturn, the Milky Way. Nothing
to see. She looked back and howled.

                                  She stooped low
and caught their souls in her hands as they fell
from the burning towers.

Loud

Parents with mutilated children have been turned away from the empty hospital and told to hire smugglers to take them across the border to Quetta, a Pakistani frontier city at least six hours away by car.
(Afghanistan, 28 October 2001)

The News had often made her shout,
but one day her voice ripped out of her throat
like a firework, with a terrible sulphurous crack
that made her jump, a flash of light in the dark.
Now she was loud.

            Before, she'd been easily led,
one of the crowd, joined in with the national whoop
for the winning goal, the boos for the bent MP, the cheer
for the royal kiss on the balcony. Not any more. Now
she could roar.

            She practised alone at home, found
she could call abroad without using the phone, could sing
like an orchestra in the bath, could yawn like thunder
watching TV. She switched to the News. It was all about
Muslims, Christians, Jews.

            Then her scream was a huge bird
that flew her away into the dark; each vast wing a shriek,
awful to hear, the beak the sickening hiss of a thrown spear.
She stayed up there all night, in the wind and rain, wailing,
uttering lightning.

    Down, she was pure sound, rumbling
like an avalanche. She bit radios, swallowed them, gargled
their News, till the words were – *ran into the church and sprayed
the congregation with bullets no one has claimed* – gibberish, crap,
in the cave of her mouth.

                     Her voice stomped through the city,
shouting the odds, shaking the bells awake in their towers.
She yelled through the countryside, swelling the rivers, felling
the woods. She put out to sea, screeching and bellowing,
spewing brine.

      She bawled at the moon and it span away
into space. She hollered into the dark where fighter planes
buzzed at her face. She howled till every noise in the world
sang in the spit on the tip of her tongue: the shriek of a bomb,
the bang of a gun,

            the prayers of the priest, the pad of the feet
in the mosque, the casual rip of the post, the mothers' sobs,
the thump of the drop, the President's cough, the screams
of the children cowering under their pews, loud, loud,
louder, the News.

History

She woke up old at last, alone,
bones in a bed, not a tooth
in her head, half dead, shuffled
and limped downstairs
in the rag of her nightdress,
smelling of pee.

       Slurped tea, stared
at her hand – twigs, stained gloves –
wheezed and coughed, pulled on
the coat that hung from a hook
on the door, lay on the sofa,
dozed, snored.

       She was History.
She'd seen them ease him down
from the Cross, his mother gasping
for breath, as though his death
was a difficult birth, the soldiers spitting,
spears in the earth;

       been there
when the fishermen swore he was back
from the dead; seen the basilicas rise
in Jerusalem, Constantinople, Sicily; watched
for a hundred years as the air of Rome
turned into stone;

                    witnessed the wars,
the bloody crusades, knew them by date
and by name, Bannockburn, Passchendaele,
Babi Yar, Vietnam. She'd heard the last words
of the martyrs burnt at the stake, the murderers
hung by the neck,

                    seen up-close
how the saint whistled and spat in the flames,
how the dictator strutting on stuttering film
blew out his brains, how the children waved
their little hands from the trains. She woke again,
cold, in the dark,

                    in the empty house.
Bricks through the window now, thieves
in the night. When they rang on her bell
there was nobody there; fresh graffiti sprayed
on her door, shit wrapped in a newspaper posted
onto the floor.

Sub

I came on in extra time in '66, my breasts
bandaged beneath my no. 13 shirt, and put it in
off the head, the back of the heel, the left foot
from 30 yards out, hat-trick. If they'd thought
the game was all over, it was now. I felt secure
as I danced in my dazzling whites with the Cup –
tampon – but skipped the team bath with the lads,
sipped my champagne in the solitary shower
as the blood and soap suds mingled to pink.
They sang my name on the other side of the steam.

Came on too in the final gasps of the Grand Slam clincher,
scooped up the ball from the back of the scrum, ran
like the wind, bandaged again, time of the month
likewise, wiggled, weaved, waved at the crowd, slipped
like soap through muddy hands, liked that, slid
between legs, nursing the precious egg of the ball,
then flung myself like breaking surf over the line
for the winning try, converted it, was carried
shoulder high by the boys as the whistle blew.
They roared my name through mouthfuls of broken teeth.

Ringo had flu when the Fab Four toured Down
Under. Minus a drummer, the gig was a bummer
till I stepped in, digits ringed, sticked, skinned,
in a Beatle skirt, mop-topped, fringed, to wink
at Paul, quip with John, climb on the drums,
clever fingered and thumbed, give it four to the bar,
give it *yeah yeah yeah*. The screams were lava,
hot as sex, and every seat in the house was wet.
We sang *Help!*, *Day Tripper*, *Money*, *This Boy*,
Girl, *She Loves You* – John, Paul, George and Moi.

It was one small step for a man for Neil
to stand on the Moon, a small hop for me
to stand in for Buzz, bounce in my moon-suit
over the dust, waving a flag. I knelt, scooped out
a hole in the powdery ground, and buried a box
with a bottle of malt, chocolates, Emily Dickinson's
poems. Ground Control barked down the line. *Houston,
we don't have a problem*, I said. It comforts me now,
the thought of them there, when I look at the moon.
Quietly there on the moon, the things that I like.

And when Beefy fell sick in the final Test,
I stepped up, two of his boxes over my chest,
and hooked a four from the first of Lillee's balls.
He bowled so fast you could hear his fingers click
as he spun off the seam. I lolled at the crease –
five months gone – and looped and hooped them about
like a dream, googlies, bosies, chinamen, zooters,
balls that dipped, flipped, nipped, whipped
at the wicket like bombs. I felt the first kick
of my child; whacked a century into the crowd.

Motherhood then kept me busy at home till my girl
started school. Not match-fit, I was talked
into management when Taylor went, caretaker role,
jacked that in after the World Cup win – Beckham
free-kick in extra time – and agreed on a whim to slim
to the weight of a boy, ride the winner at Aintree –
Bobbyjo, '99 – when the jockey dislocated his neck.
After that, I pulled right back, signed up to write
a book of my life and times, though I did play guitar
for the Band in LA when Bob gave me the call.

And when I look back – or my grandchildren ask me
what it was like to put Mohammed Ali on the deck
when Cooper was scratched from the scrap, or stand in
for Graham Hill to be Formula One Grand Champ
in the fastest recorded speed, or to dress up
as Borg in bandana and wig and steal the fifth set
at Wimbledon from under – *You cannot be serious* –
McEnroe's nose, or to kneel, best of all, first woman there,
on the Moon and gaze at the beautiful faraway earth –
what I think to myself is this:

The Virgin's Memo

maybe not abscesses, acne, asthma,
son, maybe not boils,
maybe not cancer
or diarrhoea
or tinnitus of the inner ear,
maybe not fungus,
maybe rethink the giraffe,
maybe not herpes, son,
or (text illegible)
or jellyfish
or (untranslatable)
maybe not leprosy or lice,
the menopause or mice, mucus, son,
neuralgia, nits,
maybe not body odour,
piles,
quicksand, quagmires,
maybe not rats, son, rabies, rattlesnakes,
shite,
and maybe hang fire on the tarantula,
the unicorn's lovely,
but maybe not veruccas
or wasps,
or (text illegible)
or (untranslatable)
maybe not . . .

Anon

If she were here
she'd forget who she was,
it's been so long,
maybe a nurse, a nanny,
maybe a nun –
Anon.

A girl I met
was willing to bet
that she still lived on –
Anon –
but had packed it all in,
the best verb, the right noun,
for a life in the sun.

A woman I knew
kept her skull
on a shelf in a room –
Anon's –
and swore that one day
as she worked at her desk
it cleared its throat
as though it had something
to get off its chest.

But I know best –
how she passed on her pen
like a baton
down through the years,
with a hey nonny
hey nonny
hey nonny no –
Anon.

The Laughter of Stafford Girls' High

for T.W.

It was a girl in the Third Form, Carolann Clare,
who, bored with the lesson, the rivers of England –
Brathay, Coquet, Crake, Dee, Don, Goyt,
Rothay, Tyne, Swale, Tees, Wear, Wharfe . . .
had passed a note, which has never been found,
to the classmate in front, Emily Jane, a girl
who adored the teacher, Miss V. Dunn MA,
steadily squeaking her chalk on the board –
Allen, Clough, Duddon, Feugh, Greta, Hindburn,
Irwell, Kent, Leven, Lowther, Lune, Sprint . . .
but who furtively opened the folded note,
torn from the back of the King James Bible, read
what was scribbled there and laughed out loud.

It was a miserable, lowering winter's day. The girls
had been kept indoors at break – Wet Play
in the Hall – the windows tall and thin,
sad with rain like a long list of watery names –
Rawthey, Roeburn, Skirfare, Troutbeck, Wash . . .
likewise, the sound of the laugh of Emily Jane
was a liquid one, a gurgle, a ripple, a dribble,
a babble, a gargle, a plash, a splash of a laugh
like the sudden jackpot leap of a silver fish
in the purse of a pool. No fool, Emily Jane
clamped her turquoisey hand – her fountain pen leaked –
to her mouth; but the laugh was out, was at large,
was heard by the pupil twinned to her double desk –

Rosemary Beth – the brace on whose jiggly teeth
couldn't restrain the gulping giggle she gave
which caused Miss Dunn to spin round. *Perhaps*,
she said, *We can all share the joke?* But Emily Jane
had scrunched and dropped the note with the joke
to the floor and kicked it across to Jennifer Kay
who snorted and toed it to Marjorie May
who spluttered and heeled it backwards
to Jessica Kate. *Girls!* By now, every girl in the form
had started to snigger or snicker or titter or chuckle
or chortle till the classroom came to the boil
with a brothy mirth. *Girls!* Miss Dunn's shrill voice
scraped Top G and only made matters worse.

Five minutes passed in a cauldron of noise.
No one could seem to stop. Each tried holding
her breath or thinking of death or pinching
her thigh, only to catch the eye of a pal,
a crimson, shaking, silent girl, and explode
through the nose in a cackling sneeze. *Thank you!*
Please! screeched Miss Dunn, clapping her hands
as though she applauded the choir they'd become,
a percussion of trills and whoops filling the room
like birds in a cage. But then came a triple rap
at the door and in stalked Miss Fife, Head of Maths,
whose cold equations of eyes scanned the desks
for a suitable scapegoat. *Stand up, Geraldine Ruth.*

Geraldine Ruth got to her feet, a pale girl, a girl
who looked, in the stale classroom light, like a sketch
for a girl, a first draft to be crumpled and crunched
and tossed away like a note. She cleared her throat,
raising her eyes, water and sky, to look at Miss Fife.

The girls who were there that day never forgot
how invisible crayons seemed to colour in
Geraldine Ruth, white face to puce, mousey hair
suddenly gifted with health and youth, and how –
as Miss Fife demanded what was the meaning of this –
her lips split from the closed bud of a kiss
to the daisy chain of a grin and how then she yodelled
a laugh with the full, open, blooming rose of her throat,

a flower of merriment. *What's the big joke?*
thundered Miss Fife as Miss Dunn began again
to clap, as gargling Geraldine Ruth collapsed
in a heap on her desk, as the rest of the class
hollered and hooted and howled. Miss Fife strode
on sharp heels to the blackboard, snatched up
a finger of chalk and jabbed and slashed out
a word. SILENCE. But the class next door,
Fourth Years learning the Beaufort scale with Miss Batt,
could hear the commotion. Miss Batt droned on –
*Nought, calm; one, light air; two, light breeze; three,
gentle . . . four, moderate . . . five, fresh . . . six, strong breeze;
seven, moderate gale . . .* Stephanie Fay started to laugh.

What's so amusing, Stephanie Fay? barked Miss Batt.
What's so amusing? echoed unwitting Miss Dunn
on the other side of the wall. *Precisely what's
so amusing?* chorused Miss Fife. The Fourth Years
shrieked with amazed delight and one wag,
Angela Joy, popped her head in the jaws of her desk
and bellowed *What's so amusing? What's so
amusing?* into its musty yawn. The Third Form
guffawed afresh at the sound of the Fourth
and the noise of the two combined was heard
by the First Form, trying to get Shakespeare by heart

to the beat of the ruler of Mrs Mackay. *Don't look
at your books, look at me. After three. Friends,*

Romans, Countrymen . . . What's so amusing? rapped out
Mrs Mackay as the First Years chirruped
and trilled like baby birds in a nest at a worm;
but she heard for herself, appalled, the chaos
coming in waves through the wall and clipped
to the door. Uproar. And her Head of Lower School!
It was then that Mrs Mackay made mistake number one,
leaving her form on its own while she went to see
to the forms of Miss Batt and Miss Dunn. The moment
she'd gone, the room blossomed with paper planes,
ink bombs, whistles, snatches of song, and the class clown –
Caroline Joan – stood on her desk and took up
the speech where Mrs Mackay had left off – *Lend*

me your ears . . . just what the Second Form did
in the opposite room, reciting the Poets Laureate
for Miss Nadimbaba – *John Dryden, Thomas Shadwell,
Nahum Tate, Nicholas Rowe, Laurence Eusden, Colley Cibber,
William Whitehead . . .* but scattering titters and giggles
like noisy confetti on reaching Henry Pye as Caroline Joan
belted out Antony's speech in an Elvis style –
For Brutus, uh huh huh, is an honourable man.
Miss Nadimbaba, no fan of rock 'n' roll, could scarcely
believe her ears, deducing at once that Mrs Mackay
was not with her class. She popped an anxious head
outside her door. Anarchy roared in her face
like a tropical wind. The corridor clock was at four.

The last bell rang. Although they would later regret it,
the teachers, taking their cue from wits-end Mrs Mackay,
allowed the chuckling, bright-eyed, mirthful girls

to go home, reprimand-free, each woman privately glad
that the dark afternoon was over and done,
the chalky words rubbed away to dance as dust
on the air, the dates, the battles, the kings and queens,
the rivers and tributaries, poets, painters, playwrights,
politicos, popes . . . but they all agreed to make it quite clear
in tomorrow's Assembly that foolish behaviour –
even if only the once – wasn't admired or desired
at Stafford Girls' High. Above the school, the moon
was pinned like a monitor's badge to the sky.

Miss Dunn was the first to depart, wheeling
her bicycle through the gates, noticing how
the sky had cleared, a tidy diagram of the Plough
directly above. She liked it this cold, her breath
chiffoning out behind as she freewheeled home
down the hill, her mind emptying itself of geography,
of mountains and seas and deserts and forests
and capital cities. Her small terraced house looked,
she thought, like a sleeping face. She roused it
each evening, kisses of light on its cheeks
from her lamps, the small talk of cutlery, pots
and pans as she cooked, sweet silver steam caressing
the shy rooms of her home. Miss Dunn lived alone.

So did Miss Batt, in a flat on the edge of the park
near the school; though this evening Miss Fife
was coming for supper. The two were good friends
and Miss Fife liked to play on Miss Batt's small piano
after the meal and the slowly shared carafe of wine.
Music and Maths! Johann Sebastian Bach! Miss Batt,
an all-rounder, took out her marking – essays on Henry VIII
and his wives from the Fifth – while Miss Fife gave herself up
to Minuet in G. In between Catherine Howard

and Catherine Parr, Miss Batt glanced across at Fifi's
straight back as she played, each teacher conscious
of each woman's silently virtuous love. Nights like this,
twice a week, after school, for them both, seemed enough.

Mrs Mackay often gave Miss Nadimbaba a lift,
as they both, by coincidence, lived on Mulberry Drive –
Mrs Mackay with her husband of twenty-five grinding,
childless years; Miss Nadimbaba sharing a house
with her elderly aunt. Neither had ever invited
the other one in, although each would politely enquire
after her colleague's invisible half. Mrs Mackay
watched Miss Nadimbaba open her purple door and saw
a cat rubbing itself on her calf. She pulled away
from the kerb, worrying whether Mr Mackay would insist
on fish for his meal. Then he would do his crossword:
Mr Mackay calling out clues – *Kind of court for a bounder (8)* –
while she passed him *Roget, Brewer, Pears,* the OED.

The women teachers of England slept in their beds,
their shrewd or wise or sensible heads safe vessels
for Othello's jealousy, the Wife of Bath's warm laugh,
the phases of the moon, the country code;
for Roman numerals, Greek alphabets, French verbs;
for foreign currencies and Latin roots, for logarithms, tables,
quotes; the meanings of *currente calamo* and *fiat lux* and *stet*.
Miss Dunn dreamed of a freezing white terrain
where slowly moving elephants were made of ice.
Miss Nadimbaba dreamed she knelt to kiss Miss Barrett
on her couch and she, Miss Nadimbaba, was Browning
saying *Beloved, be my wife* . . . and then a dog began to bark
and she woke up. Miss Batt dreamed of Miss Fife.

*

Morning assembly – the world like Quink outside,
the teachers perched in a solemn row on the stage,
the Fifth and Sixth Forms clever and tall, Miss Fife
at the school piano, the Head herself, Doctor Bream,
at the stand – was a serious affair. *Jerusalem* hung
in the air till the last of Miss Fife's big chords
wobbled away. *Yesterday* intoned Doctor Bream,
*the Lower School behaved in a foolish way, sniggering
for most of the late afternoon.* She glared at the girls
through her pince-nez and paused for dramatic effect.
But the First and Second and Third and Fourth Forms
started to laugh, each girl trying to swallow it down
till the sound was like distant thunder, the opening chord

of a storm. Miss Dunn and Miss Batt, Miss Nadimbaba
and Mrs Mackay leapt to their feet as one, grim-faced.
The Fifth Form hooted and howled. Miss Fife, oddly disturbed,
crashed down fistfuls of furious notes on the yellowing keys.
The Sixth Forms, upper and lower, shrieked. Señora Devizes,
sartorial, strict, slim, severe, teacher of Spanish,
stalked from the stage and stilettoed sharply down
to the back of the Hall to chastise the Fifth and Sixth.
¡Callaos! ¡Callaos! ¡Callaos! ¡Quédense! The whole school
guffawed; their pink young lungs flowering more
than they had for the hymn. *¡El clamor!* The Hall was a zoo.
Snow began falling outside as though the clouds
were being slowly torn up like a rule book. *A good laugh,*

as the poet Ursula Fleur, who attended the school,
was to famously write, *is feasting on air.* The air that day
was chomped, chewed, bitten in two, pulled apart
like a wishbone, licked like a lollipop, sluiced and sucked.
Some of the girls were almost sick. Girls gulped or sipped
or slurped as they savoured the joke. What joke?

Nobody knew. A silly joy sparkled and fizzed. Tabitha Rose,
flower monitor for the day, wet herself, wailed, wept, ran
from the Hall, a small human shower of rain. The bell
for the start of lessons rang. Somehow the school
filed out in a raggedy line. The Head Girl, Josephine June,
scarlet-faced from killing herself, was in for a terrible time
with the Head. Snow iced the school like a giant cake.

No one on record recalls the words that were said,
but Josephine June was stripped of the Head Girl's badge
and sash and sent to the Sixth Form Common Room
to demand of the prefects how they could hope to grow to be
the finest of England's daughters and mothers and wives
after this morning's Assembly's abysmal affair?
But the crowd of girls gave a massive cheer, stamping
the floor with their feet in a rebel beat and Diana Kim,
Captain of Sports, jumped on a chair and declared
that if J.J. was no longer Head Girl then no one
would take her place. *All for one!* someone yelled. *And one
for all!* Diana Kim opened the window and jumped down
into the snow. With a shriek, Emmeline Belle jumped after her,

followed by cackling Anthea Meg, Melanie Hope, Andrea Lyn,
J.J. herself . . . It was Gillian Tess in the Fifth, being lectured
by tight-lipped Señora Devizes on how to behave, who glanced
from the first-floor window and noticed the Sixth Form
bouncing around in the snow like girls on the moon.
A snowball, the size of a netball, was creaking, rolling,
growing under their hands. *Look!* Girls at their windows gaped.
It grew from a ball to the size of a classroom globe. It grew
from a globe to the size of a huge balloon. Miss Dunn,
drumming the world's highest mountains into the heads
of the First Years – *Everest, K2, Kangchenjunga, Lhoste,*
   Makalu 1 . . .

flung open her window and breathed in the passionate cold
of the snow. A wild thought seeded itself in her head.

In later years, the size of the snowball rolled by the Sixth
grew like a legend. Some claimed that the Head, as it groaned
past her study, thought that there might have been an eclipse.
Ursula Fleur, in her prose poem *Snow*, wrote that it took
the rest of the Michaelmas Term to melt. Miss Batt,
vacantly staring down as her class wrote out a list
of the monarchs of England – *Egbert, Ethelwulf, Ethelbald,
Ethelbert, Ethelred, Alfred, Edward, Athelstan, Edmund,
Eadred, Eadwig, Edgar* . . . noticed the snowball, huge and alone
on the hockey pitch, startlingly white in the pencilly grey
of the light, and thought of desire, of piano scales slowing,
slowing, breasts. She moaned aloud, forgetful of where
she was. Francesca Eve echoed the moan. The class roared.

But that night Miss Batt, while she cooked for Miss Fife,
who was opening the wine with a corkscrew
from last year's school trip to Sienna and Florence,
felt herself naked, electric under her tartan skirt, twin set
and pearls; and later, Miss Fife at the piano, stroking
the first notes of Beethoven's 'Moonlight' Sonata, Miss Batt
came behind her, placing her inked and trembling hands
on her shoulders. A broken A minor chord stumbled
and died. Miss Fife said that Ludwig could only
have written this piece when he was in love. Miss Batt
pulled Miss Fife by the hair, turning her face around, hearing
her gasp, bending down, kissing her, kissing her, kissing her.
Essays on Cardinal Wolsey lay unmarked on the floor.

Across the hushed white park, down the slush of the hill,
Miss Dunn crouched on the floor of her sitting room
over a map of Tibet. The whisky glass in her nervous hand

clunked on her teeth, Talisker sheathing her tongue
in a heroine's warmth. She moved her finger slowly
over the map, the roof of the world. Her fingers walked to Nepal,
changing the mountain *Chomolungma* to *Sagarmatha*.
She sipped at her malt and thought about Mallory, lost
on Everest's slopes with his English Air, of how he'd wanted
to reach the summit *because it was there.* She wondered
whether he had. Nobody knew. She saw herself walking
the upper slopes with the Captain of Sports towards
the foetal shape of a sleeping man . . . She turned to the girl.

*

That Monday morning Doctor Bream, at her desk,
didn't yet know that the laughter of Stafford Girls' High
would not go away. But when she stood on the stage,
garbed in her Cambridge cap and gown, and told the school
to quietly stand and contemplate a fresh and serious start
to the week, and closed her eyes – the hush like an air balloon
tethered with ropes – a low and vulgar giggle yanked
at the silence. Doctor Bream kept her eyes clenched, hoping
that if she ignored it all would be well. Clumps of laughter
sprouted among the row upon row of girls. Doctor Bream,
determined and blind, started the morning's hymn. *I vow
to thee my country* . . . A flushed Miss Fife started to play.
All earthly things above . . . The rest of the staff joined in –

*entire and whole and perfect, the service of my love,
the love that asks no questions, the love that stands the test* . . .
But the girls were hysterical, watching the Head,
Queen Canute, singing against the tide of their mirth,
their shoals, their glittering laughter. She opened her eyes –
Clarice Maud Bream, MBE, DLitt – and saw, in the giggling sea
one face which seemed to her to be worse, cheekier,

redder and louder, than all of the rest. Nigella Dawn
was fished by the Head from her seat and made to stand
on a chair on the stage. Laughter drained from the Hall. *This girl*,
boomed the Head, *will stand on this chair for as long as it takes
for the school to come to its senses. SILENCE!* The whole school
stood like a crowd waiting for news. The bell rang. Nobody

moved. Nobody made a sound. Minutes slinked away
as Nigella Dawn swayed on her creaky chair. The First Years
stared in shame at their shoes. The Head's tight smile
was a tick. *That*, she thought, in a phrase of her mother's,
has put the tin lid on that. A thin high whine, a kitten,
wind on a wire, came from behind. The school
seemed to hold its breath. Nigella Dawn shook on her chair.
The sound came again, louder. Doctor Bream looked to the staff.
Miss Batt had her head in her lap and was keening and rocking
backwards and forwards. The noise put the Head in mind
of a radio dial – *Luxembourg, Light, Hilversum, Welsh* –
as though the woman were trying to tune in to herself. Miss Batt
flung her head back and laughed, laughed like a bride.

*

Mr and Mrs Mackay silently ate. She eyed him
boning his fish, slicing it down to the backbone,
sliding the skeleton out, fastidious, deft. She spied him
eat from the right of his plate to the left, ordered, precise.
She clenched herself for his voice. *A very nice dish
from the bottomless deep.* Bad words ran in her head like mice.
She wanted to write them down in the crossword lights.
14 Across: *F . . . * 17 Down: *F . . . . . .* 2 Down: *F . . . . . .*
Mr Mackay reached for the *OED*. She bit her lip. *A word
for one who is given to walking by night, not necessarily
in sleep.* She felt her heart flare in its dark cave, hungry, blind,

open its small beak. *Beginning with N.* Mrs Mackay
moved to the window and stared at the ravenous night. Later,

awake in the beached boat of the marital bed, Mrs Mackay
slid from between the sheets. Her spouse whistled and whined.
She dressed in sweater and slacks, in boots, in her old tweed
coat, and slipped from the house with a tut of the front door snib.
Her breath swaggered away like a genie popped from a flask.
She looked for the moon, found it, arched high over the house,
a raised eyebrow of light, and started to walk. The streets
were empty, darkly sparkling under her feet, ribbons that tied
the sleeping town like a gift. A black cat glared from a wall.
Mrs Mackay walked and walked and walked, letting the night
sigh underneath her clothes, perfume her skin; letting it in,
the scented night – stone, starlight, tree-sleep, rat, owl.
A calm rhythm measured itself in her head. *Noctambulist.*

She walked for hours, till dawn's soft tip rubbed, smudged,
erased the dark. Back home, she stripped and washed
and dressed for school, moving about in the kitchen
till Mr Mackay appeared, requesting a four-minute egg
from a satisfied hen. She watched him slice off the top
with the side of his spoon, dip in his toast, savour the soft gold
of the yolk with his neat tongue. She thought of the girls,
how they'd laughed now for weeks. Panic nipped and salted
her eyes. And later that day, walking among the giggling desks
of the Third, she read Cleopatra's lament in a shaking voice
as tears shone on her cheeks: *Hast thou no care of me?
Shall I abide in this dull world, which in thy absence is
No better than a sty? O! see my women, the crown*

*o' the earth doth melt. My lord! O! withered is the garland
of the war, the soldier's pole is fall'n; young boys and girls
are level now with men; the odds is gone, and there is nothing*

left remarkable beneath the visiting moon. Carolann Clare, trapped
in a breathless, crippling laugh, seriously thought she would die.
Mrs Mackay lay down her book and asked the girls to start
from the top and carry on reading the play round the class.
She closed her eyes and seemed to drift off at her desk.
The voices of girls shared Shakespeare, line by line, the clock
over the blackboard crumbling its minutes into the dusty air.
From the other side of the wall, light breezes of laughter came
and went. Further away, from the music room, the sound
of the orchestra hooted and sneered its way through Grieg.

Miss Batt, in the staffroom, marking The War of Jenkins' Ear
over and over again, put down her pen. Music reminded her
of Miss Fife. She lay her head on the table, dizzy with lust, longed
for the four o'clock bell, for home, for pasta and *vino rosso*,
for Fifi's body on hers in the single bed, for kisses that tasted
of jotters, of wine. She picked up an essay and read:
*England went to war with Spain because a seaman, Robert
Jenkins, claimed that the Spanish thought him a smuggler
and cut off his ear. He showed the ear in the Commons
and public opinion forced the Government to declare war
on October 23, 1739* . . . Miss Batt cursed under her breath,
slashing a red tick with her pen. The music had stopped. Hilarity
squealed and screeched in its place down the corridor.

Miss Nadimbaba was teaching the poems of Yeats
to the Fifth when the girls in the orchestra laughed. She held
in her hands the poem which had made her a scribbler of verse
at twelve or thirteen. 'The Song' – she was sick of the laughter
at Stafford Girls' High – 'of Wandering Aengus.' She stared
at the girls in her class who were starting to shake. An epidemic,
that's what it was. It had gone on all term. It was now the air
that they breathed, teachers and girls: a giggling, sniggering,
gurgling, snickering atmosphere, a laughing gas that seeped

under doors, up corridors, into the gym, the chemistry lab,
the swimming pool, into Latin and Spanish and French and Greek,
into Needlework, History, Art, R.K., P.E., into cross-country runs,
into the silver apples of the moon, the golden apples of the sun.

Miss Dunn stood with her bike outside school after four,
scanning the silly, cackling girls for a face – Diana Kim's.
The Captain of Sports was tall, red-haired. Her green eyes
stared at Miss Dunn and Miss Dunn *knew*. This was a girl
who would scale a vertical wall of ice with her fingertips,
who would pitch a tent on the lip of a precipice, who would know
when the light was good, when the wind was bad, when snow
was powdery or hard. The girl had the stuff of heroines. Diana Kim
walked with the teacher, pushing her bicycle for her, hearing her
outline the journey, the great adventure, the climb to the Mother
of Earth. Something inside her opened and bloomed.
Miss Dunn was her destiny, fame, a strong hand pulling her
higher and higher into the far Tibetan clouds, into the sun.

*

Doctor Bream was well aware that something had to be done.
Laughter, it seemed, was on the curriculum. The girls
found everything funny, strange; howled or screamed
at the slightest thing. The Headmistress prowled the school,
listening at classroom doors. The new teacher, Mrs Munro,
was reading The Flaying of Marsyas to the Third: *Help!
Why are you stripping me from myself?* The girls were in fits.
Mrs Munro's tight voice struggled on: *It was possible to count
his throbbing organs and the chambers of his lungs.* Shrieks
and squeals stabbed the air. Why? At what? Doctor Bream
snooped on. Miss Batt was teaching the First Form the names
of the nine major planets: *Mercury, Venus, Earth, Mars,
Jupiter, Saturn, Uranus . . .* Pandemonium hooted and whooped.

The grim Head passed down the corridor, hearing the Fifth Form
gargling its way through the Diet of Worms. She came
to the Honours Board, the names of the old girls written in gold –
Head Girls who had passed into legend, Captains of Sport
who had played the game, prize-winning girls, girls who'd gone on
to achieve great things. Members of Parliament! Blasts of laughter
belched from the playing fields. Doctor Bream walked to her room
and stood by her desk. Her certificates preened behind glass
in the wintery light. Silver medals and trophies and cups gleamed
in the cabinet. She went to the wall – the school photograph
glinted and glowed, each face like a fingertip; the pupils
straight-backed, straight-faced; the staff upright, straight-laced.
A warm giggle burbled outside. She flung open the door.

The empty corridor winked. She could hear
a distant piano practising Für Elise . . . Señora Devizes
counting in Spanish in one of the rooms – *uno, dos, tres,
cuatro, cinco, seis, siete, ocho, nueve, diez, once, doce,
trece, catorce, quince, diez y seis, diez y siete, diez y ocho* . . .
a shrill whistle blowing outside . . . But then a burst of hysteria
came from the classroom above, rolled down the stairs,
exploded again in the classroom below. Mrs Mackay,
frantic, hoarse, could be heard pitching Portia's speech
over the hoots of the Fourth: *The quality of MERCY
is not STRAINED. It droppeth as the gentle rain from HEAVEN
upon the place BENEATH* . . . Cackles, like gunfire, crackled
and spat through the school. A cheer boomed from the Gym.

It went on thus – through every hymn or poem, catechism,
logarithm, sum, exam; in every classroom, drama room
to music room; on school trips to a factory or farm; from
First to Sixth Form, dunce to academic crème de la crème,
day in, day out; till, towards the end of the Hilary Term,

Doctor Bream called yet another meeting in the Staffroom,
determined now to solve the problem of the laughter
of the girls once and for all. The staff filed in at 4.15 –
Miss Batt, Miss Fife, Miss Dunn, Mrs Munro, the sporty
Mrs Lee, Mrs Mackay, Miss Nadimbaba, the Heads of French
and Science – Miss Feaver, Mrs Kaye – Señora Devizes,
the tuneful Miss Aherne, the part-time drama teacher
Mrs Prendergast. The Head stood up and clapped her hands.

Miss Fife poured Earl Grey tea. Miss Dunn stood by the window,
staring out. Miss Batt burned at Miss Fife. Mrs Mackay
sat down and closed her eyes. Miss Nadimbaba churned
the closing couplet of a poem in her head. Miss Feaver
crossed her legs and smiled at Mrs Lee, who twirled
a squash racquet between her rosy knees. *I think we all agree,*
said Doctor Bream, *that things are past the pale. The girls
are learning nothing. Discipline's completely gone
to pot. I'd like to hear from each of you in turn. Mrs Mackay?*
Mrs Mackay opened her eyes and sighed. And shook her head.
And then she started singing: *It was a lover and his lass,
with a hey, and a ho, and a hey nonino, that o'er
the green cornfield did pass, in the spring time,*

*the only pretty ring time, when birds do sing, hey ding
a ding, ding; sweet lovers love the spring.* A silence fell.
Miss Batt looked at Miss Fife and cleared her throat. *Miss Fife
and I are leaving at the end of term.* Miss Dunn at the window
turned. *I'm leaving then myself. To have a crack at Everest . . .*
The Head sank to a chair. Miss Nadimbaba stood. Then one by one
the staff resigned – to publish poetry, to live in Spain, to form
a tennis club, to run a restaurant in Nice, to tread the boards,
to sing in smoky clubs, to translate Ovid into current speech,
to study homeopathy. Doctor Bream was white with shock.

And what, she forced herself at last to say, *about the girls?*
Miss Batt, slowly undressing Fifi in the stockroom in her head,
winked at Miss Fife. She giggled girlishly. Miss Feaver laughed.

*

Small hours. The moon tracked Mrs Mackay as she reached the edge
of the sleeping town, houses dwindling to fields, the road
twisting up and away into the distant hills. She caught her mind
making anagrams – *grow heed*, *stab*, *rats* – and forced herself
to chant aloud as she walked. Hedgerow. Bats. Star. Her head
cleared. The town was below her now, dark and hunched,
a giant husband bunched in his sleep. Mrs Mackay climbed on,
higher and higher, keeping close to the ditch, till the road snaked
in a long S then levelled out into open countryside. *Shore,
love, steer, low, master, night loom, riven use, no.* Horse. Vole.
Trees. Owl. Stream. Moonlight. Universe. On. *Wed, loop, wand,
drib, tiles, pay thaw, god.* Dew. Pool. Dawn. Bird. Stile. Pathway.
Dog. She arrived at the fringe of a village as morning broke.

Miss Batt held Miss Fife in her arms at dawn, the small room
chaste with new light. Miss Fife began to talk in her sleep –
*The square on the hypotenuse is equal to the sum
of the squares of the other two sides.* Miss Batt slid down,
nuzzled her breastbone, her stomach, kissed down,
kissed down, down to the triangle. The tutting bedside clock
counted to five. They woke again at seven, stupid with love,
everything they knew – the brightest stars, Sirius, Canopus,
Alpha Centauri, Vega; the Roman Emperors, Claudius,
Nero, Galba, Otho, Vitellius; musical terms, *allegro, calando,
crescendo, glissando*; mathematics, the value of pi,
prime numbers, Cantor's infinities – only a jumble of words,
a jumble of words. A long deep zero groaned from Miss Fife.

Miss Dunn took out her list and checked it again. Her class
was sniggering its way through a test on Britain's largest lakes.
She mouthed her list like a prayer: socks, mittens, shirt, leggings,
hat, face mask, goggles, harness, karabiners, ice screws, pitons,
helmet, descender, ascender, loops, slings, ice axe, gaiters,
crampons, boots, jacket, hood, trousers, water bottle, urine
bottle, waste bags, sleeping bag, kit bag, head torch, batteries,
tent, medical kit, maps, stove, butane, radio, fixing line, rope,
cord, stoppers, wands, stakes and chocks and all of it twice.
A sprinkle of giggles made her look up. *Pass your test to the girl
on your left to be marked. The answers are: Lough Neagh,
Lower Lough Erne, Loch Lomond, Loch Ness, Loch Awe, Upper
Lough Erne . . .* Diana Kim climbed and climbed in her head.

Doctor Bream read through the letter to parents then signed
her name at the end. The school was to close at the end of term
until further notice. A dozen resignation notes from the staff
lay on her desk. The Head put her head in her hands and wept.
A local journalist lurked at the gates. Señora Devizes
and Miss Nadimbaba entered the room to say that the girls
were filing into the Hall for the Special Assembly. There was still
no sign of Mrs Mackay. She looked at the shattered Head
and Kipling sprang to Miss Nadimbaba's lips: *If you can force
your heart and nerve and sinew to serve your turn long after they
are gone . . .* Señora Devizes joined in: *Persiste aun no tengas
fuerza, y sólo te quede la voluntad que les dice:
¡Persiste!* The Head got to her feet and straightened her back.

And so, Doctor Bream summed up, *you girls have laughed this once
great school into the ground. Señora Devizes plans to return
to Spain.* Cries of *¡Olé! Miss Batt and Miss Fife have resigned.*
Wolf whistles. *Mrs Prendergast is joining the Theatre Royale.*
A round of applause crashed on the boards like surf. The Head stared

at the laughing girls then turned and marched from the stage,
clipped up the polished corridor, banged through the double doors,
crunched down the gravel drive to the Staff Car Park and into her car.
Elvis, shrieked Caroline Joan from the Hall, *has left the building*.
A cheer like an avalanche bounced off the roof. The Captain of Sports
slipped from her seat and followed Miss Dunn. The girls burst
into song as their mute teachers walked from the stage. *Till we
have built Jerusalem in England's green and pleasant land.*

*

The empty school creaked and sighed, its desks the small coffins
of lessons, its blackboards the tombstones of learning. The books
in the Library stiffened and yellowed and curled. The portraits
of gone Headmistresses stared into space. The school groaned,
the tiles on its roof falling off in its sleep, its windows as white
as chalk. The grass on the playing fields grew like grass
on a grave. Doctor Bream stared from her hospital window
over the fields. She could see the school bell in its tower glint
in the evening sun like a tear in an eye. She turned away. Postcards
and get-well messages from the staff were pinned to the wall.
She took down a picture of Everest from Miss Dunn: *We leave
Camp II tomorrow if the weather holds to climb the Corridor
to 21,000 feet. Both coping well with altitude. The Sherpas . . .*

Mrs Mackay walked through Glen Strathfarrar, mad, muttering,
free; a filthy old pack on her back filled with scavenged loot –
banana, bottle, blanket, balaclava, bread, blade, bible. She sat
by a stream, filled her bottle and drank. She ate the crusts,
the fruit. Kingfisher. Eagle. Heron. Red deer. Midge. The Glen
darkened and cooled like History. Mrs Mackay lay in the heather
under her blanket, mumbling lines from Lear: *As mad as the vex'd
sea; singing aloud; crowned with rank fumitor and furrow weeds,*

with burdocks, hemlocks, nettles, cuckoo-flowers, darnel...
Syllables. Syllables. Sleep came suddenly, under the huge black,
the chuckling clever stars. The Head at her window looked north
to the clear night sky, to Pollux and Castor, Capella, Polaris,
and wondered again what could have become of Mrs Mackay.

Rough lads from the town came up to the school to throw stones
through the glass. Miss Batt and Miss Fife had moved
to a city. They drank in a dark bar where women danced, cheek
to cheek. Miss Batt loved Miss Fife till she sobbed and shook
in her arms. Stray cats prowled through the classrooms, lunging
at mice. Miss Fife dreamed that the school was a huge ship
floating away from land, all hands lost, steered by a ghost,
a woman whose face was the Head's, was Miss Nadimbaba's,
then Mrs Mackay's, Mrs Lee's, Miss Feaver's, Miss Dunn's,
Mrs Munro's, Mrs Kaye's, Miss Aherne's, Señora Devizes' . . .
She woke in the darkness, a face over hers, a warm mouth
kissing the gibberish from her lips. The school sank in her mind,
a black wave taking it down as she gazed at the woman's face.

Miss Nadimbaba put down her pen and read through her poem.
The palms of her hands felt light, that talented ache. She altered
a verb and the line jumped on the page like a hooked fish. She needed
to type it up, but the poem was done. She was dying
to read it aloud to her aunt. She would open some wine.
In the hospital, a nurse brought warm milk and a pill to the Head,
who stared through the bars at the blackened hulk of the school.
By dawn, at John O'Groats, Mrs Mackay had finally run out of land.
She wrote her maiden name with a stick in the sand then walked
into the sea, steady at first, step by step, till the firm waves lifted her
under her arms and danced her away like a groom with a bride.
High above in the cold sky the seagulls, like schoolgirls, laughed.
Higher again, a teacher fell through the clouds with a girl in her arms.

A Dreaming Week

Not tonight, I'm dreaming
in the heart of the honeyed dark
in a boat of a bed in the attic room
in a house on the edge of the park
where the wind in the big old trees
creaks like an ark.

Not tomorrow, I'm dreaming
till dusk turns into dawn – *dust, must,
most, moot, moon, mown, down* –
with my hand on an open unread book,
a bird that's never flown . . . distantly
the birdsong of the telephone.

Not the following evening, I'm dreaming
in the monocle of the moon,
a sleeping *S* on the page of a bed
in the tome of a dim room, the rain
on the roof, rhyming there,
like the typed words of a poem.

Not the night after that, I'm dreaming
till the stars are blue in the face
printing the news of their old light
with the ink of space,
yards and yards of black silk night
to cover my sleeping face.

Not the next evening, I'm dreaming
in the crook of midnight's arm
like a lover held by another
safe from harm, like a child
stilled by a mother, soft and warm,
twelve golden faraway bells for a charm.

Not that night either, I'm dreaming
till the tides have come and gone
sighing over the frowning sand,
the whale's lonely song
scored on wave after wave of water
all the wet night long.

Not the last evening, I'm dreaming
under the stuttering clock,
under the covers, under closed eyes,
all colours fading to black,
the last of daylight hurrying
for a date with the glamorous dark.

White Writing

No vows written to wed you,
I write them white,
my lips on yours,
light in the soft hours of our married years.

No prayers written to bless you,
I write them white,
your soul a flame,
bright in the window of your maiden name.

No laws written to guard you,
I write them white,
your hand in mine,
palm against palm, lifeline, heartline.

No rules written to guide you,
I write them white,
words on the wind,
traced with a stick where we walk on the sand.

No news written to tell you,
I write it white,
foam on a wave
as we lift up our skirts in the sea, wade,

see last gold sun behind clouds,
inked water in moonlight.
No poems written to praise you,
I write them white.

Gambler

She goes for the sound of the words, the beauty they hold
in the movement they make on the air, the shape
of the breath of a word leaving her lips like a whistle

or kiss. So Hyperion's tips mean nothing to her, the form,
the favourites, whether the going is heavy or firm,
the horse a stinker or first-time blinkered. It's words

she picks, names she ticks. That day it was *Level Headed*
at 10–1, two syllables each to balance the musical chime
of *lev* and *head*, the echoing *el*. She backed it to win

and then on a whim went for *Indian Nectar* at 7–2
to come in next. *Indiannectar. Indiannectar.* She stood
in a trance at the counter, singing it over and over

again in her head which was why, she guessed, she decided
to pick *Sharp Spice* (5–2 fav) to gallop in third – the words
seemed to fit. Most days she sits with her stump of a pen

writing the poems of bets. And how can she lose? Just listen
to some of the names that she didn't choose – *Heiress of Meath,
Springfieldsupreme, Mavis, Shush, Birth of the Blues.*

The Light Gatherer

When you were small, your cupped palms
each held a candlesworth under the skin,
enough light to begin,

                and as you grew
light gathered in you, two clear raindrops
in your eyes,

        warm pearls, shy,
in the lobes of your ears, even always
the light of a smile after your tears.

Your kissed feet glowed in my one hand,
or I'd enter a room to see the corner you played in
lit like a stage set,

                the crown of your bowed head spotlit.
When language came, it glittered like a river,
silver, clever with fish,

                and you slept
with the whole moon held in your arms for a night light
where I knelt watching.

                Light gatherer. You fell from a star
into my lap, the soft lamp at the bedside
mirrored in you,

            and now you shine like a snowgirl,
a buttercup under a chin, the wide blue yonder
you squeal at and fly in,

            like a jewelled cave,
turquoise and diamond and gold, opening out
at the end of a tunnel of years.

The Cord

for Ella

They cut the cord she was born with
and buried it under a tree
in the heart of the Great Forest
when she was exactly the length
of her mother's nursing elbow
to the tip of her thumb.

She learned to speak and asked them,
though she was young yet,
what the cord had looked like –
had a princess spun it
from a golden spinning wheel?
Could the cord be silver? Was it real?

Real enough and hidden
in the roots of an ancient oak,
the tangled knot of a riddle
or the weird ribbon of a gift
in a poke. As she grew, she asked again
if the cord was made of rope,

then stared from the house she lived in
across the fields to the woods
where rooks spread their pages of wings
like black unreadable books
and the wind in the grass
scribbled sentences wherever she looked.

So she went on foot to the forest
and pressed her ear to the ground,
but not a sound or a movement,
not a breath or a word
gave her a hint where she should go
to hunt for her cord. She went deeper

into the forest, following a bird
which disappeared, a waving hand; shadows
blurred into one huge darkness,
but the stars were her mother's eyes
and the screech of an owl in the tree above
was the sound of a baby's cry.

Wish

But what if, in the clammy soil, her limbs
grew warmer, shifted, stirred, kicked off
the covering of earth, the drowsing corms,
the sly worms, what if her arms reached out
to grab the stone, the grooves of her dates
under her thumb, and pulled her up? I wish.
Her bare feet walk along the gravel path
between the graves, her shroud like washing
blown onto the grass, the petals of her wreath
kissed for a bride. Nobody died. Nobody
wept. Nobody slept who couldn't be woken
by the light. If I can only push open this heavy door
she'll be standing there in the sun, dirty, tired,
wondering why do I shout, why do I run.

North-West

for Frances

However it is we return to the water's edge
where the ferry grieves down by the Pier Head,
we do what we always did and get on board.
The city drifts out of reach. A huge silvery bird,
a kiss on the lip of the wind, follows our ship.
This is where we were young, the place no map
or heritage guide can reveal. Only an X on a wave
marks the spot, the flowers of litter, a grave
for our ruined loves, unborn children, ghosts.
We look back at the skyline wondering what we lost
in the hidden streets, in the rented rooms,
no more than punters now in a tourist boom.
Above our heads the gulls cry *yeah yeah yeah*.
Frets of light on the river. Tearful air.

Death and the Moon

i.m. Adrian Henri

The moon is nearer than where death took you
at the end of the old year. Cold as cash
in the sky's dark pocket, its hard old face
is gold as a mask tonight. I break the ice
over the fish in my frozen pond, look up
as the ghosts of my wordless breath reach
for the stars. If I stood on the tip of my toes
and stretched, I could touch the edge of the moon.

I stooped at the lip of your open grave
to gather a fistful of earth, hard rain,
tough confetti, and tossed it down. It stuttered
like morse on the wood over your eyes, your tongue,
your soundless ears. Then as I slept my living sleep
the ground gulped you, swallowed you whole,
and though I was there when you died,
in the red cave of your widow's unbearable cry,

and measured the space between last words
and silence, I cannot say where you are. Unreachable
by prayer, even if poems are prayers. Unseeable
in the air, even if souls are stars. I turn
to the house, its windows tender with light, the moon,
surely, only as far again as the roof. The goldfish
are tongues in the water's mouth. The black night
is huge, mute, and you are further forever than that.

falling in Love is glamorous hell.

Now no discourse, except it be of Love;
Now I can break my fast, dine, sup, and sleep
Upon the very naked name of Love.
                    Shakespeare,
        Two Gentlemen of Verona (II, iv, 137–9)

You

Uninvited, the thought of you stayed too late in my head,
so I went to bed, dreaming you hard, hard, woke with your name,
like tears, soft, salt, on my lips, the sound of its bright syllables
like a charm, like a spell.

                Falling in love
is glamorous hell; the crouched, parched heart
like a tiger ready to kill; a flame's fierce licks under the skin.
Into my life, larger than life, beautiful, you strolled in.

I hid in my ordinary days, in the long grass of routine,
in my camouflage rooms. You sprawled in my gaze,
staring back from anyone's face, from the shape of a cloud,
from the pining, earth-struck moon which gapes at me

as I open the bedroom door. The curtains stir. There you are
on the bed, like a gift, like a touchable dream.

Text

I tend the mobile now
like an injured bird.

We text, text, text
our significant words.

I re-read your first,
your second, your third,

look for your small *xx*,
feeling absurd.

The codes we send
arrive with a broken chord.

I try to picture your hands,
their image is blurred.

Nothing my thumbs press
will ever be heard.

Name

When did your name
change from a proper noun
to a charm?

Its three vowels
like jewels
on the thread of my breath.

Its consonants
brushing my mouth
like a kiss.

I love your name.
I say it again and again
in this summer rain.

I see it,
discreet in the alphabet,
like a wish.

I pray it
into the night
till its letters are light.

I hear your name
rhyming, rhyming,
rhyming with everything.

Forest

There were flowers at the edge of the forest, cupping
the last of the light in their upturned petals. I followed you in,
under the sighing, restless trees and my whole life vanished.

The moon tossed down its shimmering cloth. We undressed,
then dressed again in the gowns of the moon. We knelt in the leaves,
kissed, kissed; new words rustled nearby and we swooned.

Didn't we? And didn't I see you rise again and go deeper
into the woods and follow you still, till even my childhood shrank
to a glow-worm of light where those flowers darkened and closed.

Thorns on my breasts, rain in my mouth, loam on my bare feet, rough
bark grazing my back, I moaned for them all. You stood, waist deep,
in a stream, pulling me in, so I swam. You were the water, the wind

in the branches wringing their hands, the heavy, wet perfume of soil.
I am there now, lost in the forest, dwarfed by the giant trees. Find me.

River

Down by the river, under the trees, love waits for me
to walk from the journeying years of my time and arrive.
I part the leaves and they toss me a blessing of rain.

The river stirs and turns, consoling and fondling itself
with watery hands, its clear limbs parting and closing.
Grey as a secret, the heron bows its head on the bank.

I drop my past on the grass and open my arms, which ache
as though they held up this heavy sky, or had pressed
against window glass all night as my eyes sieved the stars;

open my mouth, wordless at last meeting love at last, dry
from travelling so long, shy of a prayer. You step from the shade,
and I feel love come to my arms and cover my mouth, feel

my soul swoop and ease itself into my skin, like a bird
threading a river. Then I can look love full in the face, see
who you are I have come this far to find, the love of my life.

Haworth

I'm here now where you were.
The summer grass under my palms is your hair.
Your taste is the living air.

I lie on my back. Two juggling butterflies are your smile.
The heathery breath of the moor's simply your smell.
Your name sounds on the coded voice of the bell.

I'll go nowhere you've not.
The bleached dip in a creature's bone's your throat.
That high lark, whatever it was you thought.

And this ridged stone your hand in mine,
and the curve of the turning earth your spine,
and the swooning bees besotted with flowers your tune.

I get up and walk. The dozing hillside is your dreaming head.
The cobblestones are every word you said.
The grave I kneel beside, only your bed.

Hour

Love's time's beggar, but even a single hour,
bright as a dropped coin, makes love rich.
We find an hour together, spend it not on flowers
or wine, but the whole of the summer sky and a grass ditch.

For thousands of seconds we kiss; your hair
like treasure on the ground; the Midas light
turning your limbs to gold. Time slows, for here
we are millionaires, backhanding the night

so nothing dark will end our shining hour,
no jewel hold a candle to the cuckoo spit
hung from the blade of grass at your ear,
no chandelier or spotlight see you better lit

than here. Now. Time hates love, wants love poor,
but love spins gold, gold, gold from straw.

Swing

Someone had looped a rope over a branch
and made a rough swing for the birch tree
next to the river. We passed it, walking and walking
into our new love; soft, unbearable dawns of desire
where mist was the water's slipping veil, or foam
boasted and frothed like champagne at the river's bend.

You asked me if I was sure, as a line of Canada geese
crowded the other bank, happy as wedding guests. Yes,
sure as the vision that flares in my head, away from you now,
of the moment you climbed on the swing, and swung out
into the silver air, the endless affirmative blue,
like something from heaven on earth, from paradise.

Rain

Not so hot as this for a hundred years.
You were where I was going. I was in tears.
I surrendered my heart to the judgement of my peers.

A century's heat in the garden, fierce as love.
You returned on the day that I had to leave.
I mimed the full, rich, busy life I had to live.

Hotter than hell. I burned for you day and night;
got bits of your body wrong, bits of it right,
in the huge mouth of the dark, in the bite of the light.

I planted a rose, burnt orange, the colour of flame,
gave it the last of the water, gave it your name.
It flared back at the sun in a perfect rhyme.

Then the rain came, like stammered kisses at first
on the back of my neck. I unfurled my fist
for the rain to caress with its lips. I turned up my face,

and water flooded my mouth, baptised my head,
and the rainclouds gathered like midnight overhead,
and the rain came down like a lover comes to a bed.

Absence

Then the birds stitching the dawn with their song
have patterned your name.

Then the green bowl of the garden filling with light
is your gaze.

Then the lawn lengthening and warming itself
is your skin.

Then a cloud disclosing itself overhead
is your opening hand.

Then the first seven bells from the church
pine on the air.

Then the sun's soft bite on my face
is your mouth.

Then a bee in a rose is your fingertip
touching me here.

Then the trees bending and meshing their leaves
are what we would do.

Then my steps to the river are text to a prayer
printing the ground.

Then the river searching its bank for your shape
is desire.

Then a fish nuzzling the water's throat
has a lover's ease.

Then a shawl of sunlight dropped in the grass
is a garment discarded.

Then a sudden scatter of summer rain
is your tongue.

Then a butterfly paused on a trembling leaf
is your breath.

Then the gauzy mist relaxed on the ground
is your pose.

Then the fruit from the cherry tree falling on grass
is your kiss, your kiss.

Then the day's hours are theatres of air
where I watch you entranced.

Then the sun's light going down from the sky
is the length of your back.

Then the evening bells over the rooftops
are lovers' vows.

Then the river staring up, lovesick for the moon,
is my long night.

Then the stars between us are love
urging its light.

If I Was Dead

If I was dead,
and my bones adrift
like dropped oars
in the deep, turning earth;

or drowned,
and my skull
a listening shell
on the dark ocean bed;

if I was dead,
and my heart
soft mulch
for a red, red rose;

or burned,
and my body
a fistful of grit, thrown
in the face of the wind;

if I was dead,
and my eyes,
blind at the roots of flowers,
wept into nothing,

I swear your love
would raise me
out of my grave,
in my flesh and blood,

like Lazarus;
hungry for this,
and this, and this,
your living kiss.

World

On the other side of the world,
you pass the moon to me,
like a loving cup,
or a quaich.
I roll you the sun.

I go to bed,
as you're getting up
on the other side of the world.
You have scattered the stars
towards me here, like seeds

in the earth.
All through the night,
I have sent you
bunches, bouquets, of cloud
to the other side of the world;

so my love will be shade
where you are,
and yours,
as I turn in my sleep,
the bud of a star.

Hand

Away from you, I hold hands with the air,
your imagined, untouchable hand. Not there,
your fingers braid with mine as I walk.
Far away in my heart, you start to talk.

I squeeze the air, kicking the auburn leaves,
everything suddenly gold. I half believe
your hand is holding mine, the way
it would if you were here. What do you say

in my heart? I bend my head to listen, then feel
your hand reach out and stroke my hair, as real
as the wind caressing the fretful trees above.
Now I can hear you clearly, speaking of love.

Rapture

Thought of by you all day, I think of you.
The birds sing in the shelter of a tree.
Above the prayer of rain, unacred blue,
not paradise, goes nowhere endlessly.
How does it happen that our lives can drift
far from our selves, while we stay trapped in time,
queuing for death? It seems nothing will shift
the pattern of our days, alter the rhyme
we make with loss to assonance with bliss.
Then love comes, like a sudden flight of birds
from earth to heaven after rain. Your kiss,
recalled, unstrings, like pearls, this chain of words.
Huge skies connect us, joining here to there.
Desire and passion on the thinking air.

Elegy

Who'll know then, when they walk by the grave
where your bones will be brittle things – this bone here
that swoops away from your throat, and this,
which perfectly fits the scoop of my palm, and these
which I count with my lips, and your skull,
which blooms on the pillow now, and your fingers,
beautiful in their little rings – that love, which wanders history,
singled you out in your time?

                                        Love loved you best; lit you
with a flame, like talent, under your skin; let you
move through your days and nights, blessed in your flesh,
blood, hair, as though they were lovely garments
you wore to pleasure the air. Who'll guess, if they read
your stone, or press their thumbs to the scars
of your dates, that were I alive, I would lie on the grass
above your bones till I mirrored your pose, your infinite grace?

Row

But when we rowed,
the room swayed and sank down on its knees,
the air hurt and purpled like a bruise,
the sun banged the gate in the sky and fled.

But when we rowed,
the trees wept and threw away their leaves,
the day ripped the hours from our lives,
the sheets and pillows shredded themselves on the bed.

But when we rowed,
our mouths knew no kiss, no kiss, no kiss,
our hearts were jagged stones in our fists,
the garden sprouted bones, grown from the dead.

But when we rowed,
your face blanked like a page erased of words,
my hands squeezed themselves, burned like verbs,
love turned, and ran, and cowered in our heads.

Cuba

No getting up from the bed in this grand hotel
and getting dressed, like a work of art
rubbing itself out. No lifting the red rose
from the room service tray when you leave,
as though you might walk to the lip of a grave
and toss it down. No glass of champagne, left
to go flat in the glow of a bedside lamp,
the frantic bubbles swimming for the light. No white towel,
strewn, like a shroud, on the bathroom floor.
No brief steam on the mirror there for a finger
to smudge in a heart, an arrow, a name. No soft soap
rubbed between four hands. No flannel. No future plans.
No black cab, sad hearse, on the rank. No queue there.
No getting away from this. No goodnight kiss. No Cuba.

Tea

I like pouring your tea, lifting
the heavy pot, and tipping it up,
so the fragrant liquid steams in your china cup.

Or when you're away, or at work,
I like to think of your cupped hands as you sip,
as you sip, of the faint half-smile of your lips.

I like the questions – sugar? milk? –
and the answers I don't know by heart, yet,
for I see your soul in your eyes, and I forget.

Jasmine, Gunpowder, Assam, Earl Grey, Ceylon,
I love tea's names. Which tea would you like? I say,
but it's any tea, for you, please, any time of day,

as the women harvest the slopes,
for the sweetest leaves, on Mount Wu-Yi,
and I am your lover, smitten, straining your tea.

Betrothal

I will be yours, be yours.
I'll walk on the moors
with my spade.
Make me your bride.

I will be brave, be brave.
I'll dig my own grave
and lie down.
Make me your own.

I will be good, be good.
I'll sleep in my blankets of mud
till you kneel above.
Make me your love.

I'll stay forever, forever.
I'll wade in the river,
wearing my gown of stone.
Make me the one.

I will obey, obey.
I'll float far away,
gargling my vows.
Make me your spouse.

I will say yes, say yes.
I'll sprawl in my dress
on my watery bed.
Make me be wed.

I'll wear your ring, your ring.
I'll dance and I'll sing
in the flames.
Make me your name.

I'll feel desire, desire.
I'll bloom in the fire.
I'll blush like a baby.
Make me your lady.

I'll say I do, I do.
I'll be ash in a jar, for you
to scatter my life.
Make me your wife.

Bridgewater Hall

Again, the endless northern rain between us
like a veil. Tonight, I know exactly where you are,
which row, which seat. I stand at my back door.
The light pollution blindfolds every star.

I hold my hand out to the rain, simply to feel it, wet
and literal. It spills and tumbles in my palm,
a broken rosary. Devotion to you lets me see
the concert hall, lit up, the other side of town,

then see you leave there, one of hundreds in the dark,
your black umbrella raised. If rain were words, could talk,
somehow, against your skin, I'd say look up, let it utter
on your face. Now hear my love for you. Now walk.

The Lovers

Pity the lovers,
who climb to the high room,
where the bed,
and the gentle lamps wait,
and disembark from their lives.
The deep waves of the night
lap at the window.

Time slips away
like land from a ship.
The moon, their own death,
follows them, cold,
cold in their blankets.
Pity the lovers, homeless,
with no country to sail to.

Fall

Short days. The leaves are falling
to the deadline of the ground, gold

as the pages of myth. I feel the cold earth
fall away from the sun, the light's heart harden.

I fall too, as if from the glinting plane overhead,
backwards, through fierce blue, though I only lie

in your arms, on our coats, the last hour of autumn,
grasping a fistful of yellowing grass as you move in me,

fall and fall and fall towards you, your passionate gravity.

Ship

In the end,
it was nothing more
than the toy boat of a boy
on the local park's lake,
where I walked with you.

But I knelt down
to watch it arrive,
its white sail shy
with amber light,
the late sun
bronzing the wave
that lifted it up,

my ship coming in
with its cargo of joy.

Love

Love is talent, the world love's metaphor.
Aflame, October's leaves adore the wind,
its urgent breath, whirl to their own death.
Not here, you're everywhere.

                      The evening sky
worships the ground, bears down, the land
yearns back in darkening hills. The night
is empathy, stars in its eyes for tears. Not here,

you're where I stand, hearing the sea, crazy
for the shore, seeing the moon ache and fret
for the earth. When morning comes, the sun, ardent,
covers the trees in gold, you walk

                            towards me,
out of the season, out of the light love reasons.

Give

Give me, you said, on our very first night,
the forest. I rose from the bed and went out,
and when I returned, you listened, enthralled,
to the shadowy story I told.

                  Give me the river,
you asked the next night, then I'll love you forever.
I slipped from your arms and was gone,
and when I came back, you listened, at dawn,
to the glittering story I told.

                  Give me, you said, the gold
from the sun. A third time, I got up and dressed,
and when I came home, you sprawled on my breast
for the dazzling story I told.

                  Give me
the hedgerows, give me the fields.
I slid from the warmth of our sheets,
and when I returned, to kiss you from sleep,
you stirred at the story I told.

                  Give me the silvery cold
of the moon. I pulled on my boots and my coat,
but when I came back, moonlight on your throat
outshone the pale story I told.

                        Give me, you howled,
on our sixth night together, the wind in the trees.
You turned to the wall as I left,
and when I came home, I saw you were deaf
to the blustering story I told.

                        Give me the sky, all the space
it can hold. I left you, the last night we loved,
and when I returned, you were gone with the gold,
and the silver, the river, the forest, the fields,
and this is the story I've told.

Quickdraw

I wear the two, the mobile and the landline phones,
like guns, slung from the pockets on my hips. I'm all
alone. You ring, quickdraw, your voice a pellet
in my ear, and hear me groan.

                        You've wounded me.
Next time, you speak after the tone. I twirl the phone,
then squeeze the trigger of my tongue, wide of the mark.
You choose your spot, then blast me

                        through the heart.
And this is love, high noon, calamity, hard liquor
in the old Last Chance saloon. I show the mobile
to the Sheriff; in my boot, another one's

concealed. You text them both at once. I reel.
Down on my knees, I fumble for the phone,
read the silver bullets of your kiss. Take this . . .
and this . . . and this . . . and this . . . and this . . .

Finding the Words

I found the words at the back of a drawer,
wrapped in black cloth, like three rings
slipped from a dead woman's hand, cold,
dull gold. I had held them before,

                              years ago,
then put them away, forgetting whatever it was
I could use them to say. I touched the first to my lips,
the second, the third, like a sacrament,
like a pledge, like a kiss,

                        and my breath
warmed them, the words I needed to utter this, small words,
and few. I rubbed at them till they gleamed in my palm –
I love you, I love you, I love you –
as though they were new.

December

The year dwindles and glows
to December's red jewel,
my birth month.

The sky blushes,
and lays its cheek
on the sparkling fields.

Then dusk swaddles the cattle,
their silhouettes
simple as faith.

These nights are gifts,
our hands unwrapping the darkness
to see what we have.

The train rushes, ecstatic,
to where you are,
my bright star.

Grace

Then, like a sudden, easy birth, grace –
rendered as light to the softening earth,
the moon stepping slowly backwards
out of the morning sky, reward
for the dark hours we took to arrive and kneel
at the silver river's edge near the heron priest,
anointed, given – what we would wish ourselves.

New Year

I drop the dying year behind me like a shawl
and let it fall. The urgent fireworks fling themselves
against the night, flowers of desire, love's fervency.
Out of the space around me, standing here, I shape
your absent body against mine. You touch me as the giving air.

Most far, most near, your arms are darkness, holding me,
so I lean back, lip-read the heavens talking on in light,
syllabic stars. I see, at last, they pray at us. Your breath
is midnight's, living, on my skin, across the miles between us,
fields and motorways and towns, the million lit-up little homes.

This love we have, grief in reverse, full rhyme, wrong place,
wrong time, sweet work for hands, the heart's vocation, flares
to guide the new year in, the days and nights far out upon the sky's
dark sea. Your mouth is snow now on my lips, cool, intimate, first kiss,
a vow. Time falls and falls through endless space, to when we are.

Chinatown

Writing it, I see how much I love the sound.
Chinatown. Chinatown. Chinatown.
We went down, the day of the Year of the Monkey,
dim sum and dragons bound.

                    Your fair head
was a pearl in the mouth of the crowd. The fireworks
were as loud as love, if love were allowed
a sound. Our wishing children pressed their incense
into a bowl of sand

                    in Chinatown, the smoke drifting off
like question marks over their heads. If I had said
what I'd wished, if I had asked you to tell me the words,
shifting up from your heart

                            for your lips to sift,
at least I'd have heard their sound uttered by you,
although then nothing we'd wished for in Chinatown,
Chinatown, Chinatown, would ever come true.

Wintering

All day, slow funerals have ploughed the rain.
We've done again
that trick we have of turning love to pain.

Grey fades to black. The stars begin their lies,
nothing to lose.
I wear a shroud of cold beneath my clothes.

Night clenches in its fist the moon, a stone.
I wish it thrown.
I clutch the small stiff body of my phone.

Dawn mocks me with a gibberish of birds.
I hear your words,
they play inside my head like broken chords.

*

The garden tenses, lies face down, bereaved,
has wept its leaves.
The Latin names of plants blur like belief.

I walk on ice, it grimaces, then breaks.
All my mistakes
are frozen in the tight lock of my face.

Bare trees hold out their arms, beseech, entreat,
cannot forget.
The clouds sag with the burden of their weight.

The wind screams at the house, bitter, betrayed.
The sky is flayed,
the moon a fingernail, bitten and frayed.

*

Another night, the smuggling in of snow.
You come and go,
your footprints like a love letter below.

Then something shifts, elsewhere and out of sight,
a hidden freight
that morning brings in on a tide of light.

The soil grows hesitant, it blurts in green,
so what has been
translates to what will be, certain, unseen,

as pain turns back again to love, like this,
your flower kiss,
and winter thaws and melts, cannot resist.

Spring

Spring's pardon comes, a sweetening of the air,
the light made fairer by an hour, time
as forgiveness, granted in the murmured colouring
of flowers, rain's mantra of reprieve, reprieve, reprieve.

The lovers waking in the lightening rooms believe
that something holds them, as they hold themselves,
within a kind of grace, a soft embrace, an absolution
from their stolen hours, their necessary lies. And this is wise:

to know that music's gold is carried in the frayed purse
of a bird, to pick affection's herb, to see the sun and moon
half-rhyme their light across the vacant, papery sky.
Trees, in their blossoms, young queens, flounce for clemency.

Answer

If you were made of stone,
your kiss a fossil sealed up in your lips,
your eyes a sightless marble to my touch,
your grey hands pooling raindrops for the birds,
your long legs cold as rivers locked in ice,
if you were stone, if you were made of stone, yes, yes.

If you were made of fire,
your head a wild Medusa hissing flame,
your tongue a red-hot poker in your throat,
your heart a small coal glowing in your chest,
your fingers burning pungent brands on flesh,
if you were fire, if you were made of fire, yes, yes.

If you were made of water,
your voice a roaring, foaming waterfall,
your arms a whirlpool spinning me around,
your breast a deep, dark lake nursing the drowned,
your mouth an ocean, waves torn from your breath,
if you were water, if you were made of water, yes, yes.

If you were made of air,
your face empty and infinite as sky,
your words a wind with litter for its nouns,
your movements sudden gusts among the clouds,
your body only breeze against my dress,
if you were air, if you were made of air, yes, yes.

If you were made of air, if you were air,
if you were made of water, if you were water,
if you were made of fire, if you were fire,
if you were made of stone, if you were stone,
or if you were none of these, but really death,
the answer is yes, yes.

Treasure

A soft ounce of your breath
in my cupped palm.
The gold weight of your head
on my numb arm.

Your heart's warm ruby
set in your breast.
The art of your hands,
the slim turquoise veins under your wrists.

Your mouth, the sweet, chrism blessing
of its kiss,
the full measure of bliss pressed
to my lips.

Your fine hair, run through my fingers,
sieved.
Your silver smile, your jackpot laugh,
bright gifts.

Sighted amber, the 1001 nights
of your eyes.
Even the sparkling fool's gold
of your lies.

Presents

I snipped and stitched my soul
to a little black dress,

hung my heart on a necklace,
tears for its pearls,

my mouth went for a bracelet,
gracing your arm,

all my lover's words
for its dangling charms,

and my mind was a new hat,
sexy and chic,

for a hair of your head on my sleeve
like a scrawled receipt.

Write

Write that the sun bore down on me,
kissing and kissing, and my face
reddened, blackened, whitened to ash,
was blown away by the passionate wind
over the fields, where my body's shape
still flattened the grass, to end as dust
in the eyes of my own ghost.

                        Or write
that the river held me close in its arms, cold fingers
stroking my limbs, cool tongue probing my mouth,
water's voice swearing its love love love in my ears,
as I drowned in belief.

                        Then write the moon
striding down from the sky in its silver boots
to kick me alive; the stars like a mob of light,
chanting a name, yours. Write your name on my lips
when I entered the dark church of the wood
like a bride, lay down for my honeymoon,
and write the night, sexy as hell, write the night
pressing and pressing my bones
into the ground.

Venus

6.19 a.m., 8th June 2004

The jet of your pupil
set in the gold of your eye –

nor can I see

the dark fruit of your nipple
ripe on your breast –

nor can I feel

the tip of my tongue
burn in the star of your mouth –

nor can I hold

the small pulse at your wrist
under my thumb –

but I can watch

the transit of Venus
over the face of the sun.

Whatever

I'll take your hand, the left,
and ask that it still have life
to hold my hand, the right,
as I walk alone where we walked,
or to lie all night on my breast,
at rest, or to stop all talk with a finger
pressed to my lips.

                I'll take your lips,
ask, when I close my eyes, as though
in prayer, that they ripen out of the air
to be there again on mine,
or to say my name, or to smile, or to kiss
the sleep from my eyes. I'll take

                              your eyes,
nothing like, lovelier under, the sun,
and ask that they wake to see, to look
at me, even to cry, so long as I feel their tears
on your face, warm rain on a rose.

Your face I'll take, asleep, ask that I learn,
by heart, the tilt of your nose; or awake, and ask
that I touch with my tongue the soft buds of the lobes
of your ears

        and I'll take them, too,
ask that they feel my breath shape
into living words, that they hear.

                        I'll take your breath
and ask that it comes and goes, comes and goes, forever,

like the blush under your cheek, and I'll even settle for that. Whatever.

Midsummer Night

Not there to see midsummer's midnight rose
open and bloom, me,
or there when the river dressed in turquoise
under the moon, you;
not there when stones softened, opened, showed
the fossils they held
or there, us, when the dark sky fell to the earth
to gather its smell.

Not there when a strange bird sang on a branch
over our heads, you
and me, or there when a starlit fruit ripened
itself on a tree.
Not there to lie on the grass of our graves, both,
alive alive oh,
or there for Shakespeare's shooting star,
or for who we are,

but elsewhere, far. Not there for the magic hour
when time becomes love
or there for light's pale hand to slip, slender,
from darkness's glove.
Not there when our young ghosts called to us
from the other side
or there where the heron's rags were a silver gown,
by grace of the light.

Not there to be right, to find our souls, we,
dropped silks on the ground,
or there to be found again by ourselves, you, me,
mirrored in water.

Not there to see constellations spell themselves on the sky
and black rhyme with white
or there to see petals fold on a rose like a kiss
on midsummer night.

Grief

Grief, your gift, unwrapped,
my empty hands made heavy,
holding when they held you
like an ache; unlooked for,
though my eyes stare inward now
at where you were, my star, my star;
and undeserved, the perfect choice
for one with everything, humbling
my heart; unwanted, too, my small voice
lost for words to thank you with; unusual,
how it, given, grows to fill a day, a night,
a week, a month, teaching its text,
love's spinster twin, my head bowed,
learning, learning; understood.

Ithaca

And when I returned,
I pulled off my stiff and salty sailor's clothes,
slipped on the dress of the girl I was,
and slid overboard.
A mile from Ithaca, I anchored the boat.

The evening softened and spread,
the turquoise water mentioning its silver fish,
the sky stooping to hear.
My hands moved in the water, moved on the air,
the lover I was, tracing your skin, your hair,

and Ithaca there, the bronze mountains
shouldered like rough shields,
the caves, where dolphins hid,
dark pouches for jewels,
the olive trees ripening their tears in our pale fields.

Then I drifted in on a ribbon of light,
tracking the scents of rosemary, lemon, thyme,
the fragrances of your name,
which I chanted again in my heart,
like the charm it was, bringing me back

to Ithaca, all hurt zeroed now
by the harm you could do with a word,
me as hero plainly absurd,
wading in, waist-high, from the shallows at dusk,
dragging my small white boat.

Land

If we were shades
who walked here once
over the heather, over the shining stones,
fresh in our skin and bones
with all of the time to come
left to be us,

if we were dust,
once flesh, where a cloud
swoons on the breast of a hill,
breathing here still
in our countable days,
the words we said,

snagged on the air
like the murmuring bees,
as we lay by the loch,
parting our clothes with our hands
to feel who we were,
we would rather be there

than where we are here,
all that was due to us
still up ahead,
if we were shades or dust
who lived love
before we were long dead.

Night Marriage

When I turn off the light
and the dark mile between us
crumples and falls,
you slip from your self
to wait for me in my sleep,
the face of the moon sinking into a cloud;

or I wake bereaved
from the long hours
I spend in your dreams,
an owl in the forest crying its soft vowels,
dark fish swimming under the river's skin.

Night marriage. The small hours join us,
face to face as we sleep and dream;
the whole of the huge night is our room.

Syntax

I want to call you thou, the sound
of the shape of the start
of a kiss – like this, thou –
and to say, after, I love,
thou, I love, thou I love, not
I love you.

        Because I so do –
as we say now – I want to say
thee, I adore, I adore thee,
and to know in my lips
the syntax of love resides,
and to gaze in thine eyes.

Love's language starts, stops, starts;
the right words flowing or clotting in the heart.

Snow

You come back,
after my three-month night,
as I knew you would, like light, light.
And though it is summer's height,
sexy with thunder, rainy heat,
you talk of snow.

           It is gathering now,
packing the freight of itself
into cold, faraway clouds,
miles out at sea,
crying upwards into the black sky;

each flake unique, that will fall on us, as we kiss,
or I tell you the poem by Louis MacNeice.
The room was suddenly rich . . .

Your Move

Now you've moved
to my neck of the woods,
let me show you around.

The name scarred
on all of the trees
is your own.

The blood poised,
red rain on the thorn
of a rose, mine.

The goblin, crouched
under that dripping bush,
your servant, ma'am.

The lightning,
frantic to touch,
means you no harm.

The thunder,
tendering huge words,
is spelling a charm.

The local news
starting as prose
ends in a rhyme.

The inns and taverns
are dusting off
their finest of wines,

and the air we breathe,
I say to myself,
is the same, the same.

Epiphany

Not close my eyes to the light
when the light
is in my head,
         or sleep
when only your, only thy warm skin
is my bed,
         or live, when days, nights,
sightless of you, sightless of thee,
are hours with the dead,
               or talk sense
when words, when words,
are the cauls of the unsaid,
                   or believe when belief
is a light gone out yet burning, gold, red.

The Love Poem

Till love exhausts itself, longs
for the sleep of words –
                      my mistress' eyes –
to lie on a white sheet, at rest
in the language –
                let me count the ways –
or shrink to a phrase like an epitaph –
                            come live
    with me –
or fall from its own high cloud as syllables
in a pool of verse –
                one hour with thee.

Till love gives in and speaks
in the whisper of art –
                dear heart,
how like you this? –
love's lips pursed to quotation marks
kissing a line –
            look in thy heart
    and write –
love's light fading, darkening,
black as ink on a page –
                  there is a garden
in her face.

Till love is all in the mind –
                    O my America!
my new-found land –
or all in the pen
in the writer's hand –
                behold, thou art fair –
not there, except in a poem,
known by heart like a prayer,
both near and far,
near and far –
             the desire of the moth
for the star.

Art

Only art now – our bodies, brushstroke, pigment, motif;
our story, figment, suspension of disbelief;
the thrum of our blood, percussion;
chords, minor, for the music of our grief.

Art, the chiselled, chilling marble of our kiss;
locked into soundless stone, our promises,
or fizzled into poems; page print
for the dried flowers of our voice.

No choice for love but art's long illness, death,
huge theatres for the echoes that we left,
applause, then utter dark;
grand opera for the passion of our breath;

and the Oscar-winning movie in your heart;
and where my soul sang, croaking art.

Unloving

Learn from the winter trees, the way
they kiss and throw away their leaves,
then hold their stricken faces in their hands
and turn to ice;

        or from the clocks,
looking away, unloving light, the short days
running out of things to say; a church
a ghost ship on a sea of dusk.

Learn from a stone, its heart-shape meaningless,
perfect with relentless cold; or from the bigger moon,
implacably dissolving in the sky, or from the stars,
lifeless as Latin verbs.

           Learn from the river,
flowing always somewhere else, even its name,
change, change; learn from a rope
hung from a branch like a noose, a crow cursing,

a dead heron mourned by a congregation of flies.
Learn from the dumbstruck garden, summer's grave,
where nothing grows, not a Beast's rose;
from the torn veil of a web;

              from our daily bread:
perpetual rain, nothing like tears, unloving clouds;
language unloving love; even this stale air
unloving all the spaces where you were.

Over

That's the wise thrush; he sings each song twice over,
Lest you should think he never could recapture
The first fine careless rapture!
                                    ROBERT BROWNING

I wake to a dark hour out of time, go to the window.
No stars in this black sky, no moon to speak of, no name
or number to the hour, no skelf of light. I let in air.
The garden's sudden scent's an open grave.
What do I have

             to help me, without spell or prayer,
endure this hour, endless, heartless, anonymous,
the death of love? Only the other hours –
the air made famous where you stood,
the grand hotel, flushing with light, which blazed us
on the night,

             the hour it took for you
to make a ring of grass and marry me. I say your name
again. It is a key, unlocking all the dark,
so death swings open on its hinge.
I hear a bird begin its song,
piercing the hour, to bring first light this Christmas dawn,
a gift, the blush of memory.

What will you do now with the gift of your loft of life?

Bees

Here are my bees,
brazen, blurs on paper,
besotted; buzzwords, dancing
their flawless, airy maps.

Been deep, my poet bees,
in the parts of flowers,
in daffodil, thistle, rose, even
the golden lotus; so glide,
gilded, glad, golden, thus –

wise – and know of us:
how your scent pervades
my shadowed, busy heart,
and honey is art.

Last Post

In all my dreams, before my helpless sight,
He plunges at me, guttering, choking, drowning.

If poetry could tell it backwards, true, begin
that moment shrapnel scythed you to the stinking mud . . .
but you get up, amazed, watch bled bad blood
run upwards from the slime into its wounds;
see lines and lines of British boys rewind
back to their trenches, kiss the photographs from home –
mothers, sweethearts, sisters, younger brothers
not entering the story now
to die and die and die.
Dulce – No – Decorum – No – Pro patria mori.
You walk away.

You walk away; drop your gun (fixed bayonet)
like all your mates do too –
Harry, Tommy, Wilfred, Edward, Bert –
and light a cigarette.
There's coffee in the square,
warm French bread,
and all those thousands dead
are shaking dried mud from their hair
and queueing up for home. Freshly alive,
a lad plays Tipperary to the crowd, released
from History; the glistening, healthy horses fit for heroes, kings.

You lean against a wall,
your several million lives still possible
and crammed with love, work, children, talent, English beer, good food.
You see the poet tuck away his pocket-book and smile.

If poetry could truly tell it backwards,
then it would.

Echo

I think I was searching for treasures or stones
in the clearest of pools
when your face . . .

                    when your face,
like the moon in a well
where I might wish . . .

                        might well wish
for the iced fire of your kiss;
only on water my lips, where your face . . .

where your face was reflected, lovely,
not really there when I turned
to look behind at the emptying air . . .

the emptying air.

Scheherazade

Dumb was as good as dead;
better to utter.
Inside a bottle, a genie.
Abracadabra.
Words were a silver thread
stitching the night.
The first story I said
led to the light.

Fact was in black and white;
fiction was colour.
Inside a dragon, a jewel.
Abracadabra.
A magic carpet took flight,
bearing a girl.
The hand of a Queen shut tight
over a pearl.

Imagination was world;
clever to chatter.
Inside a she-mule, a princess.
Abracadabra.
A golden sword was hurled
into a cloud.
A dead woman unfurled
out of a shroud.

A fable spoken aloud
kindled another.
Inside a virgin, a lover.
Abracadabra.
Forty thieves in a crowd,
bearded and bold.
A lamp rubbed by a lad
turning to gold.

Talking lips don't grow cold;
babble and jabber.
Inside a beehive, a fortune.
Abracadabra.
What was lost was held
inside a tale.
The tall stories I told
utterly real.

Inside a marriage, a gaol;
better to vanish.
Inside a mirror, an ogre;
better to banish.
A thousand and one tales;
weeping and laughter.
Only the silent fail.
Abracadabra.

Big Ask

What was it Sisyphus pushed up the hill?
I wouldn't call it a rock.
Will you solemnly swear on the Bible?
I couldn't swear on a book.
With which piece did you capture the castle?
I shouldn't hazard a rook.

When did the President give you the date?
Nothing to do with Barack!
Were 1200 targets marked on a chart?
Nothing was circled in black.
On what was the prisoner stripped and stretched?
Nothing resembling a rack.

Guantanamo Bay – how many detained?
How many grains in a sack?
Extraordinary Rendition – give me some names.
How many cards in a pack?
Sexing the Dossier – name of the game?
Poker. Gin Rummy. Blackjack.

Who planned the deployment of shock and awe?
I didn't back the attack.
Inside the Mosque, please describe what you saw.
I couldn't see through the smoke.
Your estimate of the cost of the War?
I had no brief to keep track.

Where was Saddam when they found him at last?
Maybe holed under a shack.
What happened to him once they'd kicked his ass?
Maybe he swung from the neck.
The WMD . . . you found the stash?
Well, maybe not in Iraq.

Ariel

Where the bee sucks,
neonicotinoid insecticides
in a cowslip's bell lie,
in fields purple with lavender,
yellow with rape,
and on the sunflower's upturned face;
on land monotonous with cereals and grain,
merrily,
       merrily;
sour in the soil,
sheathing the seed, systemic
in the plants and crops,
the million acres to be ploughed,
seething in the orchards now,
under the blossom
                that hangs
on the bough.

Politics

How it makes your face a stone
that aches to weep, your heart a fist,
clenched or thumping, your tongue
an iron latch with no door; your right hand
a gauntlet, a glove-puppet the left, your laugh
a dry leaf twitching in the wind, your desert island discs
hiss hiss hiss, the words on your lips dice
that throw no six.
                    How it takes the breath
away, the piss, your kiss a dropped pound coin,
your promises latin, feedback, static, gibberish,
your hair a wig, your gait a plankwalk. How it says
politics – to your education, fairness, health; shouts
Politics! – to your industry, investment, wealth; roars, to your
conscience, moral compass, truth, *POLITICS POLITICS*.

The Falling Soldier

after the photograph by Robert Capa

A flop back for a kip in the sun,
dropping the gun,
or a trip on a stone to send you
arse over tip
with a yelp and a curse?
No; worse. The shadow you cast
as you fall
is the start of a shallow grave.
They give medals, though,
to the grieving partners, mothers, daughters,
sons of the brave.

A breakdance to amuse your mates,
give them a laugh,
a rock'n'roll mime, Elvis time,
pretending the rifle's
just a guitar?
Worse by far. The shadow you shed
as you fall
is, brother, your soul.
They wrap you up in the flag, though,
blow a tune on a bugle before they lower you
into the hole.

A slide down a hill, your head thrown back,
daft as a boy,
and the rifle chucked away to the side
in a moment of joy,
an outburst?
Much worse. The shadow you throw
as you fall
is the shadow of death.
The camera, though,
has caught you forever and captured forever
your final breath.

Mrs Schofield's GCSE

You must prepare your bosom for his knife,
said Portia to Antonio in which
of Shakespeare's Comedies? Who killed his wife,
insane with jealousy? And which Scots witch
knew *Something wicked this way comes?* Who said
Is this a dagger which I see? Which Tragedy?
Whose blade was drawn which led to Tybalt's death?
To whom did dying Caesar say *Et tu?* And why?
Something is rotten in the state of Denmark – do you
know what this means? Explain how poetry
pursues the human like the smitten moon
above the weeping, laughing earth; how we
make prayers of it. *Nothing will come of nothing:
speak again.* Said by which King? You may begin.

Poetry

I couldn't see Guinness
and not envisage a nun;
a gun, a finger and thumb;
midges, blether, scribble, scrum.

A crescent moon, boomerang, smirk,
bone; or full, a shield, a stalker,
a stone. I couldn't see woods
for the names of trees – sycamore,
yew, birch, beech –

                    or bees
without imagining music scored
on the air – nor pass a nun
without calling to mind a pint of one, stout,
untouched, on a bar at the Angelus.

Achilles

Myth's river – where his mother dipped him,
fished him, a slippery golden boy –
flowed on, his name on its lips.
Without him, it was prophesied,
they would not take Troy.

Women hid him, concealed him in girls' sarongs;
days of sweetmeats, spices, silver song . . .
but when Odysseus came,
with an athlete's build, a sword and a shield,
he followed him to the battlefield,
the crowd's roar,
                      and it was sport, not war,
his charmed foot on the ball . . .

but then his heel, his heel, his heel . . .

The Shirt

Afterwards, I found him alone at the bar
and asked him what went wrong. *It's the shirt,*
he said. *When I pull it on it hangs on my back*
like a shroud, or a poisoned jerkin from Grimm
seeping its curse onto my skin, the worst tattoo.
I shower and shave before I shrug on the shirt,
smell like a dream; but the shirt sours my scent
with the sweat and stink of fear. It's got my number.
I poured him another shot. *Speak on, my son.* He did.
I've wanted to sport the shirt since I was a kid,
but now when I do it makes me sick, weak, paranoid.
All night above the team hotel, the moon is the ball
in a penalty kick. Tens of thousands of fierce stars
are booing me. A screech owl is the referee.
The wind's a crowd, forty years long, bawling a filthy song
about my Wag. It's the bloody shirt! He started to blub
like a big girl's blouse and I felt a fleeting pity.
Don't cry, I said, *at the end of the day you'll be stiff*
in a shirt of solid gold, shining for City.

Oxfam

A silvery, pale-blue satin tie, freshwater in sunlight, 50p.
Charlotte Rhead, hand-painted oval bowl, circa 1930, perfect
for apples, pears, oranges a child's hand takes without
a second thought, £80. Rows of boots marking time, £4.
Shoes like history lessons, £1.99. That jug, 30p, to fill with milk.
That mirror, £5, to look yourself in the eye. A commemoration
plate, 23 July 1986, marriage of HRH Prince Andrew
to Miss Sarah Ferguson, £2.99, size of a landmine.
Rare 1st ed. Harry Potter and the Philosopher's Stone, signed
by the author – like magic, a new school – £9000. Pen, 10p.
Pair of spectacles (longsight) £3. P/b Fieldnotes from a Catastrophe:
Report on Climate Change by Elizabeth Kolbert (hindsight) 40p.
Jade earrings and necklace, somewhere a mother, £20, brand new
gentleman's suit, somewhere a brother, £30. All Fairtrade.

The Female Husband

Having been, in my youth, a pirate
with cutlass and parrot, a gobful of bad words
yelled at the salty air to curse a cur to the end
of a plank; having jumped ship

                                        in a moonstruck port,
opened an evil bar – a silver coin for a full flask,
a gold coin for don't ask – and boozed and bragged
with losers and hags for a year; having disappeared,

a new lingo's herby zest on my tongue,
to head South on a mule, where a bandit man
took gringo me to the heart of his gang; having robbed
the bank, the coach, the train, the saloon, outdrawn

the sheriff, the deputy sheriff, the deputy's deputy, caught
the knife of an enemy chief in my teeth; having crept away
from the camp fire, clipped upstream for a night
and a day on a stolen horse,

                          till I reached the tip
of the century and the lip of the next – it was nix to me
to start again with a new name, a stranger to fame.
Which was how I came to this small farm,

                                        the love of my life
on my arm, tattooed on my wrist,
where we have cows and sheep and hens and geese
and keep good bees.

Virgil's Bees

Bless air's gift of sweetness, honey
from the bees, inspired by clover,
marigold, eucalyptus, thyme,
the hundred perfumes of the wind.
Bless the beekeeper

                who chooses for her hives
a site near water, violet beds, no yew,
no echo. Let the light lilt, leak, green
or gold, pigment for queens,
and joy be inexplicable but *there*
in harmony of willowherb and stream,
of summer heat and breeze,
                          each bee's body
at its brilliant flower, lover-stunned,
strumming on fragrance, smitten.

                          For this,
let gardens grow, where beelines end,
sighing in roses, saffron blooms, buddleia;
where bees pray on their knees, sing, praise
in pear trees, plum trees; bees
are the batteries of orchards, gardens, guard them.

Rings

I might have raised your hand to the sky
to give you the ring surrounding the moon
or looked to twin the rings of your eyes
with mine
          or added a ring to the rings of a tree
by forming a handheld circle with you, thee,
or walked with you
                where a ring of church-bells
looped the fields,
or kissed a lipstick ring on your cheek,
a pressed flower,
          or met with you
in the ring of an hour,
and another hour . . .
            I might
have opened your palm to the weather, turned, turned,
till your fingers were ringed in rain
or held you close,
           they were playing our song,
in the ring of a slow dance
or carved our names
in the rough ring of a heart
or heard the ring of an owl's hoot
as we headed home in the dark
or the ring, first thing,
            of chorusing birds
waking the house
or given the ring of a boat, rowing the lake,
or the ring of swans, monogamous, two,

or the watery rings made by the fish
as they leaped and splashed
or the ring of the sun's reflection there . . .
I might have tied
              a blade of grass,
a green ring for your finger,
or told you the ring of a sonnet by heart
or brought you a lichen ring,
found on a warm wall,
or given a ring of ice in winter
                              or in the snow
sung with you the five gold rings of a carol
or stolen a ring of your hair
or whispered the word in your ear
that brought us here,
where nothing and no one is wrong,
and therefore I give you this ring.

Invisible Ink

When Anon, no one now,
knew for sure the *cu* and *koo*
he spelled from his mouth
could put the tribe in sight
of a call they'd met before
in their ears, the air ever after was
invisible ink.

      Then, *hey nonny no*,
the poets came; rhyme, metre,
metaphor, there for the taking
for every chancer or upstart crow
in hedgerow, meadow, forest, pool;
shared words, vast same poem
for all to write.

        I snap a twig
from a branch as I walk, sense
the nib of it dip and sip, dip
and sip, a first draft of the gift –
anonymous yet – texted from heart
to lips; my hand dropping a wand
into this fluent, glittery stream.

Atlas

Give him strength, crouched on one knee in the dark
with the Earth on his back,
                         balancing the seven seas,
the oceans, five, kneeling
in ruthless, empty, endless space
                         for grace
of whale, dolphin, sea-lion, shark, seal, fish, every kind
which swarms the waters. Hero.

                         Hard, too,
heavy to hold, the mountains;
burn of his neck and arms taking the strain –
Andes, Himalayas, Kilimanjaro –
give him strength, he heaves them high
to harvest rain from skies for streams
and rivers, he holds the rivers,
holds the Amazon, Ganges, Nile, hero, hero.

Hired by no one, heard in a myth only, lonely,
he carries a planet's weight,
                         islands and continents,
the billions there, his ears the last to hear
their language, music, gunfire, prayer;
give him strength, strong girth, for elephants,
tigers, snow leopards, polar bears, bees, bats,
the last ounce of a hummingbird.

                    Broad-backed
in infinite, bleak black,
                    he bears where Earth is, nowhere,
head bowed, a genuflection to the shouldered dead,
the unborn's hero, he is love's lift;
sometimes the moon rolled to his feet, given.

John Barleycorn

Although I knew they'd laid him low,
thrashed him, hung him out to dry,
had tortured him with water and with fire,
then dashed his brains out on a stone,
I saw him in the Seven Stars
and in the Plough.
I saw him in the Crescent Moon
and in the Beehive and the Barley Mow,
my green man, newly-born, alive, John Barleycorn.

I saw him seasonally, at harvest time
in the Wheatsheaf and the Load of Hay.
I saw him, heard his laughter,
in the Star and Garter, in the Fountain, in the Bell,
the Corn Dolly, the Woolpack and the Flowing Spring.
I saw him in the Rising Sun,
the Moon and Sixpence and the Evening Star.
I saw him in the Rose and Crown,
my green man, ancient, barely born, John Barleycorn.

He moved through Britain, bright and dark
like ale in glass. I saw him run across the fields
towards the Gamekeeper, the Poacher and the Blacksmith's Arms.
He knew the Ram, the Lamb, the Lion and the Swan,
White Hart, Blue Boar, Red Dragon, Fox and Hounds.
I saw him in the Three Goats' Heads,
the Black Bull and Dun Cow,
Shoulder of Mutton, Griffin, Unicorn,
green man, beer borne, good health, long life, John Barleycorn.

I saw him festively, when people sang
for victory, or love, or New Year's Eve,
in the Raven and the Bird in Hand,
the Golden Eagle, the Kingfisher, the Dove.
I saw him grieve, or mourn, a shadow at the bar
in the Falcon, the Marsh Harrier, the Sparrow Hawk,
the Barn Owl, Cuckoo, Heron, Nightingale;
a pint of bitter in the Jenny Wren
for my green man, alone, forlorn, John Barleycorn.

Britain's soul, as the crow flies so flew he.
I saw him in the Hollybush, the Yew Tree,
the Royal Oak, the Ivy Bush, the Linden.
I saw him in the Forester, the Woodman.
He history, I saw him in the Wellington, the Nelson,
Greyfriars Bobby, Wicked Lady, Bishop's Finger.
I saw him in the Ship, the Golden Fleece, the Flask,
the Railway Inn, the Robin Hood and Little John,
my green man, legend strong, re-born, John Barleycorn.

Scythed down, he crawled, knelt, stood.
I saw him in the Crow, Newt, Stag, all weathers,
noon or night. I saw him in the Feathers, Salutation,
Navigation, Knot, the Bricklayer's Arms, Hop Inn,
the Maypole and the Regiment, the Horse and Groom,
the Dog and Duck, the Flag. And where he supped,
the past lived still; and where he sipped, the glass brimmed full.
He was in the King's Head and Queen's Arms, I saw him there,
green man, well-born, spellbound, charming one, John Barleycorn.

Hive

All day we leave and arrive at the hive,
concelebrants. The hive is love,
what we serve, preserve, avowed in Latin murmurs
as we come and go, skydive, freighted
with light, to where we thrive, us, in time's hum,
on history's breath,
                industrious, identical . . .

there suck we,
alchemical, nectar-slurred, pollen-furred,
the world's mantra us, our blurry sound
along the thousand scented miles to the hive,
haven, where we unpack our foragers;
or heaven-stare, drone-eyed, for a queen's star;
or nurse or build in milky, waxy caves,
the hive, alive, us – how we behave.

Nile

When I went, wet, wide, white and blue, my name Nile,
you'd kneel near to net fish, or would wade
where I shallowed, or swim in my element,
or sing a lament for the child drowned where I was too deep,
too fast; but once you found, in my reeds,
a boy in a basket.
                    I gushed, fresh lake, salt sea,
utterly me, source to mouth, without me, drought, nought,
for my silt civilized –
                    from my silt, pyramids.
Where I went, undammed, talented,
food, wine, work, craft, art;
no Nile, nil, null, void.
                    I poured, full spate, roared,
voiced water, calling you in from dust, thirst, burn,
to where you flourished; Pharaoh, firstborn . . .
now Cleopatra's faint taste still on my old tongue.

Water

Your last word was *water*,
which I poured in a hospice plastic cup, held
to your lips – your small sip, half-smile, sigh –
then, in the chair beside you,
                            fell asleep.

Fell asleep for three lost hours,
only to waken, thirsty, hear then see
a magpie warn in a bush outside –
dawn so soon – and swallow from your still-full cup.

Water. The times I'd call as a child
for a drink, till you'd come, sit on the edge
of the bed in the dark, holding my hand,
just as we held hands now and you died.

A good last word.
                    Nights since I've cried, but gone
to my own child's side with a drink, watched
her gulp it down then sleep. *Water.*
What a mother brings
                    through darkness still
to her parched daughter.

Drams

The snows melt early,
meeting river and valley,
greeting the barley.

*

In Glen Strathfarrar
a stag dips to the river
where rainclouds gather.

*

Dawn, offered again,
and heather sweetens the air.
I sip at nothing.

*

A cut-glass tumbler,
himself splashing the amber . . .
now I remember.

*

Beautiful hollow
by the broad bay; safe haven;
their Gaelic namings.

*

It was Talisker
on your lips, peppery, sweet,
I tasted, kisser.

*

Under the table
she drank him, my grandmother,
Irish to his Scotch.

*

Barley, water, peat,
weather, landscape, history;
malted, swallowed neat.

*

Out on Orkney's boats,
spicy, heather-honey notes
into our glad throats.

*

Allt Dour Burn's water –
pure as delight, light's lover –
burn of the otter.

*

The gifts to noses –
bog myrtle, aniseed, hay,
attar of roses.

*

Empty sherry casks,
whisky – *sublime accident* –
a Spanish accent.

*

Drams with a brother
and doubles with another . . .
blether then bother.

*

The perfume of place,
seaweed scent on peaty air,
heather dabbed with rain.

*

With Imlah, Lochhead,
Dunn, Jamie, Paterson, Kay,
Morgan, with MacCaig.

*

Not prose, poetry;
crescendo of mouth music;
not white wine, whisky.

*

*Eight bolls of malt, to
Friar John Cor, wherewith to
make aquavitae.*

*

A recurring dream:
men in hats taking a dram
on her coffin lid.

*

The sad flit from here
to English soil, English air,
from whisky to beer.

*

For joy, grief, trauma,
for the newly-wed, the dead –
bitter-sweet water.

*

A quaich; Highland Park;
our shared sips in the gloaming
by the breathing loch.

*

The unfinished dram
on the hospice side-table
as the sun came up.

*

What the heron saw,
the homesick salmon's shadow,
shy in this whisky.

Moniack Mhor

Something is dealing from a deck of cards,
face up, seven, a week of mornings, today's
revealing the hills at Moniack Mhor, shrugging off
their mists. A sheepdog barks six fields away;
I see the farm from here.

Twelve-month cards, each one thumbed, flipped,
weathered in its way – this the eighth, harvest-time,
a full moon like a trump, a magic trick.
It rose last night above this house, affirmative.
I sensed your answer – hearts.

Or a single hour is a smiling Jack, a diamond,
or a spade learning a grave; charms or dark lessons.
Something is shuffling; the soft breath of Moniack Mhor
on the edge of utterance, I know it, the verbs of swifts
riffling the air

and the road turning itself into the loch, a huge ace
into which everything folds. Here is the evening,
displayed then dropped to drift to the blazon of barley, bracken,
heather. Something is gifting this great gold gathering of cloud;
a continual farewell.

The English Elms

Seven Sisters in Tottenham,
long gone, except for their names,
were English elms.

Others stood at the edge of farms,
twinned with the shapes of clouds
like green rhymes;
or cupped the beads of rain
in their leaf palms;
or glowered, grim giants, warning of storms.

In the hedgerows in old films,
elegiacally, they loom,
the English elms;
or find posthumous fame
in the lines of poems –
the music making elm –
for ours is a world without them . . .

to whom the artists came,
time upon time,
scumbling, paint on their fingers and thumbs;
and the woodcutters, who knew the elm
was a coffin's deadly aim;
and the mavis, her filled nest unharmed
in the crook of a living, wooden arm;
and boys, with ball, bat, stumps
for a game;
and nursing ewes and lambs, calm
under English elms . . .

great, masterpiece trees
who were overwhelmed.

The Counties

But I want to write to an Essex girl,
greeting her warmly.
But I want to write to a Shropshire lad,
brave boy, home from the Army,
and I want to write to the Lincolnshire Poacher
to hear of his hare
and to an aunt in Bedfordshire
who makes a wooden hill of her stair.
But I want to post a rose to a Lancashire lass,
red, I'll pick it,
and I want to write to a Middlesex mate
for tickets for cricket.
But I want to write to the Ayrshire cheesemaker
and his good cow
and it is my duty to write to The Queen at Berkshire
in praise of Slough.
But I want to write to the National Poet of Wales at Ceredigion
in celebration
and I want to write to the Dorset Giant
in admiration
and I want to write to a widow in Rutland
in commiseration
and to the Inland Revenue in Yorkshire
in desperation.
But I want to write to my uncle in Clackmannanshire
in his kilt
and to my scrumptious cousin in Somerset
with her cidery lilt.

But I want to write to two ladies in Denbighshire,
near Llangollen
and I want to write to a laddie in Lanarkshire,
Dear Lachlan . . .
But I want to write to the Cheshire Cat,
returning its smile.
But I want to write the names of the Counties down
for my own child
and may they never be lost to her . . .
all the birds of Oxfordshire and Gloucestershire . . .

The White Horses

The earth's heart hears hooves
under hillsides,
              thunder in Wiltshire;
and the glistening rain, in wet hours,
all ears for the white horses, listens;
the wind, hoarse, gargles
breath and whinny and shriek.
The moon's chalk face pines for her foals.

But the sky swears
              the white horses
are dropped clouds;
the sea vows they came from a wave,
foamy, salt-maned, galloping inland;
death claims it will set them
to pulling a hearse,
              and love
goes riding, all night, bareback,
hunting itself.

They dreamed them, the local dead,
ghosts of war-horses,
                      warriors', heroes',
asleep in the landscape;
woke to the white horses shining
high over woods and farms;
young ancestors working the fields,
naming them his, hers, ours.
They sensed them, pulling the county
deep into England,
harnessed, history's;
                      their scent sweet on the air –
wheat, hops, hay, chalk, clay.
Then stars nailed shoes to their hooves.

The conservationists climb the hills
away from their cars,
                      new leucippotomists
with implements to scour and groom,
scrub and comb.
              On a clear day,
from twenty miles,
                  a driver sees a white horse
printing its fresh, old form on turf
like a poem.

Luke Howard, Namer of Clouds

Eldezar and Asama Yama, 1783,
erupted violently; a *Great Fogg*
blending incredible skies over Europe.
In London, Luke Howard was ten.
The sky's lad then.

          Smitten,
he stared up evermore; saw
a meteor's fiery spurt,
the clamouring stars;
what the moon wouldn't do;
but loved clouds most –
dragons and unicorns;
Hamlet's camels, weasels and whales;
the heads of heroes;
the sword of Excalibur, lit
by the setting sun.
          Mackerel sky,
mackerel sky, not long wet,
not long dry.

        And knew
love goes naming,
even a curl of hair – thus, Cirrus.
Cumulus. Stratus. Nimbus.

The Woman in the Moon

Darlings, I write to you from the moon
where I hide behind famous light.
How could you think it ever a man up here?
A cow jumped over. The dish ran away with

the spoon. What reached me were your joys, griefs,
here's-the-craic, losses, longings, your lives
brief, mine long, a talented loneliness. I must have
a thousand names for the earth, my blue vocation.

Round I go, the moon a diet of light, sliver of pear,
wedge of lemon, slice of melon, half an orange,
silver onion; your human sound falling through space,
childbirth's song, the lover's song, the song of death.

Devoted as words to things, I gaze, gawp, glare; deserts
where forests were, sick seas. When night comes,
I see you gaping back as though you hear my *Darlings,
what have you done, what have you done to the world?*

Parliament

Then in the writers' wood,
every bird with a name in the world
crowded the leafless trees,
took its turn to whistle or croak.
An owl grieved in an oak.
A magpie mocked. A rook
cursed from a sycamore.
The cormorant spoke:
      Stinking seas
below ill winds. Nothing swims.
A vast plastic soup, thousand miles
wide as long, of petroleum crap.

A bird of paradise wept in a willow.
The jewel of a hummingbird shrilled
on the air.
A stork shawled itself like a widow.
The gull said:
Where coral was red, now white, dead
under stunned waters.
The language of fish
cut out at the root.
Mute oceans. Oil like a gag
on the Gulf of Mexico.

A woodpecker heckled.
A vulture picked at its own breast.
Thrice from the cockerel, as ever.
The macaw squawked:
                    Nouns I know –
Rain. Forest. Fire. Ash.
Chainsaw. Cattle. Cocaine. Cash.
Squatters. Ranchers. Loggers. Looters.
Barons. Shooters.

A hawk swore.
A nightingale opened its throat
in a garbled quote.
A worm turned in the blackbird's beak.
This from the crane:
What I saw – slow thaw
in permafrost; broken terrain
of mud and lakes;
peat broth; seepage; melt;
methane breath.

A bat hung like a suicide.
Only a rasp of wings from the raven.
A heron was stone; a robin blood
in the written wood.
So snow and darkness slowly fell;
the eagle, history, in silhouette,
with the golden plover,
and the albatross
                  telling of Arctic ice
as the cold, hard moon calved from the earth.

Telling the Bees

When I went to read
the bulletin about broken holy beads
to the bees,
the beads were the bees themselves . . .

(though once I'd been
a bairn with a bamboo-cane,
keen to follow the beekeeper
down to the hives, tap and tell
all news – whose bride, who lied, who'd died –
and had seen the bees as a rosary, girdling,
garden by garden, the land;
or had heard their hard devotional sound
in the ears of flowers
as I barely breathed, beheld
their bold, intimate touch . . .)

for a scattered bracelet of bees
lay on the grass by their burgled hive.

So how could I tell the bees?

Black blood in the sea.
Corn buttercup brought to its knee.
No honey for tea.

Dorothy Wordsworth is Dead

who came to lose every tooth in her head;
fierce maid, who saw the crowfoot
as a spinster friend; found, in the russet fronds
of Osmunda ferns, fervour;

                              feared cows;
on all fours crawled
home through a thunderstorm;
walked five miles each way, each day,
in hope of letters; thin scrap, work-worn,
her black frock mud-hemmed;

                              Dorothy,
green gold of moss in her loose purse, gatherer,
who thought strawberry blossom *brave*
in its early grave of rock; had quick birds
for her own eyes from watching them:
the robin's blushing bounce,
the magpie's funeral chic,
the heron's grief,
                grief . . .

whose tongue travelled her empty gums
on her long lake treks;
                          but was loved yet,
sharp lass, noticer; all ears, years,
for the wind's thumb on the latch;
first to spy – *o sister* –
the moon's eye at the glass,
two stars squinting . . .

                          and cold in her bed
uttered flowers, *hepatica, daffodil, anemone,
crocus,*
      as a corpse in its manner does
in St. Oswald's churchyard under the yews
her brother planted;
and trudged or lay by him till he kindled.

Cockermouth and Workington

No folk fled the flood,
no flags furled or spirits failed –
one brave soul felled.

Fouled fortune followed,
but families filed into the fold
for a fire flared.

They were floored,
a few said fooled; no – fuelled
by fellow-feeling, hearts full.

New bridge now, small fords;
farmhands in foaled fields.

Spell

Yes, I think a poem is a spell of kinds
that keeps things living in a written line,
whatever's lost or leaving – lock of rhyme –
and so I write and write and write your name.

Simon Powell

What was your appeal, Simon Powell?
Your silver smile;
how you held your face aloft,
a trophy, when you laughed.
You had style,
swooping towards Swansea
on your Moto Morini,
brave, *bravo!*, pale rider.

Whom did you beguile, Simon Powell,
on that ferry in Liverpool?
A poetry girl. Well, well,
you were always poetry's proud pal;
she was bound to chime with you
eventually,
        vowel to pure vowel –
poetry and Simon Powell.

Our days continue to delight us, or appal,
like yours: the birth of sons,
the death of Siân;
then to your Indian wedding on a horse,
your thousand nights; blessed, you told us,
Simon Powell, in your wives,
the seeded futures of your three boys' lives;
as we by thee, dear Simon; Simon Powell.

Cold

It felt so cold, the snowball which wept in my hands,
and when I rolled it along in the snow, it grew
till I could sit on it, looking back at the house,
where it was cold when I woke in my room, the windows
blind with ice, my breath undressing itself on the air.
Cold, too, embracing the torso of snow which I lifted up
in my arms to build a snowman, my toes, burning, cold
in my winter boots; my mother's voice calling me in
from the cold. And her hands were cold from peeling
and pooling potatoes into a bowl, stooping to cup
her daughter's face, a kiss for both cold cheeks, my cold nose.
But nothing so cold as the February night I opened the door
in the Chapel of Rest where my mother lay, neither young, nor old,
where my lips, returning her kiss to her brow, knew the meaning of cold.

The Bee Carol

Silently on Christmas Eve,
the turn of midnight's key;
all the garden locked in ice –
a silver frieze –
except the winter cluster of the bees.

Flightless now and shivering,
around their Queen they cling;
every bee a gift of heat;
she will not freeze
within the winter cluster of the bees.

Bring me for my Christmas gift
a single golden jar;
let me taste the sweetness there,
but honey leave
to feed the winter cluster of the bees.

Come with me on Christmas Eve
to see the silent hive –
trembling stars cloistered above –
and then believe,
bless the winter cluster of the bees.

Decembers

The single bed
was first a wooden boat;
stars translated for me
as I drifted away –
our cargoed winter house
dark and at anchor –

and then a Russian Doll
where I stilled in my selves;
six secrets or presents
under a thrilled tree.

I saw a coffin, shouldered
through snow, shrouded
in its cold, laced sheet.
Now, delirious bells
shaking this small spare room
on Christmas morning.

Winter's Tale

Tell she is well in these arms;
synonymous, her heartbeat to mine;
the world a little room; undone
all hurt; her inbreath, breath,
love where death, where harm, hope,
flesh where stone; my line – O
she's warm! – charm, blessing, prayer,
spell; outwith dream, without time;
enchantment tell, garden from grave
to garland her; above these worms,
violet, oxlip, primrose, columbine;
she wakes, moves, prompted by her name.

Snow

Then all the dead opened their cold palms
and released the snow; slow, slant, silent,
a huge unsaying, it fell, torn language, settled;
the world to be locked, local; unseen,
fervent earthbound bees around a queen.
The river grimaced and was ice.

                                      Go nowhere –
thought the dead, using the snow –
but where you are, offering the flower of your breath
to the white garden, or seeds to birds
from your living hand. You cannot leave.
Tighter and tighter, the beautiful snow
holds the land in its fierce embrace.
It is like death, but it is not death; lovelier.
Cold, inconvenienced, late, what will you do now
with the gift of your left life?

Crunch

It's snowing! Twelve, she runs outside into the cold.
I follow from the kitchen, in my hand an apple
I was about to peel and core. She squeals, loud,
snowflakes melting on her tongue, then topples
down, cartoon joyful, brightly young. Here come the dogs,
hilariously perplexed, barking at the ghosts of plants,
biting the sky. Last weekend, burglars came – *Be drugs*,
the policeman said, *or credit crunch* – taking their chance,
the Visa, chequebook, presents underneath the tree,
laptop, TV. I watch snow deepen, settle hard,
like . . . which simile? Like debt? Like poverty? . . .
imagine some gloved hand insert my useless cards
into the wall, that other life; then *What's for lunch?*
she bawls. I throw the apple, happy, hear the crunch.

A Goldfish

I bought, on a whim, a goldfish for a good girl.
It swam in an antique bowl in the kitchen there,
creative among the lentils and the marmalade,
painting itself over and over, self-portrait in liquid;
learning its letter, O for oxygen, for only.

                                          It seemed fulfilled;
the halo of its constant swim unrolling a pond
below willow trees, an imperial palace garden
where the poet sat, floating on silence; a mouth opening
to gold: walking towards her, carrying fragrant tea,
her beloved, favourite child.

Music

Do you think they cried, the children
who followed the Piper, when the rock
closed behind them forever; or cried never,
happy to dance to his tune, lost
in the music?
              And the lame boy,
pressing his ear to locked stone
to carry an echo home in his head,
did he weep, alone, the melody gone? Tell me

who hasn't tossed a coin in a hat
for the busker on blues harmonica, heartbreak
in the rain;
              or stood in the square
by the students there, cheap violins
gleaming under their chins, the Bach Double
clapped by pigeons;
                        or smiled at the ragged choir
rattling their tins? What's music
the food of? Send over a beer
to the bow-tied piano man to play it again . . .

a child's hands
on the keys, opening a scale
like a toy of sound . . .

and who hasn't lifted the lid
to pick at a tune with a fingertip –
Perfect Day, Danny Boy, Für Elise –
recalling a name, or a kiss;
the breath our lips shared,
unsung song?

                When the light's gone,
it's what the dying choose,
the music we use at funerals –
psalms listed in roman numerals;
solo soprano singing to a grave;
sometimes the pipes, a harp.
Do you think music hath charms?
Do you think it hears and heals our hearts?

Orta St Giulio

My beautiful daughter stands by the lake
at Orta St Giulio; the evening arriving, dressed
in its milky, turquoise silks, her fortune foretold;
assonant mountains and clouds all around;
an aptness of bells from here, there, there, there. *Ella.*

I watch her film the little fish
which flop, slap, leap in the water, hear
her hiss *yes, yes,* as she zooms on fresh verbs
and my heart makes its own small flip.
I slip behind her into the future; memory.

A bat swoops, the lake a silence of dark light;
how it will be, must be.

The Dead

They're very close to us, the dead;
us in our taxis, them in their hearses,
waiting for the lights to change.
We give them precedence.

So close to us, unknown on television;
dead from hunger, earthquake, war,
suicide bomber, tsunami.
We count the numbers.

The famous dead – a double glamour –
we buy their music, movies, memoirs.
O! Elizabeth Taylor as Cleopatra
in glorious technicolor.

In Venice, we glimpse the dead
drift to the island cemetery across the lagoon.
We float our gondolas along the green canals
and do not die.

Sung

Now only words in a song,
no more than a name
on a stone,
and that well overgrown –
MAR–   –ORIS– –;

and wind though a ruined croft,
the door an appalled mouth,
the window's eye put out;

hours and wishes and trysts
less than shadows of bees on grass,
ghosts that did dance, did kiss . . .

those who would gladly die for love long dead –
a skull for a bonnie head –
and love a simile, a rose, red, red.

At Ballynahinch

I lay on the bank at Ballynahinch
and saw the light hurl down
like hammers flung by the sun
to light-stun me, batter
the water to pewter,
everything dream or myth,
my own death further upstream;
the sleeping breath now – by my side
in our wounded sprawl – of the one
who did not love me at all,
who had never loved me, no,
who would never love me, I knew,
down by the star-thrashed river at Ballynahinch,
at Ballynahinch, at Ballynahinch.

New Vows

From this day forth to unhold,
to see the nothing in ringed gold,
uncare for you when you are old.

New vows you make me swear to keep –
not ever wake with you, or sleep,
or your body, with mine, worship;

this empty hand slipped from your glove,
these lips sip never from our loving cup,
I may not cherish, kiss; unhave, unlove . . .

And all my worldly goods to unendow . . .
And who here present upon whom I call . . .

Leda

Obsessed by faithfulness,
                        I went to the river
where the swans swam in their pairs and saw how a heart
formed in the air as they touched, partnered forever.
Under the weeping trees a lone swan swam apart.

I knelt like a bride as bees hymned in the clover
and he rose, huge, an angel, out of the water,
to cover me, my billed, feathered, webbed, winged lover;
a chaos of passion beating the fair day whiter.

My hands, frantic to hold him, felt flight, force, friction,
his weird beautiful form rising and falling above –
the waxy, intimate creak –
                                as though he might fly,
turn all my unborn children into fiction.
I knew their names that instant, pierced by love
and by the song the swans sing as they die.

Valentine's

Pain past bearing, poetry's price,
to know which of the harms and hurts
dealt to you, to the day, was fatal;
a kick to the heart by the ghost of a mule
you thought to ride to your wedding-feast.

But now you can snip that shadow
from your heels for mourning-dress
or go to hell in a handcart, along
with the rest of our helpless world;
and, O, if you could, you would,
where lovers walked, sell off the trees
and not give a flying fuck for
the muted mausoleums of the bees.

The Human Bee

I became a human bee at twelve,
when they gave me my small wand,
my flask of pollen,
and I walked with the other bees
out to the orchards.

I worked first in apples,
                    climbed the ladder
into the childless arms of a tree
and busied myself, dipping and tickling,
duping and tackling, tracing
the petal's guidelines
down to the stigma.
                    Human, humming,
I knew my lessons by heart:
the ovary would become the fruit,
the ovule the seed,
fertilized by my golden touch,
my Midas dust.

I moved to lemons,
                head and shoulders
lost in blossom; dawn till dusk,
my delicate blessing.
All must be docile, kind, unfraught
for one fruit –
                pomegranate, lychee,
nectarine, peach, the rhymeless orange.
And if an opening bud
                        was out of range,
I'd jump from my ladder onto a branch
and reach.

So that was my working life as a bee,
till my eyesight blurred,
my hand was a trembling bird
                        in the leaves,
the bones of my fingers thinner than wands.
And when they retired me,
I had my wine from the silent vines,
and I'd known love,
and I'd saved some money –

but I could not fly and I made no honey.

Drone

An upward rush on stairs of air
to the bliss of nowhere, higher,
a living jewel, warm amber, her,
to be the one who would die there.

Gesture

Did you know your hands could catch that dark hour
like a ball, throw it away into long grass
and when you looked again at your palm, there
was your life-line, shining?
                         Or when death came,
with its vicious, biting bark, at a babe,
your whole body was brave;
or came with its boiling burns,
your arms reached out, love's gesture.
                                   Did you know
when cancer draped its shroud on your back,
you'd make it a flag;
or ignorance smashed its stones through glass,
light, you'd see, in shards;
paralysed, walk; traumatised, talk?
                                Did you know
at the edge of your ordinary, human days
the gold of legend blazed,
where you kneeled by a wounded man,
or healed a woman?
                  Know –
your hand is a star.
Your blood is famous in your heart.

Passing-Bells

That moment when the soldier's soul
slipped through his wounds, seeped
through the staunching fingers of his friend
then, like a shadow, slid across a field
to vanish, vanish, into textless air . . .
there would have been a bell in Perth,
Llandudno, Bradford, Winchester,
rung by a landlord in a sweating, singing pub
or by an altar-boy at Mass – in Stoke-on-Trent,
Leicester, Plymouth, Crewe, in Leeds, Stockport,
Littleworth – an ice-cream van jingling in a park;
a door pushed open to a jeweller's shop;
a songbird fluttering from a tinkling cat – in Ludlow,
Wolverhampton, Taunton, Hull – a parish church
chiming out the hour; the ringing end of school –
in Wigan, Caythorpe, Peterborough, Ipswich,
Aberdeen, King's Lynn, Malvern, Poole –
a deskbell in a quiet, dark hotel; bellringers' practice
heard by Sunday cricketers; the first of midnight's bells
at Hogmanay – in Huddersfield, Motherwell, Rhyl –
there would have been a bell in Chester,
Fife, Bridgend, Wells, Birkenhead, Newcastle,
in city and in town and countryside –
the crowded late night bus; a child's bicycle;
the old, familiar, clanking cow-bells of the cattle.

Premonitions

We first met when your last breath
cooled in my palm like an egg;
you dead, and a thrush outside
sang it was morning.
I backed out of the room, feeling
the flowers freshen and shine in my arms.

The night before, we met again, to unsay
unbearable farewells, to see
our eyes brighten with re-strung tears.
O I had my sudden wish –
though I barely knew you –
to stand at the door of your house,
feeling my heartbeat calm,
as they carried you in, home, home and healing.
Then slow weeks, removing the wheelchair, the drugs,
the oxygen mask and tank, the commode,
the appointment cards,
until it was summer again
and I saw you open the doors to the grace of your garden.

Strange and beautiful to see
the flowers close to their own premonitions,
the grass sweeten and cool and green
where a bee swooned backwards out of a rose.
There you were,
a glass of lemony wine in each hand,
walking towards me always, your magnolia tree
marrying itself to the May air.

How you talked! And how I listened,
spellbound, humbled, daughterly,
to your tall tales, your wise words,
the joy of your accent, unenglish, dancey, humorous;
watching your ash hair flare and redden,
the loving litany of who we had been
making me place my hands in your warm hands,
younger than mine are now.
Then time only the moon. And the balm of dusk.
And you my mother.

A Rare Bee

I heard tell of a tale of a rare bee,
kept in a hive in a forest's soul
by a hermit – hairshirt, heart long hurt –
and that this bee made honey so pure,
when pressed to the pout of a poet
it made her profound; or if smeared
on the smile of a singer it sweetened his sound;
or when eased on the eyes of an artist,
Pablo Picasso lived and breathed;
                                      so I saddled my steed.

No birds sang in the branches over my head,
though I saw the wreaths of empty nests
on the ground as I rode – girl, poet, knight –
deeper into the trees, where the white hart
was less than a ghost or a thought, was light
as the written word; legend. But what wasn't going, gone,
I mused, from the land, or the sky, or the sea?
I dismounted my bony horse to walk;
out of the silence, I fancied I heard
                                    the bronze buzz of a bee.

So I came to kneel at the hermit's hive –
a little church, a tiny mosque – in a mute glade
where the loner mouthed and prayed, blind
as the sun, and saw with my own eyes
one bee dance alone on the air.
I uttered my prayer: *Give me your honey,*
bless my tongue with rhyme, poetry, song.
It flew at my mouth and stung.
Then the terrible tune of the hermit's grief.
Then a gesturing, dying bee
                              on the bier of a leaf.

Alive—
Alive-oh,
the Heart's
impulse
to
cherish.

Chaucer's Valentine

for Nia

The lyf so short, the craft so long to lerne . . .
but be my valentine
                      and I'll one candle burn,
love's light a fluent tongue,
old habit young, the door ajar
to where our bed awaits,
                      not in a room
but in a wood, all thrilled with birds,
the flight of early English words to verse,
there as sweetness evermore now is,
this human kiss,
                      love's written bliss in every age . . .
hold the front page.

At Jerez

Who wouldn't feel favoured,
at the end of a week's labour,
to receive as part-wages
a pale wine
that puts the mouth in mind of the sea . . .

and not gladly be kissed
by gentle William Shakespeare's lips,
the dark, raisiny taste of his song;
bequeathed to his thousand daughters and sons,
the stolen wines of the Spanish sun . . .

then walk the cool bodegas' aisles –
where flor and oxygen
grow talented in fragrances and flavours –
to sniff, sip, spit, swallow, savour . . .

The Pendle Witches

One voice for ten dragged this way once
by superstition, ignorance.
Thou shalt not suffer a witch to live.

Witch: female, cunning, manless, old,
daughter of such, of evil faith;
in the murk of Pendle Hill, a crone.

Here, heavy storm-clouds, ill-will brewed,
over fields, fells, farms, blighted woods.
On the wind's breath, curse of crow and rook.

From poverty, no poetry
but weird spells, half-prayer, half-threat;
sharp pins in little dolls of death.

At daylight's gate, the things we fear
darken and form. That tree, that rock,
a slattern's shape ropes the devil's dog.

Something upholds us in its palm –
landscape, history, sudden time –
and, above, the gormless witness moon

below which Demdike, Chattox, shrieked,
like hags, unloved, an underclass,
eyes red, gobs gummed, unwell, unfed.

But that was then – when difference
made ghouls of neighbours; children begged,
foul, feral, filthy, in their cowls.

Grim skies, the grey remorse of rain;
cloudbreak, sunset's shame; four seasons,
turning centuries, in Lancashire,

away from Castle, Jury, Judge,
huge crowd, rough rope, short drop, no grave;
only future tourists who might grieve.

Liverpool

The Cathedral bell, tolled, could never tell;
nor the Liver Birds, mute in their stone spell;
or the Mersey, though seagulls wailed, cursed, overhead,
in no language for the slandered dead . . .

not the raw, red throat of the Kop, keening,
or the cops' words, censored of meaning;
not the clock, slow handclapping the coroner's deadline,
or the memo to Thatcher, or the tabloid headline . . .

but fathers told of their daughters; the names of sons
on the lips of their mothers were prayers; lost ones
honoured for bitter years by orphan, cousin, wife –
not a matter of football, but of life.

Over this great city, light after long dark;
and truth, the sweet silver song of a lark.

Birmingham

for Tariq Jahan

After the evening prayers at the mosque,
came the looters in masks,
                         and you three stood,
beloved in your neighbourhood,
brave, bright, brothers,
to be who you were –
a hafiz is one who has memorised
the entire Koran;
                a devout man –
then the lout in the speeding car
who purposefully mounted the kerb . . .

I think we all should kneel
                         on that English street,
where he widowed your pregnant wife, Shazad,
tossed your soul to the air, Abdul,
and brought your father, Haroon, to his knees,
his face masked in your blood
on the rolling news
                where nobody's children riot and burn.

White Cliffs

Worth their salt, England's white cliffs;
a glittering breastplate
Caesar saw from his ship;
the sea's gift to the land,
where samphire-pickers hung from their long ropes,
gathering, under a gull-glad sky,
in Shakespeare's mind's eye; astonishing
in Arnold's glimmering verse;
marvellous geology, geography;
to time, deference; war, defence;
first view or last of here, home,
in painting, poem, play, in song;
something fair and strong implied in chalk,
what we might wish ourselves.

Philharmonic

Wounds in wood, where the wind grieves
in slow breves,
                or a breeze
hovers and heals; brass,
                          bold as itself,
alchemical, blowing breath to blared gold;
all strings attached to silver sound.
This the composer found
                        in his deaf joy, despair,
and the brilliant boy; a where for time and space;
a place in endless air for perfect art –
a songbird's flight
                    through a great medieval hall
over the dancing dead.

The Beauty of the Church

Look, you are beautiful, beloved;
your eyes, framed by your hair,
are birds in the leaves of a tree,
doves in the Cedar of Lebanon;
your hair shines, a stream in sunlight
tumbling from the mountain; you are fair,
loved; your mouth, entrance; your kiss, key;
your lips, soft scarlet, opening;
your tongue, wine-sweet; your teeth, new lambs
in the pastures; your voice is for psalm, song.

I see your face; I say your face
is the garden where I sought love;
my head filled with dew; my hands
sweet with myrrh; my naked feet
in wet grasses; my mouth honey-smeared.
Your voice called at the door of my heart.

I am sick with love.
Turn away your eyes from mine,
they have overcome me.
You have ravished my heart with your eyes.
You have kissed me with the kisses of your mouth
in our green bed, under the beams of cedar,
the rafters of fir.
You are altogether lovely.
Your cheeks, spices and sweet flowers;
your breath, camphire and spikenard;
saffron; calamus and cinnamon;
frankincense and aloes;
your throat is for pearls;

your two breasts are honey and milk;
your left hand should be under my head,
your right hand embracing me.
Just to look at your hand,
I am sick with love.

You are the apple tree among the trees of the forest.
I lie under your shadow
and your fruit is sweet to my taste.
You are a cluster of camphire in the vineyards;
an orchard of ripe figs, pomegranates.
I am yours and you are mine,
until the day breaks and shadows fade.
No river to quench love, no sea to drown it.

I was in your eyes and I found favour.
I was all you desired and I gave you my loves.

I say the roof of your mouth is the best wine;
you are rose, lily, a cluster of grapes.
I looked for you at night on my bed.
I rose and walked the city streets,
searching for you.
I found you. I held you
and would not let you go,
until I had brought you to the field,
where we lay,
circled by the roes and hinds of the meadows.

I rose up to open to you
and your hands smelled of myrrh.
Your navel, a goblet which needed no wine.
How beautiful your feet.
The joints of your thighs were jewels.
Your knees were apples.

I sleep, but my heart wakes to your whisper.
You have brought me to this bed
and your banner over me is love.
Set me as a seal, beloved,
for love is strong as death,
set me as a seal upon your heart.

Shakespeare

Small Latin and less Greek, all English yours,
dear lad, local, word-blessed, language loved best;
the living human music on our tongues,
young, old, who we were or will be, history's shadow,
love's will, our heart's iambic beat, brother
through time; full-rhyme to us.
                                       Two rivers quote your name;
your journey from the vanished forest's edge
to endless fame – a thousand written souls,
pilgrims, redeemed in poetry – ends here, begins again.
And so, you knew this well, you do not die –
courtier, countryman, noter of flowers and bees,
war's laureate, magician, Janus-faced –
but make a great Cathedral, genius, of this place.

Pathway

I saw my father walking in my garden
and where he walked,
                          the garden lengthened
to a changing mile
which held all seasons of the year.
He did not see me, staring from my window,
a child's star face, hurt light from stricken time,
and he had treaded spring and summer grasses
before I thought to stir, follow him.

Autumn's cathedral, open to the weather, rose
high above, flawed amber, gorgeous ruin; his shadow
stretched before me, *cappa magna*,
my own, obedient, trailed like a nun.
He did not turn. I heard the rosaries of birds.
The trees, huge doors, swung open and I knelt.

He stepped into a silver room of cold;
a narrow bed of ice stood glittering,
and though my father wept, he could not leave,
but had to strip, then shiver in his shroud,

till winter palmed his eyes for frozen bulbs,
or sliced his tongue, a silencing of worms.

The moon a simple headstone without words.

An Unseen

I watched love leave, turn, wave, want not to go,
depart, return;
late spring, a warm slow blue of air, old-new.
Love was here; not; missing, love was there;
each look, first, last.

Down the quiet road, away, away, towards
the dying time,
love went, brave soldier, the song dwindling;
walked to the edge of absence; all moments going,
gone; bells through rain

to fall on the carved names of the lost. I saw
love's child uttered,
unborn, only by rain, then and now, all future
past, an unseen. Has forever been then? Yes,
forever has been.

Silver Lining

Five miles up, the hush and shoosh of ash,
yet the sky is as clean as a wiped slate –
I could write my childhood there. Selfish
to sit in this garden, listening to the past –
a Tudor bee wooing its flower, a lawnmower –
when grounded planes mean ruined plans, holidays
on hold, sore absences from weddings, funerals,
wingless commerce.
                  But Britain's birds
sing in this spring, from Inverness to Liverpool,
from Crieff, Caernarfon, Cambridge, Wenlock Edge,
Land's End to John O'Groats; the music silence summons,
George Herbert heard, Burns, Edward Thomas; briefly, us.

The Crown

The crown translates a woman to a Queen –
endless gold, circling itself, an O like a well,
fathomless, for the years to drown in – history's bride,
anointed, blessed, for a crowning. One head alone
can know its weight, on throne, in pageantry,
and feel it still, in private space, when it's lifted:
not a hollow thing, but a measuring; no halo,
treasure, but a valuing; decades and duty. Time-gifted,
the crown is old light, journeying from skulls of kings
to living Queen.   Its jewels glow, virtues; loyalty's ruby,
blood-deep; sapphire's ice resilience; emerald evergreen;
the shy pearl, humility. My whole life, whether it be long
or short, devoted to your service. Not lightly worn.

Lessons in the Orchard

An apple's soft thump on the grass, somewhen
in this place. What was it? Beauty of Bath.
What was it? Yellow, vermillion, round, big, splendid;
already escaping the edge of itself,
                              like the mantra of bees,
like the notes of rosemary, tarragon, thyme.
Poppies scumble their colour onto the air,
now and there, here, then and again.

                              Alive-alive-oh,
the heart's impulse to cherish; thus,
a woman petalling paint onto a plate –
cornflower blue –
as the years pressed out her own violet ghost;
that slow brush of vanishing cloud on the sky.

And the dragonfly's talent for turquoise.
And the goldfish art of the pond.
And the open windows calling the garden in.

This bowl, life, that we fill and fill.

Christmas Eve

for Ella

Time was slow snow sieved by the night,
a kind of love from the blurred moon;
your small town swooning, unabashed,
was Winter's own.

Snow was the mind of Time, sifting
itself, drafting the old year's end.
You wrote your name on the window-pane
with your young hand.

And your wishes went up in smoke,
beyond where a streetlamp studied
the thoughtful snow on Christmas Eve,
beyond belief,

as Time, snow, darkness, child, kindled.
Downstairs, the ritual lighting of the candles.

A prayer drifting as human breath, as the ghost of words.

Mrs Scrooge

Scrooge doornail-dead, his widow, Mrs Scrooge, lived by herself
in London Town. It was that time of year, the clocks long back,
when shops were window-dressed with unsold tinsel, trinkets, toys,
trivial pursuits, with sequinned dresses and designer suits,
with chocolates, glacé fruits and marzipan, with Barbie,
Action Man, with bubblebath and aftershave and showergel;
the words *Noel* and *Season's Greetings* brightly mute
in neon lights. The city bells had only just chimed three,
but it was dusk already. It had not been light all day.
Mrs Scrooge sat googling at her desk,
                          Catchit the cat
curled at her feet; snowflakes tumbling to the ground
below the window, where a robin perched,
pecking at seeds. *Most turkeys,*
bred for their meat, are kept in windowless barns,
with some containing over 20,000 birds. Turkeys
are removed from their crates and hung from shackles
by their legs in moving lines. A small fire crackled
in the grate. *Their heads are dragged under*
a water bath – electrically charged – before their necks
are cut. Mrs Scrooge pressed *Print*.
                          She planned
to visit Marley's Supermarket *(Biggest Bargain Birds!)* at four.

Outside, snowier yet, and cold! Piercing, searching, biting cold.
The cold gnawed noses just as dogs gnaw bones. It iced
the mobile phones pressed tight to ears.
                          The coldest Christmas Eve
in years saw Mrs Scrooge at Marley's, handing leaflets out.

The shoppers staggered past, weighed down with bags
or pushing trolleys crammed with breasts, legs, crowns, eggs,
sausages, giant stalks of brussels sprouts, carrots,
spuds, bouquets of broccoli, mange tout, courgettes, petits
pois, foie gras; with salmon, Stilton, pork pies, mince pies,
Christmas Pudding, custard,
port, gin, sherry, whisky,
fizz and plonk,
                all done on credit cards.
Most shook their head at Mrs Scrooge,
irked by her cry *'Find out how turkeys really die!'*
or shoved her leaflet in the pockets of their coats, unread,
or laughed and called back, *'Spoilsport! Ho! Ho! Ho!'*
Three hours went by like this.
                      The snow
                            began to ease
as she walked home.

She hated waste, consumerism, Mrs Scrooge, foraged
in the London parks for chestnuts, mushrooms, blackberries,
ate leftovers, recycled, mended, passed on, purchased secondhand,
turned the heating down and put on layers, walked everywhere,
drank tap-water, used public libraries, possessed a wind-up radio,
switched off lights, lit candles (darkness is cheap and Mrs Scrooge
liked it) and would not spend *one penny* on a plastic bag.
She passed off-licences with *6 for 5*, bookshops with *3 for 2*,
food stores with *Buy 1 get 1 free*.
                    Above her head,
the Christmas lights
            danced like a river toward a sea of dark.
The National Power Grid moaned, endangered, like a whale.

The Thames flowed on as Mrs Scrooge proceeded on her way
towards her rooms.
                        Nobody lived in the building now
but her, and all the other flats were boarded up.
Whatever the developers had offered Mrs Scrooge to move
could never be enough. She liked it where it was,
lurking in the corner of a yard, as though the house
had run there young, playing hide-and-seek,
and had forgotten the way out. She remembered
her first Christmas there with Scrooge,
                                     the single stripey sweet
he'd given her that year, and every year.
But Scrooge was dead, no doubt of that, so why,
her key turning the lock, did she see in the knocker
Scrooge's face? His face to the life, staring back at her
with living grey-green eyes and opening metal lips!
As Mrs Scrooge looked fixedly at this,
it turned into a knocker once again.

                                  Up the echoing stairs
to slippers, simple supper, candles, cocoa, cat,
went Mrs Scrooge; not scared, but oddly comforted
at glimpsing Scrooge's knockered face.
But still, she double-locked the door, put on her dressing gown
and sat down by the fire to sip her soup.
                            The fire
was very low indeed, not much on such a bitter night,
so soon enough she went to bed – night-cap, bed-socks,
Scrooge's old pyjamas, hot water-bottle, Catchit's purr . . .
and then her own soft snore.

She dreamed of Scrooge,
                    of Christmas past,
of Christmas present, Christmas yet to come; dreams
that seemed to trap her in a snowstorm bowl –
newly-married, ice-skating with Scrooge,
two necks in one long, bright red, woolly scarf;
or hanging baubles on the tree;
or being surprised by mistletoe, his kiss, the taste of him –
but then her world was shaken violently
and she was kneeling by a grave, hearing a funeral bell . . .

Midnight rang out from St Paul's. She gasped awake.
The twice-locked door was open wide
and all the room was filled with light
and smelled of tangerines and cinnamon and wine.
A cheerful Ghost was perched and grinning on her bed,
now like a child, now like a wise old man,
with silver hair and berried holly for a crown
(and yet its shimmering dress was trimmed with flowers).
'Good grief!' said Mrs Scrooge. 'Who the hell are you?'
The Ghost squealed with delight and clapped its hands
(a hard thing for a ghost to do, thought Mrs Scrooge).
'I am the Ghost of Christmas Past,' it trilled.
'Now, rise! And walk with me.'

                    It took her by the hand
then flew her through the bedroom wall. They stood at once
upon an open country road, with fields on either side.
The city had entirely gone, the darkness too;
it was a sparkling winter's day, all blinged with frost.
'I know this place!' cried Mrs Scrooge. 'I grew up here!
We're near the village of Heath Row!

My family kept an orchard close to here.'
They walked along the road, Mrs Scrooge recalling
every gate, and post, and tree.

'That way's Harmondsworth,'
she told the Ghost excitedly. *'Famous for Richard Cox,
you know, who cultivated Cox's Orange Pippin.'*
The merry Ghost conjured an apple from the air.
She crunched delightedly. *'That way's Longford village;
that way's the farm at Perry Oaks; and that way's Sipson Green!'*
They'd reached the village now, a green, a row of houses and an Inn;
two fields away a farm, beyond that farm another farm;
the landscape glittering as if it were in love with light.
A laughing local bunch of lads ran by.
Mrs Scrooge went red!
'I snogged that tall one once!' she said.

                                          'They're shadows,'
said the Ghost. *'They have no consciousness of us.'*
High in the sky there came an aeroplane, rare enough
to make the boys stand pointing at the endless, generous air
and yell out *'Merry Christmas!'* to the plane.
                                       *'This is the past,
it cannot come again,'* went on the Ghost, *'It is the gift
your soul gives to your heart.'*
Mrs Scrooge stopped in the road and turned. *'Why show
me this?'* she asked. *'Because,'* the Ghost replied,
*'Scrooge sends a message from the grave –
keep going! You shall overcome!'*
'No Runway Three!' cried Mrs Scrooge,
the breath her words made
like a ghost itself, swooning, vanishing.

                    But when she looked,
the face of Christmas Past bent down,
just like a lover stoops to steal a kiss,
and then her lips were soft, then salty,
tasting tears, her own, and then she woke,
at home, and old, and all alone.

Not quite alone,
for Catchit dozed and snuggled at her feet,
visions of robin redbreasts in his head.
                                        London's moon,
the moon of Shakespeare, Dickens, Oscar, Virginia Woolf,
shone down on silent theatres, banks, hotels,
on palaces and dosshouses and parks,
                                    on Mrs Scrooge,
who lay, wide-eyed and fretful, in the dark. She heard
a scrabbling noise inside the chimney-breast
and sat bolt upright in her bed –
                        'Who's there?' she said –
then, with a thump, a flash,
                        a figure in a crimson Santa suit
glowed in the grate, as if the fire had taken human shape
and combed itself a beard from its smoke.
'*I am the Ghost of Christmas Present,*'
boomed the Ghost. '*Now rise, and come with me!*'

Before she knew it, Mrs Scrooge sat in a sleigh,
being pulled by reindeers through the starry sky,
tying a ribbon round the earth;
the Ghost of Christmas Present talking as they flew, naming
the oceans, forests, mountain ranges far below,
until the Arctic Circle rose beneath them like a moon.

They landed,
         skidding on the ice,
in a percussion of sharp hooves and jingling bells.
Tears, like opals,
         fell, then froze,
on Mrs Scrooge's cheeks as she looked.
She stood upon a continent of ice
which sparkled between sea and sky,
                        endless and dazzling,
as though the world kept all its treasure there;
                        a scale
which balanced poetry and prayer.

But then she heard a crackling, rumbling groan
and saw huge icebergs calving from the floe
                        into the sea;
then, further out, a polar bear, floating,
                    stranded,
on a raft of ice.
            'The Polar Ice Cap melting,' said the Ghost.
'Can mankind save it?'
'Yes, we can!' cried Mrs Scrooge. *'We must!'*
'I bring encouragement from Scrooge's dust,' replied the Ghost.
*'Never give up. Don't think one ordinary human life
can make no difference – for it can!'*
The reindeers steamed and snorted in the snow.
Mrs Scrooge stretched out her hand to one,
stroking the warm, rough texture of its hide,
which seemed to alter, soften, into Catchit's fur!
The North Pole vanished like a snuffed-out flame.
She woke again.

                    '*Old fool!*'
said Mrs Scrooge to herself. '*These are just dreams.*'
She pulled her blankets up beneath her chin
and lay there, worrying about large things and small.
The wall flickered with strange shadows, shifting shapes –
a turkey, and then a bear, and then a hooded form
which pointed at her silently,
until it swelled and stood and spoke!
'*I am the Ghost of Christmas Yet to Come! Rise now,
and follow me!*'

It took her in its arms like a bride
and flew her through a winter wood
towards a clearing
                 and an open grave,
around which mourners stood,
                           then put her down.
'*My family!*' said Mrs Scrooge. '*There's Bob!
And that's his lovely wife!
There are my grandchildren! Peter! Martha! Tiny Tim!
Look! They're my dearest friends, the Fezziwigs! Their girls!
Why are we here? Who died?*'

The Spirit pointed downward to the grave.
Mrs Scrooge crept near and peeped into a wormy, loamy hole.
She saw a cardboard coffin, crayoned brightly with a name,
cartooned with flowers, faces, animals,
covered with poems, kisses, hearts.
                              She turned . . .

At once, she stood beside the Ghost
inside a huge and crowded room,
her friends and family piling in!
In came a fiddler with a music-book
who started up a jig.
                (Mrs Scrooge,
who loved a whirl,
restrained herself from dancing with the Ghost.)
In came Mrs Fezziwig, one vast substantial smile,
bearing a tray of home-made, warm mince pies; saying
'*She would have wanted it this way!*' In came
the Fezziwig girls with babies chuckling in their arms. In came
tall nephews arm-in-arm with little aunts.
                                  In came old comrades
with whom she'd marched in protest
against every kind of harm.
                        In they all came,
aglow with life and possibility, old and young;
away they went, twenty couples all at once,
gay and straight, down the middle, up and round again,
the beaming fiddler trying to saw his instrument in half!

There never was
                such a wake!
More dancing, then more music, someone sang,
several shed tears;
then mince pies, cake, mulled wine, cold beer,
more wine, more beer;
then Mrs Scrooge heard a cheer
and there was Tiny Tim, up on a chair!
There was a hush.

'*A toast!*'
cried Tiny Tim. '*To my grandmother! The best woman
who ever was! She taught us all
to value everything!*
                    *To give ourselves!
To live as if each day
                    was Christmas Day!*'
Another cheer and Mrs Scrooge's name rang out
from everybody's lips.
                    She seemed to float
above them; all the bright, familiar faces
                                        looking up,
raised glasses in the air.
She heard Bob say, '*She really had a wonderful life!*'
The Ghost of Christmas Yet to Come
                              pulled back its hood.
She looked into its smiling, loving, grey-green eyes
and understood.

            Clash, clang, hammer, ding, dong, bell!
Bell, dong, ding, hammer, clang, clash!
It was St Paul's again,
                    gargling its morning bells,
the room her own;
            and dribbling Catchit
staring down at her from her chest!
Quickly, Mrs Scrooge showered and dressed.
She flung open the window and leaned out –
a clear, bright, jovial, cold and glorious day!
The doorbell rang.
            Down she hurried,
opened wide the door,
            and in they poured,

taking the stairs two at a time – Bob, Bob's wife,
the grandchildren, the Fezziwigs,
their girls, babies, partners,
                              all shouting
'*Merry Christmas! Merry Christmas! Merry Christmas!*'

What news they had!
                    The credit crunch
had forced the property developers
to sell the empty flats below to the Fezziwig girls!
So come New Year, all three were moving in!
Hurrah! Hurrah! What did Mrs Scrooge think of that!
(And would she babysit?)
                         Bob came grinning from the kitchen
with a tray of glasses of Buck's Fizz!
Mrs Fezziwig and Mrs Scrooge
                             cuddled and wept with joy!
And that delightful boy, Tiny Tim, called out,
'*Here you are, Grandma, the sweet that Grandad gave you
every Christmas that he lived! A . . .*'
                           '*HUMBUG!*'
exclaimed Mrs Scrooge!
'*God Bless Us, Every One!*' cried Tiny Tim.

The Christmas Truce

Christmas Eve in the trenches of France,
the guns were quiet.
The dead lay still in No Man's Land –
Freddie, Franz, Friedrich, Frank . . .
The moon, like a medal, hung in the clear, cold sky.

Silver frost on barbed wire, strange tinsel,
sparkled and winked.
A boy from Stroud stared at a star
to meet his mother's eyesight there.
An owl swooped on a rat on the glove of a corpse.

In a copse of trees behind the lines,
a lone bird sang.
A soldier-poet noted it down – *a robin
holding his winter ground* –
then silence spread and touched each man like a hand.

Somebody kissed the gold of his ring;
a few lit pipes;
most, in their greatcoats, huddled,
waiting for sleep.
The liquid mud had hardened at last in the freeze.

But it was Christmas Eve; *believe*; belief
thrilled the night air,
where glittering rime on unburied sons
treasured their stiff hair.
The sharp, clean, midwinter smell held memory.

On watch, a rifleman scoured the terrain –
no sign of life,
no shadows, shots from snipers,
nowt to note or report.
The frozen, foreign fields were acres of pain.

Then flickering flames from the other side
danced in his eyes,
as Christmas Trees in their dozens shone,
candlelit on the parapets,
and they started to sing, all down the German lines.

Men who would drown in mud, be gassed, or shot,
or vaporised
by falling shells, or live to tell,
heard for the first time then –
Stille Nacht. Heilige Nacht. Alles schläft, einsam wacht . . .

Cariad, the song was a sudden bridge
from man to man;
a gift to the heart from home,
or childhood, some place shared . . .
When it was done, the British soldiers cheered.

A Scotsman started to bawl *The First Noel*
and all joined in,
till the Germans stood, seeing
across the divide,
the sprawled, mute shapes of those who had died.

All night, along the Western Front, they sang,
the enemies –
carols, hymns, folk songs, anthems,
in German, English, French;
each battalion choired in its grim trench.

So Christmas dawned, wrapped in mist,
to open itself
and offer the day like a gift
for Harry, Hugo, Hermann, Henry, Heinz . . .
with whistles, waves, cheers, shouts, laughs.

Frohe Weinachten, Tommy! Merry Christmas, Fritz!
A young Berliner,
brandishing schnapps,
was the first from his ditch to climb.
A Shropshire lad ran at him like a rhyme.

Then it was up and over, every man,
to shake the hand
of a foe as a friend,
or slap his back like a brother would;
exchanging gifts of biscuits, tea, Maconochie's stew,

Tickler's jam . . . for cognac, sausages, cigars,
beer, sauerkraut;
or chase six hares, who jumped
from a cabbage-patch, or find a ball
and make of a battleground a football pitch.

I showed him a picture of my wife.
Ich zeigte ihm
ein Foto meiner Frau.
Sie sei schön, sagte er.
He thought her beautiful, he said.

They buried the dead then, hacked spades
into hard earth
again and again, till a score of men
were at rest, identified, blessed.
Der Herr ist mein Hirt . . . my shepherd, I shall not want.

And all that marvellous, festive day and night,
they came and went,
the officers, the rank and file,
their fallen comrades side by side
beneath the makeshift crosses of midwinter graves . . .

. . . beneath the shivering, shy stars
and the pinned moon
and the yawn of History;
the high, bright bullets
which each man later only aimed at the sky.

Wenceslas

The King's Cook had cooked for the King
a Christmas Pie,
                wherein the Swan,
once bride of the river,
half of for ever,
six Cygnets circling her,
lay scalded, plucked, boned, parboiled,
salted, peppered, gingered, oiled;
and harboured the Heron
whose grey shadow she'd crossed
as it stood witness,
                grave as a Priest,
on the riverbank.
Now the Heron's breast was martyred with Cloves.

Inside the Heron inside the Swan –
in a greased cradle, pastry-sealed –
a Common Crane,
                gutted and trussed,
smeared with Cicely, Lavender, Rose,
was stuffed with a buttered, saffroned
golden Goose.
                Within the Goose,
perfumed with Fruits, was a Duck,
and jammed in the Duck, a Pheasant,
embalmed in Honey
                from Bees
                      who'd perused
the blossoms of Cherry trees.

Spring in deep midwinter;
      a year in a pie;
a Guinea-Fowl in a Pheasant;
a Teal in a Fowl.
     Nursed in the Teal,
a Partridge, purse to a Plover;
a Plover, glove to a Quail;
and caught in the mitt of the Quail,
        a Lark –
a green Olive stoppered its beak.
The Christmas Pie
for the good King, Wenceslas,
was seasoned with Sage, Rosemary, Thyme;
and a living Robin sang through a hole in its crust.

Pot-herbs to accompany this;
Roasted Chestnuts, Red Cabbage,
Celery, Carrots, Colly-flowre,
each borne aloft by a Page
       into the Hall,
where the Pie steamed on a table
in front of the fire;
     and to flow at the feast,
mulled Wine, fragrant
with Nutmeg, Cinnamon, Mace,
with Grains of Paradise.
      The Lords and Ladies
sat at their places, candlelight
on their festive faces.

Up in the Minstrels' Gallery,
the King's Musicians tuned the Lute
to the Flute
           to the Pipe
to the Shawm, the Gemshorn, the Harp,
to the Dulcimer
             to the Psaltery;
and the Drum was a muffled heart
like an imminent birth
and the Tambourine was percussion as mirth.
Then a blushing Boy stood to trill
of how the Beasts, by some good spell,
in their crude stable began to tell
the gifts they gave Emmanuel.

Holly, Ivy, Mistletoe,
                  shredded Silver,
hung from the rafters
and the King's Fool
              pranced beneath
five red Apples,
         one green Pear,
which danced in the air.
Snow at the window twirled;
and deep, crisp, even,
              covered the fields
where a fox and a vixen curled in a den
as the Moon scowled
at the cold, bold, gold glare of an Owl.

Also there,
    out where the frozen stream
lay nailed to the ground,
was a prayer
    drifting as human breath,
as the ghost of words,
    in a dark wood,
yearning to be
   Something
      Understood.
But Heaven was only old light
and the frost was cruel
where a poor, stooped man
    went gathering fuel.

A miracle then,
    fanfared in,
that the King in red robes, silver crown,
glanced outside
    from his wooden throne
to see the Pauper
    stumble, shiver,
and sent a Page to fetch him
    Hither.
Then Wenceslas sat the poor man down,
poured Winter's Wine,
and carved him a sumptuous slice
    of the Christmas Pie . . .
as prayers hope You would, and I.

Bethlehem

A mild dusk; the little town
                        snaked
on the edge between desert and farmland;
camel prints in the sand
                        like broken hearts;
the call and response of sheep
                                among dry shrub.

To the West,
            the whispering prayer of olive groves;
incense of rosemary, cedar, pine, votive
on purpling air.

Everyone there who had to be there.

*

The lamps lit; all Bethlehem
                            full;
every cave stabled with beasts, jostling for hay
in the fusty gloom;
                every room
peopled and packed from rafter to floor;
barley bread in the ovens rising . . .

and a girl's hands
                at an open door,
her blade halving a pomegranate,
its blood on her pale palms . . .

a voice from an alleyway chanting a psalm.

The moon rose; the shepherds sprawled,
                              shawled,
a rough ring on sparse grass, passing
a leather flask.
              From the town,
a swelling human sound; cooking smells braiding the hour
as lambs and fishes spat in the fires.

A hundred suppers –
                    honey, fig, olive, grape,
set before stone-cutter, potter, tent-maker, maid,
nurse, farmer, child.

Young wine in the old jars, yellow and cold.

                    *

The Inn bulged; travellers boozed,
                              bawled,
bragged, swapping their caravan tales; money-lenders
biting their gold coins; painted women
dancing on tables; mules brayed
outside in the stable;
a youth in the courtyard strummed on a harp.

The sweating Innkeeper shouted and served;
his wife counting the heads,
then making up beds on the flat roof,
in the vine-covered yard.

Above, bright news in the sky, arrived, a star.

The small hours; all living souls
                         slept
or half-slept; the night fires smouldering low
out in the scrub;
the olive oil cooling in clay lamps;
a goatherd snored in the straw
                         between two goats.

Silent night;
            a soft breeze from the desert
laying a dusting of sand on the dark road,
blessing the homes.

A donkey's slow, deliberate hooves on the stones.

                    *

Afterwards, the witnesses
                         spoke
of a singing boy, an angel,
walking the fields in the hour before dawn,
winged in his own light;
of how the shepherds fled from the sight,
lambs in their arms.

And some swore, on their lives,
on their children's lives,
that they saw an olive tree
                    turning to pure gold . . .

that the moon stooped low to gape at the world.

What's certain – the time and place:
                              heard,
three crows from the cockerel;
                      seen,
the stable behind the Inn; present,
animals, goatherd, shepherds, Innkeeper, wife . . .
then the small, raw cry of a new life.

And one wept at a miracle; another
was hoping it might be so;
                      others ran,
daft, shouting, to boast in the waking streets.

Wise men swayed on camels out of the East.

Dorothy Wordsworth's Christmas Birthday

First, frost at midnight –
Moon, Venus and Jupiter
named in their places.

Ice, like a cold key,
turning its lock on the lake;
nervous stars trapped there.

Darkness, a hand poised
over the chord of the hills;
the strange word moveless.

The landscape muted;
soft apprehension of snow,
a holding of breath.

Up, rapt at her gate,
Dorothy Wordsworth ages
one year in an hour;

her Christmas birthday
inventoried by an owl,
clock-eyed, time-keeper.

Indoors, the thrilled fire
unwraps itself; sprightly hands
opening the coal.

For she cannot sleep,
Dorothy, primed with herself,
waiting for morning . . .

gradual sure light,
like the start of a poem,
its local accent.

Striding towards dawn,
Samuel Taylor Coleridge
swigs at his port wine,

sings a nonsense rhyme,
which Helm Crag learns and echoes
at the speed of sound.

The rock formations –
old lady at piano,
a lion, a lamb.

And, out on a limb,
he skids down a silvered lane
into a sunburst;

a delight of bells,
the exact mood of his heart,
from St. Oswald's Church.

New rime on the grass
where the Wordsworths' graves will be
at another time.

Not there, then; here, now,
Dorothy's form on the road
coming to meet him,

in her claret frock,
in her boots, bonnet and shawl,
her visible breath.

Then her arm through his
on the stroll to Dove Cottage;
spiced apples baking.

Wordsworth lies a-bed
in his nightshirt and nightcap,
rhyming *cloud* with *crowd*.

The cat at his feet
licks at her black-and-white fur,
rhyming *purr* with *purr*.

The kitchen table,
set for this festive breakfast,
an unseen still-life:

cream in a brown jug,
the calmness of bowls and spoons,
one small round white loaf.

And a tame robin,
aflame on the windowsill,
its name in its song.

They walk to the lake,
where Wordsworth skates like a boy,
in heaven on earth;

a tangerine sun
illuminating the hour
into manuscript;

so Dorothy's gifts
are the gold outlines of hills,
are emblazoned trees;

Coleridge on a rock,
lighting his pipe, votive smoke
ascending the air . . .

Nowt to show more fair –
ecstatic, therefore, her stare,
seeing it all in.

Later, the lamps lit
in the parlour, hot punch fumes
in a copper pan.

The feast: mutton pie,
buttered parsnips, potatoes,
a Halifax goose.

Coleridge's flushed face,
never so vivid again
in Dorothy's mind.

Loud boots at the porch
and a stout thump on the door
as the Minstrels come,

dangling their tin cans
for a free ladle of ale
after caroling . . .

*Bring us in good ale,
for that goes down at once-oh!
Bring us in good ale . . .*

All in each other,
Miss Wordsworth and the poets,
bawling the chorus;

their voices drifting,
in 1799,
to nowhen, nowhere . . .

but Winter's slow turn,
and snow in Dorothy's hair
and on her warm tongue.

Index of titles

$ 43

A Clear Note 26
A Dreaming Week 356
A Goldfish 489
A Healthy Meal 61
A Provincial Party, 1956 40
A Rare Bee 506
A Shilling for the Sea 166
Absence 378
Absolutely 85
Achilles 447
Adultery 212
All Days Lost Days 107
Alliance 25
Alphabet for Auden 6
An Old Atheist Places His Last Bet 74
An Unseen 524
And How Are We Today? 86
And Then What 62
Anne Hathaway 256
Anon 335
Answer 407
Ape 142
Ariel 441
Art 427
Ash Wednesday, 1984 12
At Ballynahinch 495
At Jerez 512
Atlas 455

Away and See 197
Away from Home 171

Back Desk 45
Beachcomber 194
Beautiful 310
Bees 433
Before You Jump 38
Before You Were Mine 187
Bethlehem 550
Betrothal 389
Big Ask 439
Big Sue and *Now, Voyager* 106
Birmingham 516
Borrowed Memory 56
Boy 151
Bridgewater Hall 391
Brothers 186
By Heart 119

Café Royal 202
Caul 196
Chaucer's Valentine 511
Chinatown 403
Christmas Eve 528
Circe 272
Close 211
Cockermouth and Workington 480
Cold 483
Colours by Someone Else 101
Comprehensive 4
Confession 189
Correspondents 111
Crunch 488

Crush 203
Cuba 387

Dear Norman 41
Death and the Moon 365
Debt 33
December 400
Decembers 485
Delilah 254
Demeter 300
Deportation 121
Descendants 144
Dies Natalis 68
Disgrace 222
Dorothy Wordsworth Is Dead 478
Dorothy Wordsworth's Christmas Birthday 554
Drams 462
Dream of a Lost Friend 161
Dreaming of Somewhere Else 37
Drone 501
Drunk 198

Echo 436
Education for Leisure 13
Elegy 385
Eley's Bullet 152
Elvis's Twin Sister 290
Epiphany 424
Eurydice 283
Every Good Boy 90

Fall 393
Finding the Words 399
First Love 201

Following Francis 154
Foreign 108
Forest 372
Frau Freud 280
Fraud 217
Free Will 24
from Mrs Tiresias 240
Funeral 160

Gambler 359
Gesture 502
Girl Talking 3
Girlfriends 165
Give 396
Grace 401
Grief 417

Hand 383
Hard to Say 167
Havisham 214
Haworth 374
Head of English 9
History 329
Hive 459
Homesick 77
Hometown 131
Hour 375
Human Interest 36

I Live Here Now 76
I Remember Me 14
If I Was Dead 380
In Mrs Tilscher's Class 128

In Your Mind 177
Ink on Paper 49
Invisible Ink 454
Ithaca 418

Jealous as Hell 18
Job Creation 138
John Barleycorn 457

Land 419
Last Post 434
Leda 497
Lessons in the Orchard 527
Letters from Deadmen 63
Liar 150
Like Earning a Living 191
Like This 162
Lineage vii
Litany 183
Little Red-Cap 229
Liverpool 515
Liverpool Echo 44
Lizzie, Six 11
Losers 157
Loud 327
Love 395
Lovebirds 22
Lovesick 116
Luke Howard, Namer of Clouds 473

Making Money 139
Mean Time 225
Medusa 265

Midsummer Night 415
Miles Away 123
Missile 53
M-M-Memory 158
Model Village 79
Moments of Grace 200
Money Talks 93
Moniack Mhor 466
Mouth, With Soap 105
Mrs Aesop 245
Mrs Beast 296
Mrs Darwin 246
Mrs Faust 249
Mrs Icarus 279
Mrs Lazarus 274
Mrs Midas 237
Mrs Quasimodo 260
Mrs Rip Van Winkle 278
Mrs Schofield's GCSE 445
Mrs Scrooge 531
Mrs Sisyphus 247
Mrs Skinner, North Street 133
Music 490

Name 371
Naming Parts 20
Never Go Back 204
New Vows 496
New Year 402
Night Marriage 420
Nile 460
North-West 364
Nostalgia 184
November 173

Only Dreaming 118
Oppenheim's Cup and Saucer 48
Originally 127
Orta St Giulio 492
Oslo 206
Over 429
Oxfam 449

Parliament 475
Passing-Bells 503
Pathway 523
Penelope 294
Père Lachaise 159
Philharmonic 518
Pilate's Wife 244
Plainsong 122
Pluto 193
Poem in Oils 47
Poet for Our Times 136
Poetry 446
Poker in the Falklands with Henry & Jim 55
Politico 96
Politics 442
Pope Joan 292
Postcards 109
Practising Being Dead 67
Premonitions 504
Presents 410
Psychopath 87
Pygmalion's Bride 276

Queen Herod 233
Queen Kong 257
Quickdraw 398

Rain 377
Rapture 384
Recognition 83
Rings 452
River (*The Other Country*) 175
River (*Rapture*) 373
Room 224
Row 386

Salome 281
Sanctuary 72
Saying Something 17
Scheherazade 437
Scraps 97
Selling Manhattan 94
Shakespeare 522
Ship 394
Shooting Stars 57
Silver Lining 525
Simon Powell 482
Sit at Peace 130
Sleeping 209
Small Female Skull 199
Snow (*Rapture*) 422
Snow (*The Bees*) 487
Someone Else's Daughter 60
Somewhere Someone's Eyes 149
Space, Space 115
Spell 481
Spring 406
Stafford Afternoons 185
Standing Female Nude 46
Statement 92
Stealing 99

Steam 210
Strange Language in Night Fog 75
Strange Place 117
Stuffed 216
Sub 331
Sung 494
Survivor 155
Swing 376
Syntax 421

Talent 42
Talent Contest 141
Tall 324
Tea 388
Telegrams 112
Telephoning Home 114
Telling the Bees 477
Terza Rima SW19 19
Text 370
The Act of Imagination 147
The B Movie 58
The Bee Carol 484
The Beauty of the Church 519
The Biographer 219
The Brink of Shrieks 82
The Captain of the 1964 *Top of the Form* Team 181
The Christmas Truce 542
The Cliché Kid 192
The Cord 361
The Counties 469
The Crown 526
The *Darling* Letters 170
The Dead 493
The Devil's Wife 267

The Diet 317
The Dolphins 59
The Dummy 78
The English Elms 467
The Falling Soldier 443
The Female Husband 450
The Good Teachers 190
The Grammar of Light 207
The Human Bee 499
The Kissing Gate 168
The Kray Sisters 287
The Laughter of Stafford Girls' High 336
The Legend 143
The Light Gatherer 360
The Literature Act 174
The Long Queen 303
The Love Poem 425
The Lovers 392
The Map-Woman 305
The Pendle Witches 513
The Shirt 448
The Suicide 215
The Virgin's Memo 334
The Way My Mother Speaks 176
The White Horses 471
The Windows 221
The Woman in the Moon 474
The Woman Who Shopped 319
Thetis 231
This Shape 15
Three Paintings 102
Till Our Face 21
Translating the English, 1989 132
Translation 100

Treasure 409
Two Small Poems of Desire 164

Unloving 428

Valentine 208
Valentine's 498
Venus 412
Virgil's Bees 451

War Photographer 51
Warming Her Pearls 120
Water 461
We Remember Your Childhood Well 146
Weasel Words 135
Welltread 188
Wenceslas 546
What Price? 52
Whatever 413
Where We Came in 23
White Cliffs 517
White Writing 358
Who Loves You 163
Whoever She Was 35
Wintering 404
Winter's Tale 486
Wish 363
Woman Seated in the Underground, 1941 50
Words of Absolution 32
Words, Wide Night 169
Work 322
World 382
Write 411

Yes, Officer 91
You 369
You Jane 34
Your Move 423

Index of first lines

7 April 1852. 246

A body has been discussed between them. 20
A chemical inside you secretes the ingredients of fear. 40
A flop back for a kip in the sun, 443
A ghost loves you, has got inside you in the dark. 118
A mild dusk; the little town 550
A one a two a one two three four – 43
A silvery, pale-blue satin tie, freshwater in sunlight, 50p. 449
A soft ounce of your breath 409
A suspicion, a doubt, a jealousy 265
A woman's skin was a map of the town 305
Ace in the hole; ten, jack, queen on the baize. 74
After I learned to transubstantiate 292
After I no longer speak they break our fingers 57
After I've spoken to you, I walk out to the gate 168
After the evening prayers at the mosque, 516
Afterwards, I found him alone at the bar 448
Again, the endless northern rain between us 391
All day, slow funerals have ploughed the rain. 404
All day we leave and arrive at the hive, 459
All I know is this: 240
All yours, Injun, twenty-four bucks' worth of glass beads, 94
Along the ruined avenues the long gone lie 159
Although I knew they'd laid him low, 457
An apple's soft thump on the grass, somewhen 527
An upward rush on stairs of air 501
And when I returned, 418
At childhood's end, the houses petered out 229
At first, I looked along the road 294
At night I fart a Guinnes smell against the wife 34

At the end of the pier, an open-air theatre, a crowd 141
At the turn of the river the language changes, 175
Away and see an ocean suck at a boiled sun 197
Away from you, I hold hands with the air, 383

Balancing me with your hand up my back, listening 78
Because you are dead, 219
Beloved sweetheart bastard. Not a day since then 214
Beneath the earth a perfect femur glows. I recall 63
Bless air's gift of sweetness, honey 451
Blind black shark swim in me, 18
But I want to write to an Essex girl, 469
But one day we woke to disgrace; our house 222
But what if, in the clammy soil, her limbs 363
But when we rowed, 386
By Christ, he could bore for Purgatory. He was small, 245

Child, stardust, small wonder vii
Christmas Eve in the trenches of France, 542
Cold, I was, like snow, like ivory. 276
Come away into this dark cell and tell 189
Con artists, barefaced liars, clocks shuffle the hours slowly. 157
Corner of Thistle Street, two slack shillings jangled 96
Darlings, I write to you from the moon 474
Did you know your hands could catch that dark hour 502
Do Wah Diddy Diddy, Baby Love, Oh Pretty Woman 181
Do you think they cried, the children 490
Don't ask me how, but I've fetched up 82
Down by the river, under the trees, love waits for me 373
Dumb was as good as dead; 437

Eight children to feed, I worked as a nurse 26
Even barely enough light to find a mouth, 207

Fifteen years minimum, banged up inside 36
First, frost at midnight 554
First things first – 249
Firstly, his hands – a woman's. Softer than mine, 244
Firstly, I changed my name 217
Five miles up, the hush and shoosh of ash, 525
For some time now, at the curve of my mind, 155
From this day forth to unhold, 496

Girls, I was dead and down 283
Give him strength, crouched on one knee in the dark 455
Give me, you said, on our very first night, 396
Grief, your gift, unwrapped, 417

Having been, in my youth, a pirate 450
He arrives too late to tell him how it will be. 202
He remembers running to the nets, in early summer, 56
He was all night sleepless over money. 33
Her face is a perfect miniature on wide, smooth flesh, 106
Here are my bees, 433
How do you earn a life going on 221
How it makes your face a stone 442
How they can ruin a day, the funeral cars proceeding 173
However it is we return to the water's edge 364

I am Franz Schubert of Dresden. It was not easy. 45
I am the authentic language of suffering. My cold, gold eye 93
I asked him to give me an image for Love, something I could see, 167
I became a human bee at twelve, 499
I bought, on a whim, a goldfish for a good girl. 489
I came on in extra time in '66, my breasts 331
I couldn't see Guinness 446
I dream through a wordless, familiar place. 200
I drop the dying year behind me like a shawl 402

I forget. I have looked at the other faces and found 50
I found an apple. 116
I found the words at the back of a drawer, 399
I had grieved. I had wept for a night and a day 274
I have turned the newspaper boy into a diver 41
I hear your voice saying *Hello* in that guarded way 114
I heard tell tale of a rare bee, 506
I lay on the bank at Ballynahinch 495
I like pouring your tea, lifting 388
I liked being small. When I'm on my own 151
I live here now, the place where the pond 76
I made myself imagine that I didn't love you, 119
I might have raised your hand to the sky 452
I need help, Doc, and bad; I can't forget 192
I put this breve down, knowing in my head 90
I put two yellow peppers in an owl. 216
I remember peeping in at his skyscraper room 257
I run my metal comb through the D.A. and pose 87
I sank like a stone 278
I saw my father walking in my garden 523
I say her phrases to myself 176
I shrank myself 231
I snipped and stitched my soul 410
I tend the mobile now 370
I think I was searching for treasures or stones 436
I wait for your step. 22
I wake to a dark hour out of time, go to the window. 429
I want to call you thou, the sound 421
I want you and you are not here. I pause 123
I watch you undress by household candlelight. 117
I watched love leave, turn, wave, want not to go, 524
I wear the two, the mobile and the landline phones, 398
I will be yours, be yours. 389
I worry about you travelling in those mystical machines. 163

I write the headlines for a Daily Paper. 136
Ice in the trees. 233
I'd done it before 281
I'd loved them fervently since childhood. 260
If I was dead, 380
If poetry could tell it backwards, true, begin 434
If she were here 335
If we were shades 419
If you think till it hurts 194
If you were made of stone, 407
I'll take your hand, the left, 413
I'm fond, nereids and nymphs, unlike some, of the pig, 272
I'm here now where you were. 374
I'm not the first or the last 279
I'm ten years away from the corner you laugh on 187
Imagine living in a strange, dark city for twenty years. 108
In his darkroom he is finally alone 51
In St Austin's and Sacré Coeur the accents of ignorance 12
In that town there was a different time. 131
In the bar where the living dead drink all day 204
In the convent, y'all, 290
In the end, 394
It felt so cold, the snowball which wept in my hands, 483
It happened like this. I shall never forget. Da 92
It was a courtship of postcards 109
It was a girl in the Third Form, Carolann Clare, 336
It was about the time of day you mention, yes. 91
It was late September. I'd just poured a glass of wine, begun 237
It was winter. Wilson had just said 134
It's snowing! Twelve, she runs outside into the cold. 488

Ladies, for argument's sake, let us say 280
Lap dissolve. You make a man speak crap dialogue, 58
Learn from the winter trees, the way 428

It was explained to Sir Robert Armstrong that 135
Living 107
Lock the door. In the dark journey of our night, 211
Look, you are beautiful, beloved; 519
Love is talent, the world love's metaphor. 395
Love's time's beggar, but even a single hour, 375

maybe not abscesses, acne, asthma, 334
Milk bottles. Light through net. No post. Cat, 133
Minims have one eye, crotchets, breves . . . quavers wink 102
Most of us worked in the Lancashire vineyards all year and a
 few freak redheads died. 144
My beautiful daughter stands by the lake 492
My poem will be a fantasy about living in a high-rise flat, 174
Myth's river – where his mother dipped him, 447

Next to my own skin, her pearls. My mistress 120
No, I don't remember the thing itself. 196
No folk fled the flood, 480
No getting up from the bed in this grand hotel 387
No vows written to wed you, 358
Nobody hurt you. Nobody turned off the light and argued 146
Not a red rose or a satin heart 208
Not close my eyes to the light 424
Not long ago so far, a lover and I 210
Not only the dark, 75
Not so hot as this for a hundred years. 377
Not there to see midsummer's midnight rose 415
Not tonight, I'm dreaming 356
Now only words in a song, 494
Now you've moved 423

Obsessed by faithfulness, 497
old lovers die hard, as in the restaurant 23
On our Eid day my cousin was sent to 3

On the other side of the world, 382
Once, I slept in a bed with these four men who share 186
One chair to sit in, 224
One voice for ten dragged this way once 513
Only art now – our bodies, brushstroke, pigment, motif; 427
Only there, the afternoons could suddenly pause 185
Out walking in the fields, Eley found a bullet 152
Over this Common a kestrel treads air 19

Pain past bearing, poetry's price, 498
Pat Hodges kissed you once, although quite shy, 44
Pity the lovers, 392

Say milky cocoa we'd say, 160
Scooping spilt, soft, broken oil 158
Scratching at the air *(There's nothing there)* 60
Scrooge doornail-dead, his widow, Mrs Scrooge, lived by herself 531
See the cows placed just so on the green hill. 79
Seven Sisters in Tottenham, 467
She asked me to luncheon in fur. Far from 48
She clings to life by a rosary, 32
She didn't shit, she *soiled* or *had a soil* 105
She goes for the sound of the words, the beauty they hold 359
She made things up: for example, that she was really 150
She was born from an egg, 310
She woke up old at last, alone, 329
She wore gloves, red to the elbow, sipped 100
Short days. The leaves are falling 393
Silently on Christmas Eve, 484
Six hours like this for a few francs. 46
Small dark hours with a bitter moon buffed by the smudgy clouds 215
Small Latin and less Greek, all English yours, 522
Some days, although we cannot pray, a prayer 226
Some keep them in shoeboxes away from the light, 170

Some say it was seven tons of meat in a thick black hide 143
Someone had looped a rope over a branch 376
Something is dealing from a deck of cards, 466
Somewhere on the other side of this wide night 169
Somewhere someone will always be leaving open 171
Spring's pardon comes, a sweetening of the air, 406
Stop. Along this path, in phrases of light, 122
Suddenly the rain is hilarious. 198
Sweetheart, this evening your smell is all around 101

Teach me, he said 254
Tell she is well in these arms; 486
Tell us what these tough words have done to you. 38
Thank you. Yes please. After you. Don't mind 85
That hot September night, we slept in a single bed, 165
That moment when the soldier's soul 503
That Thursday, it seemed they were part of the rain, 97
That's him pushing the stone up the hill, the jerk. 247
The bed we loved in was a spinning world 256
The cat is itself. 53
The cathedral bell, tolled, never could tell; 515
The clock slid back an hour 225
The country in her heart babbled a language 24
The crown translates a woman to a Queen 526
The Devil was one of the men at work. 267
The diet worked like a dream. No sugar, 317
The earth's heart hears hooves 471
The gourmet tastes the secret dreams of cows 61
The heart is placid. The wireless makes 49
The jet of your pupil 412
The King's Cook had cooked for the King 546
The little people in the radio are picking on me 86
The little sounds I make against your skin 164
The Long Queen couldn't die. 303

The lyf so short, the craft so long to lerne . . . 511
The moon is nearer than where death took you 365
The most unusual thing I ever stole? A snowman. 99
The News had often made her shout, 327
The night before, our host had pointed out the Building 156
The older she gets, 203
The other country, is it anticipated or half-remembered? 177
The single bed 485
The snows melt early, 462
The soundtrack then was a litany – *candlewick* 183
The year dwindles and glows 400
Then, in the writers' wood, 475
Then, like a christening gift or wish arriving 324
Then, like a sudden, easy birth, grace 401
Then all the dead opened their cold palms 487
Then the birds stitching the dawn with their song 378
Then with their hands they would break bread 62
There are not enough faces. Your own gapes back 14
There go the twins! geezers would say 287
There is a male silverback on the calendar. 142
There is something to be said but I, for one, 115
There were flowers at the edge of the forest, cupping 372
These myths going round, these legends, fairytales, 296
These strange stone birds are smashed 37
These were his diaries. Through the writing we may find 52
They cut the cord she was born with 361
They have not been kind here. Now I must leave, 121
They have shipped Gulliver up north. 138
They see me always as a flickering figure 35
They're very close to us, the dead; 493
Things assume your shape; discarded clothes, a damp shroud 17
Things get away from one. 83
This is the word *tightrope*. Now imagine 42
This morning you are not incurable, not yet, can walk 72

This shape is a rose, protect it, it's pure. 15
Those early mercenaries, it made them ill 184
Thought of by you all day, I think of you. 384
Till love exhausts itself, longs 425
Time was slow snow sieved by the night, 528
To feed one, she worked from home, 322
Today I am going to kill something. Anything. 13
Today we have a poet in the class. 9
Turnover. Profit. Readies. Cash. Loot. Dough. Income. Stash. 139
Tutumantu is like hopscotch, Kwani-kwani is like hide-and-seek. 4

Under the Act, the following things may be 147
Under the dark warm waters of sleep 209
Uninvited, the thought of you stayed too late in my head, 369
URGENT WHEN WE MEET COMPLETE STRANGERS DEAR STOP 112

Waking, with a dream of first love forming real words, 201
Watch me. I start with a low whistle, twist it, 154
We came from our own country in a red room 127
We first met when your last breath 504
We three play poker whilst outside *the real world* 55
Wear dark glasses in the rain. 212
Welcome to my country! We have here Edwina Currie 132
Welltread was Head and the Head's face was a fist. Yes, 188
went out with a silver shilling, willing to buy, bought 319
What are you doing? 11
What I have learnt I have learnt from the air, 47
What if there had been a painter – he was drunk – equal 149
What she has retained of herself is a hidden grip 25
What was it Sisyphus pushed up the hill? 439
What was your appeal, Simon Powell? 482
What you do. Follow the slow tram 206
What's an elephant like? I say 191
When Anon, no one now, 454

When did your name 371
When I awoke 193
When I turn off the light 420
When I was cat, my mistress tossed me sweetmeats 68
When I went, wet, wide, white and blue, my name Nile, 460
When I went to read 477
When the words have gone away 6
When they gave you them to shell and you sat 130
When we love, when we tell ourselves we do, 77
When you come on Thursday, bring me a letter. We have 111
When you die in the city where everyone was young, 162
When you were small, your cupped palms 360
Where I lived – winter and hard earth. 300
Where the bee sucks, 441
Whispers weave webs amongst thighs. I open 21
who came to lose every tooth in her head; 478
Who wouldn't feel favoured, 512
Who'll know then, when they walk by the grave 385
With some surprise, I balance my small female skull in my hands. 199
World is what you swim in, or dance, it is simple. 59
Worth their salt, England's white cliffs; 517
Wounds in wood, where the wind grieves 518
Write that the sun bore down on me, 411
Writing it, I see how much I love the sound. 403

Yes, I think a poem is a spell of kinds 481
You come back, 422
You could travel up the Blue Nile 128
You get a shilling if you see it first. 166
You must prepare your bosom for his knife, 445
You run round the back to be in it again. 190
You were dead, but we met, dreaming, 161
Your last word was *water,* 461
Your own ghost, you stand in dark rain 67